The Panama Canal

The Panama Canal

The Crisis
in Historical Perspective

Expanded Edition

Walter LaFeber

OXFORD UNIVERSITY PRESS
Oxford   New York   Toronto   Melbourne

OXFORD UNIVERSITY PRESS
Oxford   London   Glasgow
New York   Toronto   Melbourne   Wellington
Ibadan   Nairobi   Dar es Salaam   Cape Town
Kuala Lumpur   Singapore   Jakarta   Hong Kong   Tokyo
Delhi   Bombay   Calcutta   Madras   Karachi

First published by Oxford University Press, New York, 1978

First issued as an Oxford University Press paperback, in an expanded
edition, 1979

Library of Congress Cataloging in Publication Data

LaFeber, Walter.
   The Panama Canal.

   Bibliography: p.
   Includes index.
   Appendix (p.   ): The Treaty of 1903.—The
treaties of 1978.
      1.   United States—Foreign relations—Panama.
2.   Panama—Foreign relations—United States.
3.   Panama Canal—History.   I.   United States.   Treaties,
etc., 1901–1909 (Roosevelt) Panama canal. 1979.
II.   United States. Treaties, etc. Panama, Sept. 7,
1977. Panama canal treaties. 1979.   III.   Title.
E183.8.P2L33 1979   327.730 7 287   78-12247

ISBN 0-19-502511-3

Printed in the United States of America

For Scott and Suzanne

Preface

In January 1964, four United States soldiers died, 85 others were wounded, and 24 Panamanians were killed with nearly 200 wounded during four days of warfare between the troops and Panamanian mobs. Most North Americans soon forgot about the killings. Vietnam, inflation, and Watergate pre-empted headlines for the next ten years. But Panamanians did not forget. The riots had been triggered by their determination to exercise some control over the great waterway that divides their country and dominates the economy. During the following decade they worked incessantly to gain that control. North Americans were consequently surprised in 1974 when Secretary of State Henry Kissinger, acquiescing to Panamanian pressure, suddenly agreed in principle to return the Canal Zone.

Intense debate broke out in the United States. Thirty-eight Senators, four more than needed to defeat a new treaty, publicly announced their opposition to surrendering any control over the Canal. They were joined by conservative organizations which began concerted letter-writing campaigns to newspapers and politicians, and by the Zonians —

some 10,000 North Americans living in the Zone — who feared loss of jobs, or at least security, if Panama operated the waterway.

On the other side, the State Department began systematic lobbying and education efforts designed to convince Congress and the public that it was in their best interest to share control with Panama. The Panamanian government bought the services of a high-powered public relations firm to take its case directly to the North Americans. By mid-1977, the United States and Panama agreed on the treaty's essential points, but the debate within the United States continued.

Observers estimated that despite the Department of State's efforts, Senate opposition to a new pact grew in early 1977. Secretary of State Cyrus Vance admitted in June that while treaty negotiations progressed, the Carter administration lacked the votes to pass the agreement through the Senate. Knowledgeable Panamanians and North Americans agreed that if the treaty did not pass, large-scale, anti-United States rioting could erupt in Panama, causing more deaths, leading to a sabotaging and closing of the Canal, and poisoning relations between Washington and Latin America.

Strangely, the historic debate had to be conducted amidst vast ignorance about how and why the post-1964 crisis developed. Discussion was shaped more by gut feelings than by historical knowledge. As a Canal Zone official told me in the summer of 1976, "We believe that 80 percent of Americans agree with us that we must keep the Canal under our control. Unfortunately, half of those Americans are not sure where the Panama Canal is located."

The crisis can only be understood by comprehending its historical development. The history does not begin in 1974 or 1964, nor can it be understood by learning simply about Theodore Roosevelt's boast of 1911 that "I took the Canal." The problem developed over three-quarters of a century, and this history, especially the growing dependence of Panama upon the waterway, is inseparable from the crisis itself.

Yet there is no full-length survey of relations between the United States and Panama, and no adequate study exists in either English or Spanish of Panamanian political and economic history since 1903. A host of well-written and beautifully illustrated books has appeared on the glamorous era of canal building, but little on the development of the current crisis.

This book attempts to fill that void and contribute to the debate by emphasizing the forces of the past which shaped the 1974-77 treaty negotiations. About one-quarter of the work analyzes the post-1968 years, but that period is undecipherable without the larger historical context provided in the first five chapters. The book is only a survey. It is to be hoped that scholars will amplify and correct parts of it in longer analyses; in this way one gap in United States diplomatic history will be filled.

Out of the survey four themes emerge. First, contrary to a prevalent belief, Panama did not magically materialize at Theodore Roosevelt's command. The drive for Panamanian independence, the development of a demanding, often chauvinistic nationalism, long preceded Roosevelt. Panama is not an artificial nation created solely by North American beneficence.

Second, the United States did not buy the Canal area in 1903 and does not own it. This is not well understood, particularly after Republican presidential candidate Ronald Reagan emphasized, with notable success, that North American claims to the Canal and Texas were equally valid. Reagan, incidentally, received important advice on the question from Arnulfo Arias, exiled to Miami by the Panamanian military regime which overthrew his government in 1968. Arias is one of the more important and colorful characters in this account. Contrary to Reagan's statements, from the beginning Washington officials claimed control but not full ownership of the Zone. Negotiations between the 1930s and 1970s were marked by a notable North American reluctance to discuss the point. Washington found the status quo satisfactory.

Unfortunately for the United States, a long-term status quo in international relations is a contradiction in terms. A third thesis attempts to place Panamanian-United States relations within the ever changing international and particularly Latin American context. Those relations cannot be understood without realizing that since 1945 the United States has waged not one, but three types of Cold Wars. The first (1945-56) involved the United States and Russia. The second (1945-early 1970s) was waged by many nations; it is discussed in Chapter IV. The third (the post-1973 years) has been marked by a relative decline in United States power to deal with a fragmented world, and particularly with the peoples of the southern hemisphere. This Third Cold War is discussed in detail in Chapter VI. The second and third of these wars, the book argues, helped shape both Panama's aspirations and its power to deal effectively with the United States.

Finally, the problems of the 1970s must be analyzed within the context of long-term developments within Panama itself. Those developments have been strongly influenced by an informal United States colonial policy exerted over the entire Isthmus, not merely the Canal Zone. The difference between North American domination of the country and Washington's control of the Zone, the book argues, is that in the former the colonialism is informal and indirect, while in the latter it is formal and direct. Panamanian history has also been molded by a racism that afflicts natives as well as foreigners living on the Isthmus, and by the country's almost total dependence on the Canal for its economic salvation. Politically, the emergence of the National Guard (the Panamanian army and police) has been most important. The Guard replaced an elite, wealthy, familial-based, and highly irresponsible oligarchy which long mismanaged the nation. The relative decline of the oligarchy and the corresponding rise of the militaristic, United States-trained Guard are, along with a vigorous and sometimes radical student movement, the most notable political characteristics of contemporary Panama.

This book resulted from a National Endowment of the Humanities grant to the Cornell History Department for experimental undergraduate seminars. Michael Kammen developed the plan, and I am indebted to him for many things, including his suggestion that I teach one of the seminars. In preparing for that course no full-length treatment of United States-Panamanian relations could be found that brought the story into the mid-1970s, hence the idea for this book. That idea led to a trip in 1976 to Panama with Professor Thomas Holloway of Cornell. Holloway was a U.S. Army translator in Panama during the 1964 riots. His help in introducing me to Panama and its people, as well as his criticism of this manuscript, have been especially important. As always, Professors Lloyd Gardner of Rutgers, and Joel Silbey and Richard Polenberg of Cornell, have been candid critics, a necessary part of being the best of friends. The book owes much to conversations with Professor Thomas McCormick of the University of Wisconsin regarding his work on United States-Latin American relations. Chris Muenzen performed bibliographical work and some research as an undergraduate research assistant at Cornell. For two years his work has been invaluable. Between 1976 and 1978 the Cornell freshmen and sophomores enrolled in the NEH-sponsored seminar not only uncovered fresh materials and sources, but were a pleasure to work with. It was a class the professor, at least, looked forward to meeting.

Zbigniew Brzezinski, National Security Advisor on the White House Staff, and the staffs at the Lyndon Johnson Presidential Library in Austin, Texas, and the Dwight D. Eisenhower Presidential Library in Abilene, Kansas, helped declassify documents from the 1950s and 1960s, as has the Freedom of Information Office in the Department of State. William Rogers, Chaplain at Cornell and expert on Latin American affairs; Jeff Bialos, a Cornell Honors student; Eric Edelman, now at Yale Graduate School; and the superb Cornell University Library staff (particularly Caroline Spicer and Barbara P. Berthelsen) were generous with information and their discoveries of materials on United States-

Panamanian affairs. Pat Guilford typed much of the final manuscript with a good humor which neither it nor I deserved. I am indebted to persons in Panama and to Panamanian and United States officials in this country who provided information. For various reasons they are sometimes not cited by name in this account. Finally, without the confidence and help of Sheldon Meyer, Editor at Oxford University Press, Gerry McCauley, Marie Noll, and, above all, Sandra, the past year would have been considerably more leisurely, but less interesting, and I am grateful to them.

W.L.

Ithaca, New York

Contents

The Panama Canal

CANAL ZONE

CARIBBEAN SEA

Colon
Cristobal
Fort Gulick
Fort Davis
GATUN LOCKS
GATUN DAM
Chagres R.
Gatun Lake

REPUBLIC OF PANAMA
CANAL ZONE
PANAMA R.R.

Chagres R.
L. Madden
MADDEN DAM
CONTINENTAL DIVIDE

Gamboa
Gaillard Cut
(formerly Culebra Cut)
PEDRO MIGUEL LOCKS
MIRAFLORES LOCKS
L. Miraflores
Fort Clayton
Albrook Air Force Base
Ancon
Balboa
PANAMA CITY
Howard Air Force Base

REPUBLIC OF PANAMA
CANAL ZONE

INTER-AMERICAN HIGHWAY

BAY OF PANAMA

LEGEND
Canal Zone Boundary
Panama Canal
Highway
Railroad
Military Installations

Scale
0   1   5   10   15 Kms
0   5   10 Miles

1 Balboa, de Lesseps, and Cromwell

Panama was a crossroads of global trade, the keystone of the great Spanish Empire, a century before the first white settlers struggled ashore at Massachusetts Bay. From its beginnings, the Isthmus was destined to be "the center of the universe," to use the later phrase of the Latin American liberator, Simón Bolívar. The prize has been neither easily seized nor cheaply held. Spanish explorer Rodrigo de Bastidas first landed in the area during the spring of 1501, wandered through a hundred-mile zone desperately searching for treasure, and returned empty-handed to his ship. Bastidas became the first of many who sought fame and fortune in Panama and departed with neither.

A member of his crew, however, found fame if not fortune. Vasco Nuñez de Balboa decided to settle in Hispaniola (Santo Domingo), but in 1510 hurriedly traveled to Panama as a stowaway to escape creditors. He became one of the nearly 800 Spaniards who settled on the Isthmus. Then one by one they began to die, of what they did not know. The Spaniards greatly feared the many poisonous snakes which infest the country's jungles, but their killer was doubtless the tiny mosquito that carried yellow fever and malaria. Soon only sixty Spaniards remained. The stowaway seized command of the group despite protests from the King's appointed agents. Balboa promptly restored discipline and hope. The Spaniards replenished their supplies through brutal raids on Indian settlements, but Balboa, who was considerably more enlightened and humane than most European conquerors, took the radical step of befriending Indians.

His rewards were immediate, among them the beautiful daughter of a chief for a mistress, and information about a great "South Sea" washing shores stocked with gold. After an epic march of nearly a month, Balboa stood atop a peak in eastern Panama on September 25, 1513, and was the first European to see the Pacific. The Indians designated the "South Sea" correctly. The Pacific lies to the south of part of the country. (From certain points, it is even possible to watch the sun rise over the Pacific.) The natives, however, were less than accurate about the gold to be found.

As a good Spaniard, Balboa nevertheless took no chances. He claimed the water and all the shores it touched for the King of Castile. Perhaps he hoped that in return for the Pacific Ocean the King might forgive his seizure of power in the settlement. But Balboa delayed sending the good news to Spain, and he soon lost his power to the jealous governor of Darien, Pedro Arias Dávila. History records Dávila as "Pedrarias the Cruel," and with good reason. He probably killed or enslaved—or both—as many as two million Indians. (The figure leads to speculation that when Balboa landed, Panama's population was larger than it is in the 1970s—one measure of the area's importance before 1500 and the impact of slaughters thereafter.) After convicting him on trumped-up charges of treason, Pedrarias the Cruel had Balboa publicly strangled by the official executioner. The explorer's grave has never been found.

The name "Panama" apparently derived from an Indian term meaning "many fish." But it could also have come from the word "panaba," or "far away," the reply

Indians usually gave explorers who demanded the location of the nearest gold mine.[1] Balboa doubtless would have thought the second term more appropriate.

Pedrarias the Cruel expanded his domains by founding the City of Panama on the Pacific shore in 1519. That success triggered the first survey in 1534 for building a canal between the new city and Nombre de Dios, the major Spanish port on the Caribbean coast (renamed Portobelo in the 1590s). For thirty years Spanish officials pondered the idea of a waterway until finally deciding against it, in part because the King concluded, after much consultation with his religious advisers, that if God wanted the oceans to meet He would have built the canal Himself. The Spanish instead linked the two port cities with a "Royal Road," a narrow, stone trail wide enough only for two loaded mules to pass. A few yards of smooth, partly buried stones can still be seen. Longer parts of the trail are regularly explored four centuries later by Boy Scout troops from the Canal Zone.

The Destruction of the Spanish Empire

Along this rough highway mule trains carried gold and silver from the port at Panama City across to Nombre de Dios, where the riches were packed aboard galleons for the Atlantic crossing. The Spanish extracted as much as 200,000 tons of silver from their holdings, and uncountable amounts of gold. Panama City was one of the three richest centers in the new world (Lima and Mexico City were the other two). Nombre de Dios became a key port for the Spanish Empire and the site of annual trade fairs whose riches strained even Spanish imaginations. By 1572, however, Spain's holdings were both too opulent and relatively un-

1. Jules B. Billard, "Panama, Link Between Oceans and Continents," *National Geographic*, CXXXVII (March 1970), 430–431; excellent background is in David Howarth, *Panama, Four Hundred Years of Dreams and Cruelty* (New York, 1966), esp. pp. 30–40.

armed, an easy target for the British pirate Francis Drake. His privateers seized Spanish galleons, raided the rich trading areas, and finally established a base off the Panamanian coast so they could more systematically loot the defenseless Spanish colonies.

For commiting such theft, Queen Elizabeth bestowed a knighthood on Drake. But in the larger sense, Drake's appearance suddenly transformed Panama into an arena for a struggle to the death between an established empire and an aspiring empire. Appropriately, Drake died of the fever in 1596 while in Portobelo preparing to loot Spanish treasure ships. Others quickly took his place, and their robberies helped build the foundations of the British Empire. In 1671 Henry Morgan hit the Spanish jugular, Panama City. After Spanish officials and most of the inhabitants fled, powder stores exploded. A month later Morgan left the incinerated city with hundreds of prisoners and 175 muleloads of treasure.

The Spanish never attempted to rebuild the ruins. They moved to a better fortified area several miles west, where the present Panama City was founded in 1673. Today in the old city the roofless, crumbling walls of a once-majestic cathedral face toward the ocean. On one side stand barracks of the Panamanian army, the National Guard; on another, attendants clean the stables for the Guard's horses; and on the third side are hovels holding refugees from Panama City slums who use the 300-year-old ruins of the cathedral as one side of their own tarpaper or aluminum-sheet shacks.

The Appearance of a New North American Empire

Panama's fortunes were roped to the fast sinking Spanish Empire. In 1739 Portobelo was finally destroyed by a British fleet commanded by Edward Vernon (after whom a young North American, Lawrence Washington, named his estate in Virginia colony). Spain terminated Portobelo's port monopoly and destroyed Panama's autonomy by attaching it to the Viceroyalty of New Granada (now known as Colombia). Panamanians began a century-and-a-half long struggle to regain their independence, but the main colonial conflict was occurring in the north, where the British eliminated the French as a rival in 1763. Twenty years later, Great Britain in turn was defeated by a large, newly born empire. In 1800 the United States moved its seat of government to the new Washington City, which, like old Panama City of 300 years before, was built amidst swamps and fever. During the next twenty years officials of Washington City paid close attention to the Caribbean region.

They watched the Latin Americans taking advantage of Spain's struggle for survival in Europe's Napoleonic Wars to crumble the remaining shell of the Spanish Empire and delare independence. Fighting for political autonomy, plagued by centuries of corrupt Spanish administrators, lacking an economic base, the Central American area seemed to lie open before aggressive North American and British empire-builders. Great Britain, conqueror of both Napoleon and the secrets of the steam engine, held the greatest economic and military power in history. Quite often where the Manchester businessman gained a foothold, London governmental officials followed to extend the mixed blessings of an imperial bureaucracy. The new Latin America had escaped Spanish rule only to face the danger of being victimized by expansionists from the north and empire-builders from the east.

In 1823 United States President James Monroe warned that the British should not again try their luck at empire-building in the Western Hemisphere. The Monroe Doctrine admonished Europeans to plant no more colonies and refrain from interfering with American interests in the new world. In return, the President carefully promised "not to interfere in the internal concerns" of Europeans. The United States consequently committed itself to containing the expansion of the world's greatest power. It seemed a mismatch, for the North Americans had few manufactured products with which to compete in the new markets, no navy to protect their interests (the British fleet had more ships than the United States Navy had cannon), and shared less of a common heritage with Latin America than geography seemed to indicate. As Monroe's Secretary of State, John Quincy Adams, explained in 1821, there was "no prospect that [Latin Americans] would establish free or liberal institutions of government. . . . They have not the first elements of good or free government. Arbitrary power, military and ecclesiastical, was stamped upon their habits, and upon all their institutions."[2] Nor did Adams believe that commerce would link North and South America in the foreseeable future.

Adams changed his mind about Latin America's importance, although not about its talents for "free government." No one more feared British expansionism, or was more sensitive to the political implications of England's commercial conquests, than Adams. In 1819 he forced Spain to surrender Florida. Suddenly North American territory was washed by the Caribbean. Merchants from Baltimore and New York had a new foothold from which to exploit Latin American markets. In the same 1819 treaty, Adams obtained Spanish claims to the Pacific coast of North America. The United States now possessed a strength not even England enjoyed: rapidly growing trading posts spreading along the shore of the eastern Pacific which served as bases for merchants and whalers who plied South and North American coasts. But these settlements were so far separated from the cities of the East Coast that a passage through the Isthmus and up along the Pacific shores became a necessity for the United States.

The interest of North Americans in Panama consequently grew naturally out of their quest for continental and commercial empire. Their initial involvement in the

---

2. Charles Francis Adams, ed., *Memoirs of John Quincy Adams*, 12 vols. (Philadelphia, 1874–77), V, 323–326.

Isthmus occurred in 1825–26, at the midpoint of the most expansionist half-century in United States history. A group of wealthy and politically influential New York business-men, claiming Central American support, announced the creation of a canal company to build an isthmian passage-way. The announcement was premature and the investment capital moved into less riskier ventures closer to home, but it was the private businessmen and promoters, mostly northeastern Whigs involved in commercial expansion abroad, who kept alive the spark of interest in a canal for the next twenty years. Washington officials were preoccu-pied with more immediate foreign policy problems.[3]

The United States government did make one an-nouncement of consequence for a future canal. In 1825 the Latin American nations planned to meet in Panama City to develop common commercial and political policies. An in-vitation was sent to Washington, much against the wishes of Simón Bolívar who believed—correctly—that the United States did not desire to cooperate politically. After long debates, Adams (now the President) and Congress accepted the invitation, but Adams instructed the two North Ameri-can delegates not to enter into any type of alliance with the other nations. The two emissaries failed to reach the confer-ence in time, but a policy had been set: Washington offi-cials were determined to maintain complete freedom of ac-tion in handling Latin America. The call for a separate hemispheric system sounded grand in the Monroe Doc-trine, but in reality Monroe and his successors never al-lowed their hands to be tied by Latin Americans when deal-ing with either problems or opportunities in the Caribbean.

Interest in a canal intensified during the next twenty years. When the President of New Granada offered con-tracts on a possible rail or ship crossing through the Isth-mus, President Andrew Jackson, at the request of the Sen-ate, sent Charles A. Biddle to investigate the possibilities in

3. The best account is Harvey E. Wilkinson, "Early American Interest in an Isthmian Canal," Unpublished Honors Thesis, Cornell University, 1977.

both Panama and Nicaragua, the only other route which seemed to have the potential of Panama's. Biddle succumbed to a disease common in such situations: he began to bargain with the New Granada government for his own private concession to build the passageway. Jackson admired agressive, self-made men (like himself), but he had to call Biddle home in disgrace. Other groups tried unsuccessfully to pick up Biddle's plan. Then in 1846 a breakthrough occurred.

By that time the British had established settlements along the Nicaraguan coast where a possible eastern terminus of a canal might be built. In 1846 rumor spread through the Caribbean that London businessmen next planned to conquer Panama. The United States diplomatic representative in Colombia, Benjamin Bidlack, was under instructions to thwart any attempt by another power to gain special rights in Panama. As Colombian fear of Britain intensified, Bidlack seized the opportunity to negotiate a treaty in which the United States guaranteed both the rights of transit across the Isthmus and Colombian control over the area. In return, the North Americans received a guarantee of free access to any future canal. With fast footwork and ambiguous language, President James K. Polk sent the treaty to the Senate with the assurance that no entangling alliance was involved. He warned that if the United States failed to seize the opportunity, the British surely would move to control the Isthmus. In the 1840s such a warning usually proved as catalytic as an anti-Soviet appeal would be a century later. In this case, however, the Senate intermittently debated the treaty for one-and-a-half years before accepting its historic responsibility on the Isthmus.

As the Senators understood, the United States was venturing into dangerous territory. The British were not only consolidating their hold on the eastern Nicaraguan coast, but selecting sites on the Pacific side for a possible canal. The United States and England seemed on a collision course in Central America. John M. Clayton, Secretary of State in Zachary Taylor's Whig administration during 1850, searched for alternatives. The slave controversy so divided the North Americans that a united front against Great Britain was difficult to form. As a Whig and a native of Delaware, moreover, Clayton had long been interested in extending his nation's commerce while avoiding conflict with the British navy, whose cannons could destroy that commerce in short order. Yet a clash seemed possible, particularly after United States interest in the Isthmus area increased with the discovery of gold in California during the late 1840s. By 1850 thousands of overly hopeful North Americans moved through Panama and Nicaragua to find their fortune in California.

Clayton asked the British if a deal could be made. The London Foreign Office was cool. It preferred simply to strengthen its hold in Central America. The Secretary of State then played his high card. United States diplomats had negotiated treaties with Nicaragua and Honduras giving Washington exclusive rights to build canals in those two nations. Clayton not only threatened to send these pacts to the Senate for ratification, but told the British (and stretched the truth to good effect), that some Central American states "have offered and asked to be annexed to the United States already." The British quickly became interested in defusing the issue. As finally written, the Clayton-Bulwer treaty of 1850 provided that the two nations would cooperate in building any isthmian canal, and neither would try to fortify or control it exclusively. Militant Democrats predictably condemned Clayton for not shoving the British out of Nicaragua entirely, but in retrospect the treaty was clearly a triumph of North American diplomacy. It prevented possible war with the world's most formidable power, made the United States an equal partner in any canal enterprise, and—most importantly—it gave Washington time to solve internal problems of slavery, time to develop its own military power, time to become so strong in the Caribbean that it could someday push the British aside and build the canal alone.

The discovery of California gold telescoped that

time. A railroad across the 3000-mile-wide United States would not be completed until 1869, but between 1851 and 1855 New York City financiers built a transcontinental railway by laying 48 miles of rails between Panama City and the Atlantic side of the Isthmus. No one could doubt that the United States was the dominant foreign power in the Colombian province. But it was nevertheless "foreign," and when the Pacific Mail Company named the Atlantic terminal "Aspinwall" after its president, the Colombians insisted on "Colon" and made their point stick by returning any mail addressed to Aspinwall with the stamp "Destination unknown." Thus the North Americans lost the first of several battles over nomenclature to Latin American nationalism.

The railroad was not built cheaply. Nine thousand laborers died in the swamps during the five years of construction, "a life for every railroad tie," as the saying went. For the owners, of course, the price was not unbearable; they did not die of yellow fever. They indeed became very rich. During the fourteen years after the line opened in 1855, 600,000 travelers used it and as much as $750 million in gold bullion moved from California to the eastern United States along the Panama Railroad. Through 1905 it paid nearly $38 million in dividends to the owners, returned prosperity to Panama after more than a century of decline, and made the Isthmus once again crossroads of the Western world.

In retrospect, however, two other results were of greatest significance. First, United States interests held a hammerlock on the Isthmus. No one could doubt this after the completion of the railroad and the simultaneous landing of American troops to restore order after the failure of a traveler to pay for a piece of watermelon led to a riot and then the so-called "Watermelon War." This marked the first landing of United States forces under the 1846 treaty. Second, nationalism flourished with the railroad's fortunes. The first daily newspaper appeared (*The Panama Star and Herald*, still in existence), and Panamanians began to wonder why their new wealth had to be shared with the faraway Colombians. Not coincidentally, one of the bloodiest of Panamanian uprisings against Colombian control occurred in the mid-1850s. But of equal significance historically, the "Watermelon War" turned into the first of many anti-Yankee riots in Panama.

De Lesseps

During the last half of the nineteenth century, Panamanian nationalism continued to ripen, but North American control was suddenly challenged in 1878. Ferdinand de Lesseps, famed builder of the Suez Canal, announced he would build a sea-level canal across Panama. President Rutherford B. Hayes solemnly warned the United States would never accept a canal under non-American control. To make his point, Hayes dispatched warships to the Panamanian coast as a warning that the 1846 treaty prohibited de Lesseps' venture. The Colombians paid little attention and de Lesseps began digging. The Frenchman, however, made fatal mistakes. Attempting to emulate his Suez success, he determined to build a sea-level passageway across Panama instead of a multi-tiered lock system. After a decade he had completed less than half of what he planned to accomplish in six years. French engineers could not stop mud and rock slides from filling the newly dug cuts.

But worse, de Lesseps failed in waging all-out warfare against malaria and yellow fever, the "black vomit" that claimed victims in twenty-four hours. Workers wrote their wills before leaving for Panama, a few had the foresight to bring their coffins with them from France. As one reporter described Colon, it was

> a foul hole, by comparison, the ghettoes of White Russia, the slums of Toulon, Naples, and old Stamboul . . . deserve prizes for cleanliness. There are neither sewers nor street cleaners . . . toilets are quite unknown, all the rubbish is thrown into the swamps or onto rubbish heaps.

> Toads splash in the liquid muck . . . , rats infest the solid
> filth . . . , snakes hunt both toads and rats; clouds of mos-
> quitoes swarm into the homes.[4]

As many as 20,000 died before de Lesseps gave up in 1889.
Panama had ruined his and his son's fortunes and reputa-
tions. French courts found them and several associates
guilty of fraud and bribery in raising funds for the canal.
The son went to jail, and was allowed out only to visit his
father, a broken man who spent days staring at the fire,
gazing at a three-year-old newspaper, and trying vainly
to recognize his son. Left behind was a partially dug canal
and a small French cemetery outside Panama City where, as
a later visitor said, "little crosses corrode in the tropic air."[5]
De Lesseps joined the growing ranks of those who, like
Balboa and Drake, had tried and failed to tame the Isthmus.
    The North Americans meanwhile never let up in
their pressure against France or the Clayton-Bulwer treaty.
They followed the lead of Secretary of State William Seward who had fit Panama into his spectacular vision of global commercial empire by telling a group of New York
capitalists in 1869 that they must lead in building a canal.
Since "we are Americans," Seward proclaimed, "we are
charged with responsibilities of establishing on the American continent a higher condition of civilization and freedom" than has existed elsewhere. But "that destiny can
only be attained" by cutting a canal which could carry the
earth's goods cheaply by navigation. Seward had sounded
the theme: since North Americans enjoyed the freest of all
governmental systems, and since that system rested on
booming production and commercial exchanges, the world
would be served by a canal that made the exporting of both
the system's freedoms and goods easier and cheaper.[6] The

---

4. Quoted in Sheldon B. Liss, *The Canal: Aspects of United States-
Panamanian Relations* (Notre Dame, Ind., 1967), p. 16.
    5. Billard, "Panama," p. 414.
    6. George E. Baker, ed., *The Works of William H. Seward*, 5 vols. (Boston,
Mass., 1853–83), V, 590.

future of civilization hinged on an American-built canal. Given that assumption, de Lesseps' challenge was immoral as well as a strategic threat, and the Clayton-Bulwer treaty an impediment rather than an obligation.

One modest State Department message to London in 1881 stated that North Americans must single-handedly control a canal in order to claim "our rightful and long-established claim to priority on the American continent."[7] As United States power developed, so did the passion for freedom to expand as Washington saw fit. When the British rejected such an argument, the North Americans nevertheless went ahead and signed a treaty in 1884 which gave them rights to build a canal in Nicaragua—without British participation. Due in part to political party jealousies, the United States Senate refused to ratify the pact.

The 1890s Watershed

But the pressure did not abate. Indeed, interest in a canal leaped ahead during the 1890s, as an economic panic marked the nadir of a two-decade downturn in prices. Businessmen and governmental officials feared class warfare in the slum-ridden urban areas, and in 1894 Secretary of State Walter Quintin Gresham worried deeply over "symptoms of revolution" which were appearing, symptoms which he believed could be eradicated only if jobs were created by shipping the glut of United States iron, steel, and agricultural products to foreign markets. As the business periodical *Bradstreet's* observed in 1895, a canal would give the country "a decided advantage over other nations" in the "future development of the South American and Oriental countries."[8]

Similar words were sounded by the powerful Demo-

7. U.S. Department of State, *Papers Relating to the Foreign Relations of the United States, 1881* (Washington, D.C., 1882), p. 555. (Hereafter cited: *FRUS*, followed by year and volume.)

8. *Bradstreet's*, December 28, 1895, p. 820; the Gresham quote is analyzed in Walter LaFeber, *The New Empire* (Ithaca, N.Y., 1963), pp. 197–201.

cratic Senator from Alabama, John T. Morgan, and Chambers of Commerce representatives. The National Nicaraguan Canal Convention called for an isthmian passage so, in Morgan's words, the United States could have "access to the eastern Asiatic countries for our cotton." When the British landed troops in Nicaragua in 1894 to collect an indemnity for the arrest of a diplomatic official, the State Department and the North American press were in an uproar. London officials backed down, so much so that they finally released their grip on Mosquitia and the potential canal entrances. When a revolt erupted in Nicaragua during 1896, U.S. Marines, not British sailors, landed to protect foreign citizens and property. The old order was passing, and Monroe's doctrine was realized as the North Americans accelerated their drive for a canal.

In 1893–94 a giant step was taken when a government dominated by white planters seized control of Hawaii and asked Washington to annex the islands. In 1898 the William McKinley administration did so. The new territory served both as a naval base to protect Pacific entrances to a canal, and as a port for ships that sailed through a canal en route to Asian markets.

During the 1890s the first giant battleships of the modern U.S. Navy were built. According to the theories of Alfred Thayer Mahan, the best-known military strategist of the time, a canal was essential if the ships were to move quickly from one ocean to the other in order to protect both coasts and American markets worldwide. A canal, Mahan argued, would "enable the Atlantic coast to compete with Europe, on equal terms as to distance, for the markets of Asia," and reduce the distance to the western coast of Latin America by half.[9] The need for a passageway became dramatically apparent during the war against Spain in 1898. The battleship *Oregon* spent 68 days sailing from the West Coast of the United States to battle stations in Cuba *via* the

9. Alfred Thayer Mahan, "The Isthmus and Sea Power," *Atlantic Monthly*, LXXII (October 1893), 470–472.

tip of South America, a trip that would have taken one-third the time if a canal had existed.

The 1898 war introduced the United States as a great world power. Specifically, the conflict made the nation supreme in the Caribbean region. The country emerged from "the splendid little war," as Secretary of State John Hay aptly called it, with Cuba, Puerto Rico, a great (if little tested) fleet, and British recognition that the days of the Clayton-Bulwer treaty were numbered. The cry for a canal intensified. Brooks Adams, John Quincy Adams's brilliant if eccentric grandson, and close friend of arch-expansionists Theodore Roosevelt and Senator Henry Cabot Lodge, had prophesied North American "economic supremacy" in world markets. The apparent fulfillment of that prophecy after 1898, Adams bragged, "knocked the stuffing out of me." "America has been irresistibly impelled to produce a large industrial surplus," he argued. "The expansion of any country must depend on the markets for its surplus product." Since "China is the only region which now provides almost boundless possibilities of absorption," an isthmian canal "to the Pacific must be built."[10]

President William McKinley was equally direct in his Annual Message of December 1898. A canal, McKinley observed, was "demanded by the annexation of the Hawaiian Islands and the prospective expansion of our influence and commerce in the Pacific." He emphasized the waterway must be controlled by the United States.[11] Brooks Adams and other acute observers believed Great Britain actually had little choice but to become the junior partner in an Anglo-Saxon empire. Not only did United States power appear awesome, but the London government was increasingly preoccupied with a rising Germany and a rebellion in South Africa where the Boer farmers were unexpectedly humiliating British troops.

With Great Britain busy elsewhere, in 1900 the

10. Quoted in Charles S. Campbell, The Transformation of American Foreign Relations, 1865–1900 (New York, 1976), p. 154.
11. Ibid. , p. 314.

United States Senate considered a bill that would build a Nicaraguan canal without regard for the Clayton-Bulwer treaty. That threat prodded British officials to negotiate with Secretary of State Hay (a noted Anglophile), to work out an alternative. Hay finally agreed with British Ambassador Lord Pauncefote that under a new treaty the United States could build and control a canal, but would not fortify it. The Senate rebelled against the non-fortification pledge, as did a hero of the 1898 war, a self-proclaimed expansionist, and Republican candidate for Vice-President of the United States in 1900, Theodore Roosevelt. Though a close friend of Hay, Roosevelt warned that a fresh treaty was necessary. The Secretary of State threatened to resign, muttering privately that "There will always be 34 percent of the Senate on the blackguard side of every question," then thought better of it and negotiated a second treaty with Pauncefote. Hay warned friends that in dealing with the Senate one should not underrate "the power of ignorance and spite, acting upon cowardice," but this time he had nothing to fear. The agreement directly abrogated the 1850 pact and implicitly gave the United States the sole right to fortify a canal. The treaty was negotiated during the weeks that President William McKinley, who had been shot, lingered near death, and then passed away. The White House was now in the hands of that "wild man," as one of McKinley's advisers called Theodore Roosevelt.

The only remaining question concerned the location of the passageway. Since the 1870s most knowledgeable observers had assumed the site would be Nicaragua. In 1901 the Walker Commission, a group of engineers named by McKinley to examine the prospects for a canal, also reported favorably on the Nicaraguan route. That conclusion received strong endorsement from Senator Morgan. But the Walker Commission made the recommendation reluctantly, believing the Nicaragua river system too shallow for a large canal. The Commission agreed with most engineers (and Theodore Roosevelt) that the Panama route was preferable, especially since de Lesseps had completed part of the work on the Isthmus. The Commission nevertheless concluded that building the canal in Panama would be considerably more expensive than the Nicaraguan route, for the New Panama Canal Company—a group of Frenchmen who had bought out the ruined de Lesseps company—was asking $109 million for its assets and concessionary rights to build in Panama.

The Titans: Cromwell and Bunau-Varilla

At this juncture two remarkable men reversed the movement toward the Nicaraguan route. William Nelson Cromwell headed a New York City law firm prestigious in 1900 (and even more prestigious a half-century later when two of Sullivan and Cromwell's senior partners, John Foster Dulles and Arthur Dean, became important United States diplomats in the Cold War). In 1896 Cromwell emerged as the New Panama Canal Company's agent in the United States and served as legal counsel for the Panama Railroad Company. Four years later the forty-eight-year-old lawyer miraculously prevented the inclusion in the Republican Party platform of a plank favoring the Nicaraguan canal. His means for working the miracle were direct: he contributed $60,000 to the party through the party chairman, and confidant of McKinley, Senator Mark Hanna of Ohio.[12] Cromwell later charged this and other expenses to the Canal Company and apparently collected nearly a million dollars in fees.

The exact amount of money involved in the canal transactions will never be known. Cromwell burned many of his papers and most of the remainder, particularly those relating to Panama, were destroyed by several of his surviving law partners, including Dulles.[13] Cromwell neverthe-

12. William Roscoe Thayer, The Life and Letters of John Hay, 2 vols. (Boston, Mass., 1915), II, 307.
13. Erhard to Dulles, June 16, 1954, Papers of John Foster Dulles, Princeton University.

less deserved whatever he was paid, for between 1896 and 1902 he single-handedly fended off the commitment to the Nicaraguan route. In 1913 the head of a congressional investigation into the canal transactions called Cromwell "the most dangerous man the country has produced since the days of Aaron Burr." His abilities were apparent in a description written by a New York reporter in 1908:

> Mr. Cromwell is about 5 feet 8 inches high, and medium in build. . . . He can smile as sweetly as a society belle and at the same time deal a blow at a business foe that ties him in a hopeless tangle of financial knots. . . . He is a wizard with figures and a shorthand writer of wonderful skill. . . . He is one of the readiest talkers in town. . . . He talks fast, and when he wishes to, never to the point. . . . [He] has an intellect that works like a flash of lightning, and it swings about with the agility of an acrobat.[14]

In November 1901 Cromwell's wizardry with figures and politics convinced the anxious New Panama Canal Company in Paris to drop its price from $109 million to $40 million, thereby making the Panama route less expensive than the Nicaraguan. The Walker Commission now recommended Panama to the Senate as the better buy.

The New Panama Canal Company's decision to lower the price occurred after bitter debate. Arguments became so heated that Parisian police were called in to calm one meeting. In the end, however, a faction led by Phillipe Bunau-Varilla triumphed. "A somewhat picturesque personage," as a contemporary described him, the vain and trimly mustached Bunau-Varilla viewed "the earth . . . like a school globe which he, the teacher, made to revolve at his pleasure."[15] At twenty-six, Bunau-Varilla was chief engineer on the de Lesseps project in Panama before falling victim to the fever. After returning to Paris he embarked upon a ca-

14. Quoted in Dwight C. Miner, *The Fight for the Panama Route* (New York, 1940), pp. 76–77.
15. Thayer, *Hay*, II, 315.

reer of building railroads in the Belgian Congo, constructing flood controls in Rumania, serving as an editor of Le Matin in Paris, and, in 1893, playing a central role in the formation of the New Panama Canal Company.

Realizing that the company's rights would expire in 1904, Bunau-Varilla raced against time. In the mid-1890s he tried to convince Russians to buy the claims and build the canal. After all, he told them, if the Anglo-Saxons controlled Panama as well as Suez, they would rule the world's commerce. When the Czar's government did not respond, he used the same argument in discussions with the British, only transforming the reference to Anglo-Saxons into North Americans. Busy elsewhere, London officials were preparing to leave the Caribbean in Washington's hands. The second Hay-Pauncefote treaty made this clear to Bunau-Varilla, and in 1902 he left Paris to join Cromwell in the United States. Just before the Frenchman arrived, however, the House passed, by an overwhelming vote of 308–2, a bill sponsored by William P. Hepburn of Iowa which ordered the canal to be built in Nicaragua. The pro-Nicaragua lobby, led by Senator Morgan, had scored an impressive victory.

Reaching Washington in late January 1902, Bunau-Varilla joined Cromwell and Senator Hanna in pushing for an amendment sponsored by Republican Senator John C. Spooner of Wisconsin. When attached to the Hepburn bill, the Spooner amendment instructed President Roosevelt to buy the Canal Company's claims for $40 million and build the passageway in Panama if he could obtain a treaty from Colombia. If he failed, Roosevelt was to deal with Nicaragua. Within six months Bunau-Varilla, Cromwell, and Hanna collected the votes to pass the Spooner amendment. The trio was even blessed by an act of God. In May a volcano erupted on the Caribbean island of Martinique, covering a city of 30,000 inhabitants with hot lava. Bunau-Varilla immediately notified all Senators that Nicaragua could suffer the same disaster.

Nicaraguan authorities made the mistake of claiming publicly that no active volcanoes had shaken their country

since 1835. Bunau-Varilla, however, knew that Momotombo had erupted just several months before, and that in
1901 the Nicaraguan government even issued a postage
stamp showing Momotombo magnificently belching lava.
The Frenchman bought out the Washington dealers' supply
of these stamps, then placed one on each Senator's desk
with the simple notation, "Official testimony regarding vol-
canic activity in Nicaragua." The Senate and House passed
the Spooner amendment (the House so totally reversing itself that it passed the Panama bill 260–8), and Roosevelt
signed the new measure into law on June 28.[16]

Happily following instructions, Roosevelt and Hay
opened negotiations with Colombia. In January 1903, after a
good deal of arm-twisting, Hay convinced the Colombian
ambassador in Washington to sign a treaty that gave the
United States a 99-year lease on a six-mile-wide canal zone.
In return, the United States would pay Colombia $10 mil-
lion plus an annual payment of $250,000. The United
States Senate ratified the pact, but in August 1903 the Colombian Senate not only rejected it, but did so unanimously. The Bogotá government wanted more money. A
leading Colombian historian later wrote that his nation
feared the loss of sovereignty in Panama to the powerful
North Americans, and believed itself entitled to a larger
sum, particularly since the United States-owned isthmian
railroad had earned millions in profits of which Colombia
received nothing.[17] Left unsaid was that the Colombians
hoped to stall until October 1904 when the Canal Company's rights would expire. Colombia could then collect all
of the $40 million ticketed for Bunau-Varilla's and Crom-
well's organization.

Roosevelt was livid. During the next several months
he exhausted his rich vocabulary, calling the Colombians

16. The best account of the lobbying effort is Charles D. Ameringer, "The
Panama Canal Lobby of Philippe Bunau-Varilla and William Nelson Cromwell," American Historical Review, LXVII (January 1963), 345–363.
17. Germán Arciniegas, Caribbean: Sea of the New World (New York,
1946, 1954), p. 437.

everything from "inefficient bandits" to "a corrupt pithe-
coid community." The sardonic Hay hid an equal anger
behind his condescending smile and sarcastic words. At
one time in 1902 he considered outright purchase of Panama from Colombia, then dropped the scheme, agreeing
with a visitor's comment that Colombians viewed Panama
"as a financial cow to be milked for the benefit of the country at large."[18] In August 1903 the Secretary of State wondered whether he should turn to deal with Nicaragua or
instead begin "the far more difficult and multifurcate
scheme of building the Panama Canal *malgré* Bogotá."[19]

Roosevelt's mind began to move in the same direction. He would be "delighted" if Panama became independent, TR wrote a friend in October, but "I cast aside the
proposition made at this time to foment the secession of
Panama. Whatever other governments can do, the United
States cannot go into the securing by such underhand
means, the secession."[20] As usual, he worked more directly.
Roosevelt began drafting a message to Congress suggesting
that the simpler method would be to send the navy to seize
the Isthmus.

The New Four-Hundred-Year-Old Panama

Roosevelt never sent that particular message, for
Panamanian nationalists had long been awaiting such an
opportunity. These nationalists, contrary to North American myths too long propagated in textbooks, did not suddenly spring up full-grown at Roosevelt's command. The
belief that Panama should exist as a separate, independent
country was neither artificially created suddenly in 1903
nor propagated in Washington before it took hold in Panama City. The Panamanian nationalism of 1902–03 formed

18. Thayer, *Hay*, II, 303–304.
19. Dana G. Munro, *Intervention and Dollar Diplomacy in the Caribbean,
1900–1921* (Princeton, 1964), p. 49.
20. Elting E. Morison, ed., *The Letters of Theodore Roosevelt*, 6 vols. (Cambridge, Mass., 1951), III, 628.

only one part of an ancient story, although, as it turned out, the most important chapter.

The point demands emphasis. Nothing is more important in understanding the 1960s–70s crisis in United States-Panamanian relations than to realize that Panamanians are acutely conscious of their four centuries' long history, and that their ardent nationalism arising from this consciousness developed at the same time United States expansionism conquered a continent and, while building a worldwide empire, laid claims on Panama itself. Throughout the nineteenth century, the two nationalisms were on a collision course.

After Colombia declared its independence from Spain in 1821, it was never able to control Panama completely. In part this failure was due to the type of person the Isthmus attracted—the rootless, lawless, transient who obeyed no authority. This element remained in Panama, as a later observer noted, becoming "a community of gamblers, jockeys, boxers, and cockfighters."[21] At the other end of the social spectrum a small propertied elite—an "oligarchy"—developed that resembled the North American elite of 1776: both developed valuable economic and political interests apart from the mother country, and neither saw any reason to share their wealth with colonizers. Colombia, moreover, was separated from the Isthmus as the United States was from England. The mountains and jungles in eastern Panama that bordered Colombia were so dense that in 1903 North Americans could reach Panama more easily and quickly by steamer than Colombians could by horse. In the 1970s, despite new technology, the Inter-American Highway had not breached those jungles after thirty years of intermittent effort.

Separated from the supposed mother country, holding a mobile, rebellious, independent population, Panama never developed the quasi-feudal, mercantilist characteris-

21. Jan Morris, "A Terminal Case of American Perpetuity," *Rolling Stone*, Jan. 1, 1976, p. 47.

tics of neighboring Latin American nations. Movement and trade were freer, liberalism seemed more natural. The land-owning oligarchs notably profited from such laissez-faire sentiment, but it also shaped the thought of most politically active Panamanians.[22] They were individualistic, national-istic, and ripe for revolt.

They first rebelled against Colombia (then New Gra-nada), in 1830, again in 1831, and as many as fifty times between 1840 and 1903. In 1840 one of Panama's great historical figures, Colonel Tomás Herrera, led the move-ment to create an independent state. A Panamanian Con-gress ruled the area until 1842 when Colombia regained the Isthmus by making extensive promises to grant Panama more autonomy. Four years later, Colombia signed the Bid-lack treaty, an act, a later Panamanian historian argued, which sharply reduced Colombian sovereignty since the pact allowed the United States to guarantee transit rights across the Isthmus.[23]

These first rebellions were accompanied—indeed partially caused—by the development of an ideology that nurtured Panamanian nationalism thereafter. Comprised of certain European philosophies (particularly Benthamism), anti-Colombian feeling, and historical memories of the once-magnificent Panamanian past, its critical ingredient was "the geographical myth"—the belief that Panamanians were predestined to control the crossroads of the world. In the hands of Justo and Pablo Arosemena, the ideology also assumed strong anti-imperialist feelings, focused initially against Colombia, then as early as the 1850s against the United States. Panamanians were not immune to the strong currents of nationalism that swept through the Western

22. Ricaurte Soler, *Formas Ideológicas de la Nación Panameña* (San José, Costa Rica, 1972), pp. 16, 83–84.
23. Ramon M. Valdes, "La Independencia del Istmo de Panama; Sus Ante-cedentes, Sus Cause y su Justificacion," November 1903, in Buchanan to Hay, Dec. 28, 1903, Dispatches, Panama, National Archives, Record Group 59 (hereafter NA, RG 59), Microfilm. State Department translation. Frank Otto Gatell, "Canal in Retrospect—Some Panamanian and Colombian Views," *Americas*, XV (July 1958), 26–27.

world in the mid-nineteenth century, and it is striking that
their new ideology, with its anti-imperialist conponent,
was shaped at the same time North Americans constructed
their own "Manifest Destiny"—a conviction that they were
predestined to conquer a continent and exploit such vital
hemispheric areas as Panama.[24]

A major collision seemed imminent as early as
1855–56 when, during a rebellion against Colombia, Panamanian mobs threatened United States citizens and property. Washington was watching over its Caribbean interests
closely, especially in the isthmian area that was carrying
the riches of California eastward on a North-American-
owned railroad. The Navy Department instructed its commander in the area that Colombia must maintain order; if it
did not, he could use force whenever necessary.[25] The uprising won new rights from Colombia, and Panama ran its
internal affairs until the Bogotá regime cracked down again
in 1863. The Panamanians, however, had tasted independence and wanted more.

Revolts occurred sporadically until 1884–85 when rebels seized control of the Isthmus. They made the mistake of
attacking the Panama Railroad and United States shipping.
President Grover Cleveland's administration was known for
its anti-imperialist, "little America" policies, but Cleveland
vividly demonstrated that on canal issues he ranked with
Seward and other noted expansionists: the President sent
eight warships and landed 400 men in Panama to stop the
revolt and protect North American interests. The railroad
reopened after United States troops fitted out two flatcars
with a Gatling gun, cannon, and a howitzer behind a shield
of boiler iron. The rebels understandably refused to duel
with this moving fortress. Cleveland successfully completed
the largest landing operation undertaken by United States
forces between the Mexican War of the 1840s and the War of

24. Ricaurte Soler, *Pensamiento Panameño y Concepción de la Nationali-
dad durante el Siglo XIX* (Panama, 1954), pp. 99–101, 120, 125.
25. Kenneth J. Hagan, *American Gunboat Diplomacy and the Old Navy,
1877–1889* (Westport, Conn., 1973), p. 144.

1898 against Spain.[26] Colombia's authority further deteriorated. Equally important, Panamanian rebels learned they
needed the United States with them, not against them.

Colombia tried to recoup its losses by imposing a
new constitution that theoretically placed Panama directly
under Bogotá's rule. The theory dissolved between 1899
and 1902 when Colombian liberals, exiled in Nicaragua,
attacked the Bogotá regime in the "War of a Thousand
Days." More than 100,000 Colombians died, guerrilla warfare terrorized the country, and amidst the ruins Panamanian nationalism blossomed. In 1902 Colombia finally was
reduced to asking the United States for help in reclaiming
the Isthmus. A truce was worked out aboard the *U.S.S.
Wisconsin* in the Bay of Panama at the same moment, ironically, that the Colombian government was beginning to tell
Hay that its control over Panama allowed it to demand better terms from the United States.

Colombia's claim had been proven wrong throughout
the nineteenth century. Indeed the Bogotá government itself had admitted failure. At least four times (some histori-
ans say six) between 1846 and 1903 Colombia asked the
United States to restore order on the Isthmus. The settlement of the Thousand Days' War aboard a United States
warship in November 1902 was only the last in a long line
of North American interventions into affairs between Colombia and its raucous, hell-bent-for-independence province. A distinguished Panamanian diplomat later remarked
that his country emerged as an independent nation because
of its geography, economy, history, and "the interest and
the sentiments of the people of Panama"—not "the arbi-
trariness of Theodore Roosevelt."[27] And Panamanian historian Ricaurte Soler has observed that by 1903 "a nation
already existed and a Panamanian consciousness had already been formed."[28]

26. *Ibid.*, pp. 170–188.
27. Ricardo J. Alfaro, *Media Siglo de Relaciones entre Panama y los Estados Unidos* (Panama, 1959), p. 14.
28. Soler, *Formas Ideológicas*, p. 125.

That was one important lesson to be drawn from four hundred years of Panamanian experience. There were others. Panama's prosperity historically depended on traffic through the Isthmus. When the Spanish Empire prospered or the new railroad flourished, so did Panama, but at other times the country stagnated. Without vast arable lands or mineral wealth, the people's fortunes rose and fell with the use outsiders made of the major resource— geographical location. The Panamanians have been historically conditioned to think of this as the key to their welfare. That perception has been sharpened by the nationalist, anti-imperialist ideology that began to take hold in the mid-nineteenth century. In the end, Colombia could not control a nationalism that was rooted in the historical memory of four centuries and expressed in the demands of a revolutionary elite.

As Colombia's grip slipped, Roosevelt's hand began to close around the Isthmus. A long list—Balboa and Spain, Drake and England, de Lesseps and France, as well as many Colombian leaders — tried to claim this crossroads of the world. All failed. Roosevelt and the United States, with the confidence peculiar to expanding empires, now determined to try their luck.

2 Roosevelt, Bunau-Varilla, and Taft

With an isthmian canal virtually within his grasp, Roosevelt refused to allow those "contemptible little creatures" in Colombia to frustrate his grand plan. But TR could not decide how to deal with the Colombians. He apparently held little hope the deadlock would be broken by a successful Panamanian revolt. As the President searched desperately for alternatives, Bunau-Varilla and the Panamanian nationalists were devising a solution. That solution, together with a 1904 agreement negotiated between Washington and Panama City by Secretary of War William Howard Taft, created the framework for sixty years of relations between the two countries and shaped the crisis of the 1970s.

Bunau-Varilla, with considerable help from top State Department officials, took the lead in solving Roosevelt's dilemma. During September and October 1903, the Frenchman held a series of talks with Hay, Assistant Secretary of State Francis B. Loomis (whom Bunau-Varilla had known since a meeting in Paris two years before), and John Bassett Moore, a former Assistant Secretary of State, renowned international lawyer, and confidant of TR. Out of the conversations grew Bunau-Varilla's conviction that if the Panamanians tried to declare their independence the United States would use force, ostensibly to uphold its 1846 commitment to maintain transit rights across the Isthmus, but in reality to prevent Colombia from quashing the revolution.

As early as August, Moore sent a memorandum to Roosevelt arguing that the 1846 pact gave the United States the right to construct a canal. Loomis, who spent many hours with Bunau-Varilla, apparently inspired the memorandum; in any case, it completely reversed Moore's previous opinion of the 1846 treaty.[1] Later in the autumn Bunau-Varilla asked Loomis how the United States would respond to an outbreak on the Isthmus. The Assistant Secretary of State said he "could only venture to guess that this Government would probably do as it had done in the past under like circumstances." Bunau-Varilla agreed, hoping that the North Americans "might freely do more rather than less." The Frenchman received the same reply from Moore and on October 10, 1903, probably heard similar words from the ultimate authority, Roosevelt. As the President later remarked, Bunau-Varilla "would have been a very dull man had he been unable to make such a guess."[2] The Frenchman was many things, including devious, scheming, ambitious, and money-hungry, but he was certainly not dull.

And if he had been, Bunau-Varilla needed no more hints after a candid talk with Hay in the privacy of the latter's home. "I expressed my sentiments on the subject some days ago to President Roosevelt," the Frenchman began, "the whole thing will end in a revolution. You must take your measures. . . . " Hay played the game perfectly: "Yes, that is unfortunately the most probable hypothesis. But we shall not be caught napping. Orders have been given to naval forces on the Pacific to sail towards the Isth-

1. Stanford University Libraries, *Francis Butler Loomis and the Panama Crisis* (Stanford, 1965), p. 6.

2. *Ibid.*, p. 7; an account of the Roosevelt conversation is in Philippe Bunau-Varilla, *Panama: The Creation, Destruction, and Resurrection* (London, 1913), pp. 311–312.

mus." As Bunau-Varilla later editorialized, "It only remained for me to act."[3]

He first contacted the head of the revolutionary junta, Dr. Manuel Amador Guerrero, a physician closely associated with the Panama Railroad, now owned by the New Panama Canal Company. Amador happened to be in New York City to obtain money and support for the plot. Bunau-Varilla contacted Amador none too soon, for the Panamanian had just discovered that Cromwell, the New Panama Canal Company's lawyer, was growing fearful that the revolution would abort and his company's concessions seized by a vengeful Colombia. The story of Cromwell getting cold feet has been embroidered by Bunau-Varilla and so is highly suspect; in his memoirs the Frenchman, with spectacular condescension and malice, always calls him "the lawyer Cromwell." Much of the malice doubtlessly resulted from Bunau-Varilla's fear that Cromwell would someday receive as many lines in history texts as he. But it does seem that his report to Amador of the TR and Hay conversations revived sagging Panamanian hopes.

Plans again moved forward on the Isthmus. The revolutionaries comprised an odd but not illogical assortment, for a number of them had one association in common. Other than Amador (the Panama Railroad's physician), the group included José Agustín Arango (the railway's attorney), James R. Shaler (superintendent of the railway), and James R. Beers (the railway's freight agent). It might have been Beers who first assured Arango that a Panamanian revolt would be supported by the United States. Amador and Arango were joined by the oligarchy's leaders: C. C. Arosemena, Ricardo Arias, Federico Boyd, and Tomás Arias. Once free of Colombian control—once they could develop their already extensive economic and political power according to their own interests and without concern for Bogotá—these oligarchs, their sons, and grandsons dominated Panama for sixty years. The motives varied, but for good reasons the railway offi-

3. Bunau-Varilla, *Panama*, pp. 317–319.

cials and the Panamanian nationalists remained closely allied. As Roosevelt understood, "You don't have to foment a revolution. All you have to do is take your foot off and one will occur."[4]

As the zero hour approached, however, TR displayed more optimism than did people in Panama. In early October the commander of the *U.S.S. Nashville* visited Colon, then reported to Washington that although three-quarters of the people would support a leader who would build a canal, "such a leader is now lacking, and it isn't believed that in the near future these people will take any initiative steps."[5] The junta was preparing to provide the leadership, but the timing would be crucial. Closely following ship movements in the newspapers, Bunau-Varilla learned on October 30 that the *Nashville* was leaving Jamaica for an unspecified port. He correctly guessed it was heading for Colon and would arrive in two or three days. Given the intimacy between the Frenchman and Loomis, this was perhaps a mere deduction, not a lucky guess. Bunau-Varilla wired this news to Amador, who had returned to the Isthmus to lead the revolt. Both men now believed the United States was moving into a position to support their revolution. Loomis, however, jumped the gun and the result was nearly farce. "Uprising on the Isthmus reported," the Assistant Secretary anxiously cabled the United States Consul in Panama on November 3. "Keep department promptly and fully informed." Maintaining his composure, the Consul replied, "No uprising yet. Reported will be in the night. Situation critical."

Late that day the Panamanians struck, quickly seizing control of the Isthmus. The governor appointed by Colombia to rule the province, José Domingo de Obaldía, had

---

4. Charles D. Ameringer, "Philippe Bunau-Varilla: New Light on the Panama Canal Treaty," *Hispanic American Historical Review*, XLIV (February 1966), 30–32; Liss, *The Canal,* p. 19; Miles P. DuVal, Jr., *Cadiz to Cathay* (Stanford, 1940), pp. 273–276.

5. Richard D. Challener, *Admirals, Generals, and American Foreign Policy, 1898–1914* (Princeton, 1973), pp. 154–155.

long been sympathetic to Panamanian autonomy and gladly joined the revolutionaries. For his understanding he became one of Panama's first Vice-Presidents. Colombian army detachments were apparently bought off by Cromwell and the New Panama Canal Company; the commander received $30,000, other officers $10,000, and rank-and-file $50 each in gold.[6]

Commander Hubbard aboard the *Nashville* received no orders regarding the uprising until late on November 2. Roosevelt and Loomis apparently did not trust the navy with their plans. Thus when 2500 Colombian soldiers appeared off Colon on November 2 to prevent the rumored revolution, a confused Hubbard allowed them to land. Shaler, the superintendent of the railway, saved the situation. He first moved his cars to the Pacific side of the Isthmus, 48 miles from Colon, so the Colombians could not use the railway. Then he talked the Colombian officers into traveling to Panama City, assuring them that their troops would soon follow. In reality, the soldiers next saw their commanders when all were packed aboard ships for the return trip to Bogotá.[7] The next day U.S. sailors finally landed to ensure that the Colombian troops behaved. An independent Panama had already been proclaimed by Amador. A new nation the size of South Carolina was born, and the labor pains had been easy. None of the belligerents was killed. The only deaths were a Chinese citizen who had gotten trapped in some desultory shelling, a dog, and, according to some reports, a donkey.

The Rewards of Revolution

Roosevelt justified his aid to the revolutionaries by citing the 1846 commitment, a justification that had no

6. William Henry Harbaugh, *Power and Responsibility: The Life and Times of Theodore Roosevelt* (New York, 1961), pp. 208–209.

7. Ameringer, "Philippe Bunau-Varilla," pp. 33–34; Ernesto J. Castillero Reyes, *Episodios de la Independencia de Panama* (Panama, 1957), pp. 102–105, 110–118.

legal or historical basis. The treaty certainly did not give
the United States the right to use force against Colombia,
with whom the pact had been made, in order to build a
canal. Nor did it require Colombia to allow a canal to be
constructed. The treaty indeed justified United States
intervention in order to preserve Colombia's sovereignty
on the Isthmus. TR intervened, however, to destroy that
sovereignty.

But Roosevelt clung to the 1846 pact since he had
little else. He was consequently interested when Oscar
Straus, a New York lawyer and adviser of the President,
suggested the 1846 treaty required the United States to intervene because it was not made merely with Colombia, but
was "a covenant running with the land"—regardless of
who happened to control the land. With delight, and doubtless a sense of relief, Roosevelt immediately ordered Hay to
use this argument. The United States held to this interpretation even though John Bassett Moore (certainly the State
Department's most distinguished lawyer) exploded Straus's
sophistry and suggested that in TR's hands it actually
amounted to a "covenant running (away!) with the land!!"[8]

The President later argued that the seizure had been
for the sake of "civilization," thereby adopting the proposition that since North American actions were justified morally they were justified legally. His Attorney-General, Phi-
lander C. Knox, offered the appropriate reply: "Oh, Mr.
President, do not let so great an achievement suffer from
any taint of legality."[9] Knox's caustic advice was better
than he knew, for soon Roosevelt began a campaign, backed
by force, to compel Latin American governments to uphold
their own legal obligations as he defined those obligations.

In one sense, TR acted quite uncharacteristically: he

8. Quoted in David S. Patterson, *Toward a Warless World: The Travail of
the American Peace Movement, 1887–1914* (Bloomington, Ind. 1976), pp.
124–125.
9. The best discussion is Munro, *Intervention and Dollar Diplomacy*, pp.
57–58; and Albert K. Weinberg, *Manifest Destiny* (Baltimore, 1935), pp.
155–156.

aided a revolution. For a man whose central political tenet was stability, and for a nation that had fought revolutionaries and secessionists at least since 1861, unleashing revolution marked an abrupt change. It was also a short-lived change. Roosevelt possessed his canal territory and recognized the new Panamanian government led by Amador, Pablo Arosemena, and Obaldía on November 6. But when the Panamanian army attempted to land at Colon to claim the city, TR stopped it.[10] A little revolution was sufficient. Washington needed time to sort things out. The Panamanian government would have to wait a while before its army could enter the country's second largest city. In the first moments after recognition, Panama and the United States were at loggerheads.

Nor did Roosevelt try to reconcile the Colombians. On November 6 he told them he had intervened because "treaty obligations" and the "interest of civilization" required that the Isthmus not endure "a constant succession of . . . wasteful civil wars." TR urged Bogotá to recognize the new government. Colombia responded by sending to Washington its most distinguished citizen and former president, General Rafael Reyes, in an attempt to revive the Hay-Herrán treaty—the same pact which the Colombian Senate unanimously rejected several months before. Reyes was now prepared to lower the price. The welcome in Washington was cool. Hay advised Roosevelt that "the sooner you see him, the sooner we can bid him good-bye." But Reyes was a forceful, popular figure, and hired one of the most adept lobbyists in Washington to fight against a treaty with an independent Panama. Hay wrote TR, "I told [Secretary of War Elihu] Root I was going to see Reyes. He replied, 'Better look out. Ex-Reyes are dangerous.' Do you think that, on my salary, I can afford to bear such things?" Hay need not have worried. As Roosevelt later noted, he viewed Colombians as similar to "a group of Sicilian or Calabrian bandits. . . . You could no more make an agree-

10. Liss, *The Canal*, pp. 18–19.

ment with the Colombian rulers than you could nail currant jelly to a wall."[11]

TR and Hay focused on arranging the canal treaty with the Panamanians, or, more precisely, the Frenchman who had taken the opportunity to represent Panama. Bunau-Varilla engaged in a mini-power struggle with Arango, Tomás Arias, and Federico Boyd for control over negotiations in Washington. Since the three Panamanians were not yet in the United States, and because Bunau-Varilla convinced them he knew the political situation and financial channels, the Frenchman was empowered to initiate talks with Hay. Amador and Boyd left Panama on November 10 to join Bunau-Varilla.

The new government meanwhile instructed the Frenchman that the negotiations were to be guided by three principles. First, no deals could be made that affected "the sovereignty of Panama, which [was] free, independent, and sovereign." Second, the United States should pledge to uphold the new nation's "sovereignty, territorial integrity, and public order." That clause would place North American troops, if necessary, between Panama and a vengeful Colombia. Third, a canal treaty would be drafted, but only after consultation with Amador and Boyd. "You will proceed in everything strictly in agreement with them," the Frenchman was told.[12]

The instructions did not reach Bunau-Varilla in time, nor did Amador and Boyd. The minister made certain of that. On Friday the 13th of November he began talks with Roosevelt and Hay. Bunau-Varilla emphasized that time was all-important. If the treaty was not rushed to completion, he argued, a number of events would occur, all of them bad: a restless United States Senate, under Morgan's lashing, might turn back to Nicaragua; Colombia

11. Thayer, *Hay*, II, 319–327.
12. This and the following discussion of the negotiations rely upon unpublished State Department documents and the excellent discussions in Ameringer, "Philippe Bunau-Varilla," especially pages 36–44; and Munro, *Intervention and Dollar Diplomacy*, pp. 45–47.

might seduce Panama back into the fold (the suave Reyes was on his way to Panama City); and isthmian politics might turn chaotic, forcing delays in the talks. Implicitly, but obviously, Bunau-Varilla also wanted to pocket the $40 million for his New Panama Canal Company as quickly as possible. Nor would he mind going down in history as the lone negotiator on the Panamanian side who signed the epochal pact.

Heartily sharing the Frenchman's mistrust of the Senate, Hay quickly prepared a treaty draft. It was largely the Hay-Herrán agreement that Colombia had rejected. The draft explicitly recognized Panamanian sovereignty in a canal zone, and even went further than the Hay-Herrán agreement by increasing Panama's judicial authority in a zone. Panamanian troops would protect the canal, and United States forces would be used in the area only with Panama's consent. The proposed treaty would run 99 years, or until about 2002.

Then, in what proved to be one of the most momentous twenty-four-hour periods in American diplomatic history, Bunau-Varilla worked all night and all day on November 16 to rewrite Hay's paper. The minister was afraid that the draft would not sufficiently appease the Senate, at least not enough to have the body act quickly on the treaty. Bunau-Varilla also wanted to complete the treaty before Amador and Boyd arrived. They were in New York City, but Cromwell, for purposes of his own, had detained them. On November 17, Bunau-Varilla told the two Panamanians to remain in New York for another day, then rushed to the State Department to consummate the deal.

Hay could hardly believe his eyes. Bunau-Varilla's treaty ensured the canal's neutrality, proposed payment to Panama of an amount equal to that which the United States would have paid Colombia, and guaranteed Washington's protection of Panama's independence. The United States was to assume a virtual protectorate over the new country. But in return, the treaty gave the United States extensive powers in the Canal Zone, for Washington would have "all the rights, power, and authority within the zone . . . which the United States would possess and exercise if it were the sovereign of the territory within which said lands and waters are located to the entire exclusion of the exercise by the Republic of Panama of any such sovereign rights, power, and authority."

That was the most radical change, a change that has caused continual crises in U.S.-Panamanian relations for the next three-quarters of a century. But there was more. Bunau-Varilla surrendered Panamanian judicial power in the Zone, widened the zone area from ten kilometers (or six miles) to ten miles, and lengthened Hay's 99-year lease to "perpetuity." The astonished Secretary of State made only one change (the United States "leases in perpetuity" phrase was transformed into the more direct wording that Panama "grants to the United States in perpetuity the use, occupation, and control" of a canal zone). At 6:40 p.m. on November 18, the treaty was signed by the two men. Amador and Boyd arrived in Washington three hours later. Bunau-Varilla met them at Union Station, showed them the pact, and Amador nearly fainted on the train platform.

The Panamanian goverment angrily protested "the manifest renunciation of sovereignty" in the treaty. That protest echoed down through the years, becoming ever more magnified. If the new government rejected the pact, however, it faced bitter alternatives: the United States might seize the canal area without either paying for it or undertaking to protect the new republic, or Roosevelt might build in Nicaragua and leave the Panama City revolutionaries to the tender mercies of the Colombian army. In truth, the Panamanians had no choice.

They had leaped across an abyss to gain their independence, were hanging on the other side by their fingertips, and the United States held the rescue rope. Having helped put them in that position, Bunau-Varilla dictated the terms under which they could be pulled up to safety. Hay and Bunau-Varilla were too powerful and sophisticated to allow Panama to claim it accepted the treaty under duress, a claim that if declared legally valid could void the acceptance. Panama, however, did accept under duress. Having a French citizen disobey the Panamanian government's instructions, and then having no choice but to accept the Frenchman's treaty, compounded the humiliation. In the 1970s a documentary film made in Panama about the 1903 affair was entitled, "The Treaty that No Panamanian Signed."

The Debate in the United States

For the revolutionaries humiliation was nevertheless preferable to hanging. Throughout the negotiations Bunau-Varilla had kept them informed of rising indignation in the United States over his and Roosevelt's management of the affair. The President soon had another revolt on his hands; this one was in the Senate and the country at large.

It was not a massive revolt, but a surprising number of Senators and important newspapers condemned TR's action. The division was partially along party lines. William Randolph Hearst's Democratic papers attacked the President's action as "nefarious." Hearst's Chicago *American* called it "a rough-riding assault upon another republic over the shattered wreckage of international law and diplomatic usage." Such widely circulated urban dailies as the *New York Times*, New York *Evening Post*, Philadelphia *Record*, Memphis *Commercial Appeal*, and *Springfield Republican* agreed with Hearst's assessment.

In the Senate the powerful Maryland Democrat, Arthur Pue Gorman, organized opposition to the treaty. That Gorman was an avowed candidate for the 1904 presidential run against Roosevelt made his opposition doubly significant. Holding 33 of the 90 Senate seats, the Democrats could theoretically prevent the necessary two-thirds of the Senate from ratifying the pact. And with Senator Morgan holding out for the Nicaraguan route, Gorman's chances for success seemed reasonable. Even the newspapers and pub-

lic spokesmen who supported TR refused to justify his action on moral grounds. Instead, as *Public Opinion* noted,
since the majority of the country wanted "an isthmian canal above all things," it was willing to overlook moral
issues in order to justify taking the canal as strictly "a business question."[13]

Roosevelt refused to take that approach. As have
most rulers who aggressively used naked force, he wanted
it masked with morality. In an outspoken special message
to the Senate on January 4, 1904, the President submitted
the treaty and justified his actions in November on the
grounds of the 1846 pact, "our national interests and safety," and the usual Rooseveltian claim of "the interests of
collective civilization." He suffered no doubts that the
United States had "received a mandate from civilization" to
build a canal, although he could not tell exactly how that
mandate had been expressed. One problem, of course, was
that "the interests of collective civilization" had never been
seen or defined (was Colombia, for example, a part of "collective civilization"?). Like many Rooseveltian phrases, the
term better fit the President's prejudices than any international legal or moral standard.

Yet TR won and Gorman lost. The prospects of a
United States-controlled canal caused flutters of patriotism
in too many hearts and the prospect of rich satisfaction in
too many pocketbooks. In the Senate the Democrats split,
with many southerners, who had long sought the project,
joining the President. Led by the prestigious Atlanta *Constitution*, southern papers crossed party lines formed during the Civil War in order to back the treaty. Even Gorman
admitted he wanted a canal constructed; he simply disliked Roosevelt's methods. Some skeptics were won over
by the President's message. Noting that he had denied any
wrong-doing, the Detroit *Free Press* believed that the word
of a United States President "is as good as anybody else's
word." The *New York Times*, the New York *Evening Post*,

13. *Public Opinion*, XXV (Nov. 19, 1903), 643.

and the *Washington Post,* however, never surrendered, and the Chicago *Chronicle* (a Democratic paper) summarized their feelings by calling Roosevelt's appeal to "civilization" a "pitiful and alarming chapter in American government," a "tyrant's plea of necessity." The opponents were equally bitter over the South's defection to the President's side. As the *New York Times* editorialized, "This is the southern spirit of the slavery days," for like slavery, the canal to the South is "purely a question of profit in dollars and cents."[14]

As Roosevelt and the Senate Republican leadership intensified the pressure, Gorman admitted his effort had "ended in smash." On February 23, 1904, he watched sixteen, or nearly half the Senate Democrats, join the Republicans to sweep the treaty through 66–14. Opposition came almost entirely from the Northeast, the Middle States, and pockets of the South. The Midwest, West, and much of the South supported the President. Gorman's presidential hopes sunk with his effort to stop the treaty.[15] Running eight months later against the colorless Democrat, Alton B. Parker, Roosevelt understood how the opposition had been silenced. "Can you not tell our speakers to dwell more on the Panama Canal?" he wrote a campaign manager. "We have not a stronger card."[16]

After early 1904, politicians who opposed United States control of the canal were committing political suicide. Bunau-Varilla had triumphed. Although, as the *Pittsburgh Post* remarked, TR's methods in Panama "were subversive of the best principles of the republic,"[17] the Frenchman had made the treaty so attractive that the United States, as he hoped, quickly chose power over principle.

---

14. *Ibid.,* XXVI (Jan. 7, 1904), p. 6.
15. John R. Lambert, *Arthur Pue Gorman* (Baton Rouge, 1953). pp. 297–308.
16. Roosevelt to Senator Nathan Ray Scott, Oct. 9, 1904, in Morison, ed., *Letters of Theodore Roosevelt,* IV, 978.
17. *Public Opinion,* XXXVI (March 3, 1904), 260–261.

"Titular Sovereignty": What Did the Treaty Mean?

The Senate ratification marked a beginning, not the end, of the struggle over the treaty. With Article I placing them under Washington's protection ("The United States guarantees and will maintain the independence of the Republic of Panama"), the Panamanians immediately began protesting the mushrooming North American control over their country. A first clash occurred in early 1904 when the State Department insisted that Panama must acknowledge in its new constitution (and not merely in the treaty), the United States right of intervention. William Buchanan, the U.S. Minister, wanted the widest possible power to control "pests" through Panama, and brought great pressure to bear on the Panamanian constitutional convention.[18] Finally, Article 136 gave the United States the right to "intervene, in any part of Panama, to reestablish public peace and constitutional order." The North Americans could apparently unilaterally determine when public peace and order were jeopardized. But this Article squeaked through the convention 17–14; leading Panamanians were already trying to contain United States influence. As Buchanan told Hay, "The fact that fourteen . . . voted against it," together with the appearance on the streets of handbills and newspapers condemning Article 136, "amply justified the wisdom of our having secured" it.[19]

Article III of the treaty, however, has most disrupted relations. It gave the United States the rights, powers, and authority in the zone "as if it were the sovereign of the territory." From the outset Panama argued that it remained the actual sovereign in the area. Bunau-Varilla agreed, perhaps out of conscience. "The United States, without becoming the sovereign, received the exclusive use of the rights of

18. Buchanan to Hay, Jan. 4 and 5, 1904, Dispatches, Panama, NA, RG 59.
19. Buchanan to Hay, Jan. 28, 1904, Dispatches, NA, RG 59.

sovereignty," the Frenchman wrote, "while respecting the sovereignty itself of the Panama Republic."[20]

Such an arrangement was not unprecedented in 1903, although from the United States point of view the precedents were not happy. When Germany, France, and Russia forcibly took territory from an enfeebled China during the late 1890s, the treaties stipulated (to quote the words of the German-Chinese pact), that "in order to avoid the possibility of conflicts, the Imperial Chinese Government will abstain from exercising rights of sovereignty in the ceded territory during the term of the lease, and leaves the exercise of the same to Germany."[21] The precedent was not a happy one, for Washington had vigorously opposed those treaties.

Yet the United States wanted to compromise none of the vast powers Bunau-Varilla wrote into Article III. Attempting to placate the Panamanians while retaining all the power, in 1904 John Hay coined the phrase "titular sovereignty" to describe Panama's rights in a canal zone.[22] The phrase became a widely used and condescending description of Panama's sovereignty in the zone, but on October 18, 1904, Roosevelt recognized the limitations of United States rights in the canal area when he instructed Secretary of War William Howard Taft:

> We have not the slightest intention of establishing an independent colony in the middle of the State of Panama, or exercising any greater governmental functions than are necessary to enable us conveniently and safely to construct, maintain and operate the canal, under the rights given us by the treaty. Least of all do we desire to interfere with the business and prosperity of the people of Panama. . . . In asserting the equivalent of sovereignty over the

20. Quoted in Helen C. Low, "Panama Canal Treaty in Perspective," Overseas Development Council Monograph Series, #29 (1976).
21. Lyman M. Tondel, Jr., ed., *The Panama Canal: Background Papers and Proceedings of the Sixth Hammarskjold Forum* (Dobbs Ferry, N.Y., 1965), p. 12.
22. *Ibid.*, p. 13.

canal strip, it is our full intention that the rights which we exercise shall be exercised with all proper care for the honor and interests of the people of Panama.[23]

Roosevelt's term, "the equivalent of sovereignty," and the limitations placed upon United States power before and after the phrase, indicated that the President interpreted his nation's rights in the Canal Zone to be short of sovereignty itself.

After looking into the matter in Panama, Taft, who possessed a notable judicial mind, thought the issue inconsequential. His report to Roosevelt of December 19, 1904, became the standard view of the question:

> The truth is that while we have all the attributes of sovereignty necessary in the construction, maintenance and protection of the Canal, the very form in which these attributes are conferred in the Treaty seems to preserve the titular sovereignty over the Canal Zone in the Republic of Panama, and as we have conceded to us complete judicial and police power and control of two ports at the end of the Canal, I can see no reason for creating a resentment on the part of the people of the Isthmus by quarreling over that which is dear to them, but which to us is of no real moment whatever.[24]

Taft thus admitted the United States did not have full sovereignty over the new Canal Zone. It had "complete judicial and police power and control" at the vital points, but the "titular sovereignty" or residual sovereignty resided with the Panamanians. Some North Americans who insisted on total control over the Zone during the 1960s and 1970s argued that their country was "sovereign" in the Zone. They were wrong, if Hay, Roosevelt, and Taft, the three Washington officials who constructed the Panamanian-

23. Instructions to Taft, Oct. 18, 1904, Morison, ed., *Letters of Theodore Roosevelt*, IV, 986.
24. Quoted, with good commentary, by Ralph E. Minger, "Panama, the Canal Zone, and Titular Sovereignty," *Western Political Quarterly*, XIV (June 1961), 544–554.

United States relations, are to be believed. From the start the question was not whether Panama had residual sovereign rights in the Zone, for it did, but what would happen in the distant future if the Panamanians tried to exert those rights against the full control exercised by the United States.

The North Americans, of course, never had sovereignty over the Canal Zone as they do over Alaska or Texas. They must pay an annual fee to Panama for the use of the Zone, and children born of non-North American parents in the Canal Zone are not automatically United States citizens as they are if born in Texas or Alaska.[25] The $10 million paid to Panama in 1903 was for treaty rights, not the purchase of territory as in the Louisiana acquisition of 1803 or the Alaskan purchase of 1867.

The clash over sovereignty initially occurred because the United States acted as if it were sovereign throughout parts of Panama *outside* the Canal Zone. Article II of the treaty gave the United States the right "in perpetuity" to occupy and control any lands outside the Zone which it thought necessary for building or maintaining the canal. Related provisions of the treaty were breath-taking in their sweep of power granted Washington. Article IV gave the United States "in perpetuity" the right "to use rivers, streams, lakes, and other bodies of water" for any purpose relating to the canal. Article V granted the United States a "monopoly" over "any [sic] system of communication" in Panama. Article VII provided the power to take by right of eminent domain needed lands, buildings, or water rights in Panama City and Colon, and to intervene in those cities, if necessary, to preserve public order. The same article granted the United States the authority to create and enforce sanitary regulations in the two cities, a power which actually gave Washington the dominant voice in their political and financial affairs. Article XII surrendered to the Canal Company control over Panama's immigration.

25. *Wall Street Journal,* April 29, 1976, p. 14:5.

These provisions made Panama a potential colony of the United States. Article II—giving Washington officials the right "in perpetuity" to occupy and control any lands outside the Zone which, in their own opinion, they needed—was a virtual blank check. The cost of the lands would be determined by a joint U.S.-Panamanian commission, but under no circumstances could it delay canal construction while deliberating. The North Americans seized large chunks of Panamanian territory. Numerous requests for additional land were made between 1908 and 1930. Fourteen military bases were ultimately established, ostensibly to protect the Canal although some were for purposes outside Panama; several of the bases occupied land outside the Zone. Panamanian protests grew with the development of the military complex, particularly when United States-owned land later prevented orderly growth of Panama City and Colon.

Panama officials also objected to the $10 million fee and the $250,000 annual annuity. They noted that in contrast with their $10 million, the redoubtable Bunau-Varilla and his company received $40 million, and they further observed in the 1920s that the United States apologetically paid Colombia $25 million (although, admittedly, Congress found the courage to pacify the Colombians only after Roosevelt died). The $250,000 annuity merely equaled the amount Washington paid Colombia for the railroad rights alone before 1903. Panamanians interpreted each North American demand for additional land as fresh evidence they were being cheated.

As the Twig is Bent

In May 1904 Roosevelt created an Isthmian Canal Commission to build the canal. The Commission was placed under the supervision of Secretary of War Taft. Within three months, the military members of the Commission clashed with the State Department representatives in Panama. In Panama the questions of sovereignty and the right of United States intervention coalesced to create the first major crisis between the two countries. The events of 1904 were not only a portent. They left an indelible mark on Panamanian political life.

The initial controversy involved policy-making within the Washington bureaucracy. The State Department has continually battled with the War Department (after 1947, the Department of Defense), and the military officers who operated and defended the Canal Zone. A first clash occurred in 1904 when the Panamanian government strongly protested the United States use of its ports as if they belonged to the North Americans. U.S. Minister John Barrett attempted to dampen the dispute and believed he was making progress until Admiral J. G. Walker of the Isthmian Canal Commission arrived in Panama. When the Panamanian Foreign Minister invited both Walker and Barrett to discuss the port problem, Walker bluntly told Barrett not to come along. As did later military officials, the Admiral viewed Panama more as a North American base than a sovereign country. He wished to handle the talks alone. He did, and despite the Minister's warnings, Walker insisted in undiplomatic language that Panama totally yield on the port issue. The Foreign Minister was enraged. Forced to clean up after Walker's indiscretions, Barrett then started again from scratch to settle the issue.[26]

He made little headway, especially after the problem was complicated by a host of disputes. In August 1904 Panama protested that within the Canal Zone United States post offices accepted mail at rates lower than those in Panama. In Colon and Panama City, moreover, the North Americans were collecting unfair tariff rates on goods coming into the Zone from Panama itself. Businessmen from the United States escaped payment of tariffs by setting up shops in the Zone, then underselling Panamanian merchants. Hay initially wanted to claim the United States could do whatever it pleased. Roosevelt, however, took the longer view. He instructed Secretary of War Taft to work

26. Barrett to Hay. Aug. 16. 1904. Dispatches. Panama. NA. RG 59.

out the problems in Panama. Before Taft could board ship
for the Isthmus, the Panamanian situation suddenly approached a flash point.

Soon after independence, the nation's politics divided into two parties, the Conservatives, led by Amador
who controlled the government, and the Liberals, a group
convinced that it represented a majority of the country. In
certain respects that conviction was probably true. The
Conservatives included the white minority of Panama, but
the Liberals were closer to the mulattoes and mestizos who
comprised most of the population. Elections were due in
late 1904, but neither party was experienced in the compro-
mises and delicacies of democratic politics. The Liberals
hoped to overcome such shortcomings by working with
General Esteban Huertas. The aged general was a national
hero; during the revolution he and his troops had joined
the junta rather than remain loyal to Colombia. The Liberals
considered putting him into power through a *coup* if necessary. Huertas needed little convincing. He was highly susceptible to flattery, alcoholic beverages, and money. As the
moment of the rumored *coup* arrived in November, the
frightened Amador locked himself in his house. United
States officials then took matters into their own hands.

When they talked with Amador he called his own
army a "Frankenstein," and declared that only the North
Americans could control it. The officials told the State Department that the "Panama Army of about 250 men is a
continual menace to the peace of the Republic. It will always be a handy tool to be used by either party and a
continual source of unrest until it is paid off and disbanded. Among the 250 soldiers there are from 20 to 30
small boys, many of whom are not more than eleven years
old." The "more substantial element" was scared of such
an irresponsible and unpredictable force.[27] Several weeks
later the Legation added, "It would be far better for Panama
if the army could be disbanded and four or five good brass

27. Lee to Hay, Nov. 1, 1904, Dispatches, Panama, NA, RG 59.

bands established in this city so that there might be plenty of music every day. This would amuse, interest and occupy the minds of the people and also save much money for the Panama Treasury."[28]

Several days before Taft was due to arrive, Minister Barrett and the Canal Zone Governor, George W. David, decided to short-circuit Huerta's presidential aspirations. They demanded that he resign from the army and the force be disbanded. Barrett later gave a fascinating account of how he single-handedly dismissed the Panamanian army. A later Panamanian historian claimed that Tomás Arias played an important role in subduing the army. Perhaps, but Barrett's dispatch nevertheless illustrated the colonial control which the North Americans were beginning to exercise over Panama:

> It was finally arranged that the soldiers were to report at the Government house at one o'clock Saturday, to be paid off upon the terms of the Government. By two o'clock, they had not put in an appearance and President Amador sent for me to know what was the best thing to do. He was afraid the army might have decided to resist his terms. Upon my arrival at Government house I advised the President to wait half an hour more. . . .
>
> Just before the half hour expired the first detachment of some fifty soldiers came marching, unarmed, to the Government house, followed by a great crowd. When they halted, they sent up word to the President, evidently not knowing that I was there, to the effect that they would not accept the Government's terms of two payments [of cash for their dismissal], but they demanded the whole pay at that moment. The President was naturally much disturbed at this ultimatum, and asked me what he should do. I immediately told him to be absolutely firm and yield in no way to their demands, emphasizing that they had already been guilty of gross insubordination and that, if they were soldiers in the United States, they would be shot or court-marshalled [sic], and that it was no time now for temporiz-

28. Lee to Hay, Nov. 14, 1904, Dispatches, Panama, NA, RG 59.

ing. This word was sent to them but they still persisted in their position and muttered threats against the President.

When this word came up from the street, I saw that there must be no further delay in bringing matters to an end, and taking General Guardia, the Minister of Foreign Affairs and War, with me, I went down stairs and out upon the sidewalk in front of the soldiers who were there assembled. In brief words I told General Guardia to say to them that the United States, with its forces, stood back of the Government in this crisis, and that they must accept the terms of the Government, or accept the consequences. They were warned that if they did not accept these terms, and engaged in any acts of insurrection, riot, or mutiny, they would be dealt with in a most summary way, and that if necessary, the Naval forces in the Bay, and the marines at Ancon and Empire [in the Canal Zone] would be used to maintain order, with the severest punishment for those who were responsible for disorder. This warning had the desired effect and the soldiers immediately declared that they would accept the terms of the Government. . . .

The business community, and the Government, are most grateful for the attitude and action of the Legation during this crisis.[29]

Panamanian arms and ammunition were placed in the Canal Zone under U.S. control. For the next quarter-century, the country depended on a 700- to 1000-member police force and the United States military for its internal security.

Taft approved this action when he landed. His decision was hardly surprising. He earlier wrote his brother that since the 1903 treaty "permits us to prevent revolutions," he would "advise them that we'll have no more." Panama, after all, was only "a kind of Opera Bouffe republic and nation." Since "we have four hundred marines and a fleet on one side and three naval vessels on the other," the Secretary of War thought matters could be arranged satisfactorily.

29. Barrett to Hay, Nov. 22, 1904, Dispatches, Panama, NA, RG 59; Arias's role is described in Ernesto J. Castillero Reyes, *Historia de Panama* (Panama, 1955), p. 162. The issue of "colonial control" is defined and discussed in chapter III below.

For Taft the top priority was tranquility so canal construction would not be interrupted. The Conservative was therefore the preferred party, he told Roosevelt, for it included the propertied white families which had a stake in maintaining order. The Liberals, on the other hand, depended on blacks and mixed races who were "much less worthy" than the Conservatives. If the Liberals grasped power, a "large Negro influence" would appear, and since Taft believed Panamanian blacks less intelligent than North American blacks, the Isthmus could become a festering, unsettled trouble spot similar to Haiti.[30]

With the military and political situations in hand, the Secretary of War turned to tariff and postal disputes. Refusing to wilt in the damp Panamanian heat, the three-hundred-pound Taft energetically worked out a compromise that limited the Zone's imports to items needed only for the Canal or Canal employees. He quickly settled the postal problem to Panama's satisfaction while keeping the post offices in the Zone under United States direction. The series of agreements between Taft and the Panamanians became law in December 1904 when Roosevelt issued Executive orders and Panama announced decrees to put them into effect.[31]

Taft's mission was a landmark. By maintaining the Zone's right to a wide range of economic privileges, including selling goods to Panamanians working in the Zone, Taft only scotched, not ended, the complaints of Panamanian merchants outside the Zone. Those complaints later led to important modifications of the 1903 treaty. In stopping the ridiculous Huerta, the United States crippled the opposition political party, destroyed the Panamanian army, and made the government reliant upon Washington for protec-

30. The notes to Taft's brother and to Roosevelt are quoted in Minger, "Panama, the Canal Zone, and Titular Sovereignty," pp. 546–547, 550–554.
31. The text of the agreements, as well as the texts of other major reports and treaties of the 1826 to 1954 years, can be found in Diogenes A. Arosemena, *Documentary Diplomatic History of the Panama Canal* (Panama, 1961), pp. 303–316.

tion against external enemies. More important, the United States assumed responsibility for protecting the government against internal enemies. If, for example, the Conservatives urgently asked for help, Washington had some obligation to respond—that is, to maintain the oligarchy in power.

In a country possessing little experience in democratic politics, but of which democratic procedures were somehow expected, the United States placed an elite white oligarchy firmly in control. Washington officials helped create the conditions for an economically bipolarized, undemocratic, and potentially unstable country. When Panama later appeared as bipolarized, undemocratic, and unstable, North Americans could not understand why.

"Police the Surrounding Premises"

The implications of Bunau-Varilla's treaty were outrunning even Roosevelt's fertile imagination. It should be stressed, however, that the implications made a greater impact on Panama than on United States policy. Roosevelt was extremely active in the Caribbean region during these years, but his activity was not due solely to the newly acquired canal area. TR's policy was the logical continuation of a century-long North American involvement that was turning Washington into a self-appointed policeman in the Caribbean.

Since the eighteenth century the United States had been driving southward, first to conquer a continent, then, after the Civil War, to seize economic and strategic prizes. Its financial power increasingly penetrated the Caribbean area after the 1870s. Victory in the War of 1898 brought Puerto Rico and the Cuban naval base of Guantanamo. The Caribbean was becoming a North American lake, and obtaining the Canal Zone marked one more step in that direction.

Within a year after construction of the Canal began, however, Roosevelt announced a new policy, the so-called Roosevelt Corollary to the Monroe Doctrine. In his Annual

Messages to Congress in 1904 and 1905, the President hoped that Latin American nations would be happy and prosperous, but he believed they could not share such joys "unless they maintain order within their boundaries and behave with a just regard for their obligations towards outsiders." To help them, the United States would become the policeman throughout the area. (Roosevelt privately understood that the primary police work would be in the smaller Caribbean and Central American countries, not the large nations on the South American continent.) The policeman, TR proclaimed, would ensure that the countries met their "obligations," so the "outsiders" would have no excuse to intervene.[32] The "outsider" most feared in Washington was Germany, whose businessmen, diplomats, and naval officers seemed overly ambitious in the Western Hemisphere. Great Britain possessed a greater fleet, but it apparently had made its peace with North American expansion southward, most notably by agreeing to the second Hay-Pauncefote treaty.

The Roosevelt Corollary triggered the most ignoble chapter in United States-Latin American relations. Believing, as TR said, that "a civilized nation" such as the United States possessed the right to stop "chronic wrongdoing," North Americans sent troops into a half-dozen Caribbean nations during the next twelve years, and within two decades dominated at least fourteen of the twenty Latin American countries through either financial controls or military power—and, in some instances, through both.

Officials at the time argued that the Roosevelt Corollary was necessary to protect the new canal. As John Hay's successor in the State Department, Elihu Root, wrote a friend in 1905, "The inevitable effect of our building the Canal must be to require us to police the surrounding premises."[33] It became an early version of the domino theory: if

32. James Daniel Richardson, ed., *Messages and Papers of the Presidents* (New York, 1897–1914), XVI, 7375–7376.
33. Quoted in William Everett Kane, *Civil Strife in Latin America: A Legal History of U.S. Involvement* (Baltimore, 1972), pp. 66–67.

unfriendly, powerful Europeans settled in one part of the Caribbean, their influence could spread until the Canal would be endangered.

Root's explanation of the Roosevelt Corollary cannot withstand historical analysis. That the Canal increased United States interest in the Caribbean cannot be disputed. But the Corollary's principles were formed long before the Isthmus was seized—as early as the 1870s, 1880s, and 1890s, when such Washington officials as Ulysses S. Grant, "Jingo Jim" Blaine, and Richard Olney bluntly told Europeans that the Caribbean should be considered a North American lake. And the Corollary evolved quite independently of Canal Zone policy. To misunderstand this relationship is to misunderstand a most important chapter in United States-Latin American affairs.

TR's inspiration to act as a "civilized" policeman occurred before the Canal Zone was seized, and quite independently of events on the Isthmus. In 1900–1901, for example, the United States imposed on Cuba the Platt Amendment, giving Washington the right to intervene any time at its discretion to maintain order in the newly independent island. The provision established a precedent and a rationale for the later Corollary. In 1902–03 Germany and Great Britain intervened in Venezuela to collect overdue debts. An uproar resulted in the United States, and the British shrewdly suggested to Roosevelt that if he did not want the Europeans to protect their legal rights in the Western Hemisphere, he should do it for them. Grumbling that "These wretched republics cause me a great deal of trouble," TR believed a second foreign intervention "would simply not be tolerated here. I often think that a sort of protectorate over South and Central America is the only way out."[34]

34. Dexter Perkins, *Hands Off: A History of the Monroe Doctrine* (Boston, 1941, 1963), pp. 232–234. My interpretation of the Corollary is taken from Lloyd Gardner's work in Lloyd Gardner, Walter LaFeber, and Thomas McCormick, *Creation of the American Empire* (Chicago, 1976), chapter 14. For the long pre-1904 development of the Corollary, see the important essay by J. Fred Rippy, "Antecedents of the Roosevelt Corollary of the Monroe Doctrine," *The Pacific Historical Review*, IX (September 1940), 267–279.

His opportunity finally arose in Santo Domingo. For over five years New York City bankers had fought French and German financiers for control of the country's resources. By early 1904 Santo Domingo seemed to be moving toward a state of permanent revolutionary instability. Roosevelt ordered the navy to seize the country's customs houses, pay off the foreign debt, and under no circumstances allow any revolutionary activity to interrupt the country's development. He publicly rationalized the seizure by announcing the Roosevelt Corollary.

These affairs in Cuba, Venezuela, and Santo Domingo had little or nothing to do with the Isthmus. Taking the Canal Zone by no means led to the Roosevelt Corollary. Instead, Roosevelt's Panama policy can be interpreted as fitting into a larger Latin American policy that was evolving long before the Panamanian revolution. To confuse the Canal as the cause of the Corollary, therefore, is to confuse fundamental motivations of American foreign policy.

Two motives shaped Roosevelt's Corollary. First, he hated disorder, especially disorder that might lead to political bipolarization or an opportunity for European economic and/or political intervention. The Monroe Doctrine might act as a shield for Latin Americans against European imperialists, but Roosevelt would not allow the Doctrine "to be used as a warrant for letting any of these republics remain as small bandit nests of a wicked and inefficient type."[35] That premise of the Corollary was easily extended to Panama. Taft's intervention in 1904 (and again in 1908), rested in part on that premise, and both the President and his Secretary of War would have agreed with a leading naval strategist in Washington who argued that "so-called revolutions in the Caribbean are nothing less than struggles between different crews of bandits for the possession of the customs houses—and the loot."[36] A second motivation was

35. Roosevelt to Cecil Arthur Spring Rice, July 24, 1905, Morison, ed., Letters of Theodore Roosevelt, IV, 1286.
36. Quoted in Challener, Admirals, Generals, and American Foreign Policy, p. 20.

Roosevelt's belief that the United States had been entrusted with a "civilizing" mission which it should bear proudly. This belief seemed particularly applicable to the Caribbean, including Panama, where the people were largely a mixture of Indian, Spanish, and black. This motivation, of course, had its ironies. As sociologist William Graham Sumner observed at the time, "We talk of civilizing lower races, but we have never done it yet. We have exterminated them."[37]

If Taft and Roosevelt were so concerned about the Canal Zone's security (instead of their "civilizing mission" of imposing order on Latin America), they might have allowed the United States Navy to build a chain of bases in the isthmian area. They did not. After the Panamanian revolution, naval officials asked for three bases around the Zone, bases they had long sought from Colombia. Roosevelt rejected the request. When fortifications were planned for each end of the Canal, two military boards concluded that these, along with the Guantanamo base in Cuba, sufficiently protected the passageway. As President, Taft later upheld this decision and refused to spend $4 million on army barracks in Panama. If war began, he reasoned, troops could move to the Isthmus quickly enough from the United States. Taft thought the fortifications along the Canal primarily useful for stopping any unhinged Latin American dictator who might try to seize the waterway.[38]

Building the Panama Canal did not cause the announcement of the Roosevelt Corollary. TR instead used the Isthmus as one of several areas for the exercise of his police powers. The President's Panama policy was a symptom, not a cause, of his larger Caribbean plans. The evolution of United States policy in Panama can consequently be interpreted as another manifestation of his racial, economic, and military views. How such perceptions affected Panamanians and helped create their growing animosity toward

37. Quoted in David Healy, *U.S. Expansionism; the Imperialist Urge in the 1890s* (Madison, Wis. 1970), pp. 151–153, also 237–238.
38. Challener, *Admirals, Generals, and American Foreign Policy*, pp. 324–327.

North Americans should be considered separately, not
filtered through a supposed preoccupation on Roosevelt's
part to provide security for a canal.

The failure to understand the demands, dynamics,
and confusions of nationalism is hardly peculiar to TR, yet
historical circumstances made him President precisely at
the point when the European-dominated world system,
which he so admired, was disintegrating.[39] In 1904–05 Japan's dramatic victory over Russia surprised the white
races and encouraged non-whites, especially those who
lived in Asian and African colonial areas. The Chinese,
Turkish, and Russian revolutions formed roots in those
years. Roosevelt prided himself on his understanding of
historical change and his sensitivity to the nuances of a
global balance of power, but he never comprehended the
significance of these shattering events. TR was unable to
see that the world was comprised of more than simply the
"civilized" versus the "wicked and inefficient types."

After he intervened in Panama in 1903, Roosevelt pain-
stakingly explained his actions to the Cabinet, then demanded to know whether the explanation would silence his
opponents. "Have I defended myself?" he asked. "You certainly have," replied a brave Elihu Root. "You have shown
that you were accused of seduction and you have conclu-
sively proved that you were guilty of rape."[40] Roosevelt
never understood how his policies and explanations worsened the problems in the Caribbean area that he tried to stabilize. He, Taft, and Bunau-Varilla were making Panama as
well as the Canal Zone a virtual colony of the United States,
but the North American leaders refused to assume even the
responsibilities of enlightened colonialism, save that of using force or the threat of force to maintain order. That solution worsened, not ameliorated, Panama's problem and, consequently, Panamanian relations with the United States.

39. See the pioneering discussion by Geoffrey Barraclough, *Introduction to
Contemporary History* (New York, 1965), pp. 101–103.
40. Richard W. Leopold, *Elihu Root and the Conservative Tradition* (Boston, 1954), p. 178.

3 Wilson, Arias, and Roosevelt

During the post-1964 crisis, Panamanians picked out two targets for attack: the oligarchy which had long manipulated the country's politics while exploiting its resources, and the United States which dominated Panama through informal colonialism. Both the oligarchy and the colonial power were firmly established by 1914 when the Canal opened. But tensions were developing. Within a generation the oligarchs and the colonial authority were challenged by a new middle class that revitalized Panamanian nationalism. The 1905 to 1939 years served as the spawning ground for the tensions that exploded in 1964 and after.

Man's Greatest Liberty with Nature

The tensions were not apparent until World War I. In August 1914 world attention focused on Austria-Hungary, where a political assassination was leading to war among Europe's greatest powers. The opening of the Panama Canal that month nevertheless commanded headlines. It was "the greatest liberty Man has ever taken with Nature," Great Britain's statesman-historian James Bryce remarked. The builders, as Roosevelt prophesied in 1904, had completed "the most important and also the most formidable engineering feat that has hitherto been attempted."

In a decade the North Americans had finished what others merely dreamed of for four hundred years. The result was a waterway equal to a channel dug ten feet deep and fifty-five feet wide from Maine to Oregon.[1] While engineers commanded by George W. Goethals bisected the Isthmus, North American medical teams under the direction of Dr. William Gorgas conquered yellow fever and tamed malaria, the two destroyers of de Lesseps' enterprise thirty years before.

The engineering and the materials were of such quality that the mechanisms controlling the locks in 1914 remained in perfect working order sixty-four years later. ("It is a splendid antique," a Zonian noted with pride in 1976.) Ships passed through six huge but delicate locks which raised vessels eighty-five feet above sea level at the Continental Divide before lowering them at the other end of the Isthmus.

A ship entering from the Pacific side passed by the present site of Balboa (now the Canal Zone's main city), and Panama City before Miraflores Locks' two-step mechanism raised it fifty-four feet. Sailing through Miraflores Lake, it entered Pedro Miguel Lock and its one-step chamber for the remaining thirty-one-foot rise. The ship then moved through narrow Gaillard Cut, the channel which posed the greatest engineering problems since the deep cut and sheer mountain sides created sudden landslides that could close the waterway. That problem was not satisfactorily solved until the 1930s. But as late as 1974, 250,000 cubic yards of dirt slid into the Cut, reducing the Canal to one-way traffic and costing $2 million for removal.[2]

1. Morris, "A Terminal Case of American Perpetuity," p. 47.
2. U.S. Congress, House, 93d Cong., 2nd Sess., *Report on the Activities of the Merchant Marine and Fisheries Committee* (Washington, D.C., 1975), p. 143; an excellent analysis of the passage and the toll problem is Norman J. Padelford and Stephen R. Gibbs, *Maritime Commerce and the Future of the Panama Canal* (Cambridge, Md., 1975).

Moving from the Cut into Gatun Lake, the ship began the downhill side of the journey. Gatun Lake, created by a gigantic dam, was a key to the Canal's success. Its water, captured from Panama's heavy mountain rainfall, allowed the locks to fill with water. The dam creating the lake became one of the waterway's most sensitive points, for if it were destroyed by nature or sabotage, Gatun Lake would empty into the sea and at least two years of rain would be required to refill the lake and make the Canal usable. After passing through Gatun Lake, a vessel was lowered through Gatun Locks, sailed seven miles into Cristobal Harbor, and at Colon entered the Atlantic.

The lock systems were miracles of engineering. One thousand feet long and one hundred and ten feet wide, the locks could handle anything that sailed until the 1930s. Water from the lakes filled each chamber in the lock system by force of gravity. No pumps were installed, thereby saving parts and fuel. If a malfunctioning chamber refused to open while the water continued to flow in, a control tower operator had approximately one minute to rush down next to the locks and turn the huge valves of the chamber by hand to release the water. If the operator did not move quickly enough, he and the operators of the "mules" (the engines which guided the vessel through the locks), could be drowned. That has never happened; indeed, serious problems of any kind have been rare, although each ship passing through the entire system requires fifty-two million gallons of fresh water, about the amount used each day by a city of a half-million people.

Not only is passage through the locks highly delicate, but at points the channel is breathtakingly narrow. Those obstacles together with the islands that dot the passage through Gatun Lake, make the Canal pilots the Zone's aristocracy. Because of the navigational hazards, the Canal is one of the few waterways on earth where the pilot has authority over the vessel's own captain. Despite the hazards, in the 1970s the system can handle a ship that has a 975-foot length, 106.9-foot beam, 39.5-foot draft, and 65,000 long tons of cargo.

Ship tolls are based on tonnage. The cheapest voyage was paid for in 1928 by adventurer Richard Haliburton who swam the Canal and paid 36¢ toll. In a conscious policy of subsidizing North American shipping, the United States did not raise tolls between 1914 and 1973. Expanding costs were absorbed by increased tonnage passing through the Canal. The low tolls and the nearly 8000 miles cut from a trip between New York City and San Francisco enabled a ship's owner to spend for Canal charges only one-tenth the amount required to move the vessel around the tip of South America.[3] Most important in 1914, the Canal allowed the growing United States Navy to sail easily from one ocean to the other, while putting the gigantic industrial complexes in the Northeast thousands of miles closer to the mineral wealth of South America's western coast and the supposedly bottomless markets of Asia.

Theodore Roosevelt, who needed little encouragement, could justifiably feel proud. Characteristically, however, he overdid it. Speaking at the University of California stadium in 1911, TR bragged: "If I had followed traditional conservative methods," the Canal debate "would have been going on yet; but I took the Canal Zone and let Congress debate, and while the debate goes on the Canal does also." For an out-of-power politician, particularly a Republican positioning himself to challenge the incumbent Republican President for the White House in 1912, the words were not wise, although they were accurate. The House of Representatives ordered a full investigation of the 1903 revolution. The inquiry revealed in detail for the first time the roles played by Bunau-Varilla, Cromwell, and Roosevelt.

Roosevelt's speech produced one other notable and rather embarrassing result. In 1914 Woodrow Wilson's administration indirectly tried to apologize for TR's bragging by expressing "sincere regret" to Colombia and offering to pay a $25 million indemnity. The treaty was on its way to congressional passage when Roosevelt emerged from a sa-

3. Billard, "Panama," p. 414; Liss, The Canal, p. 26.

fari in Brazilian jungles where he had nearly died from
fever. Wilson's apology acted as a wonderful tonic for the
self-righteous TR. In full throat, he attacked this "crime
against the United States" with typical Rooseveltian en-
ergy. Wilson's handiwork, TR cried, could "only be justified upon the ground that this nation has played the part of
a thief or of a receiver of stolen goods." He used the treaty
as a springboard for an all-out attack upon Wilson—whom
he condemned as a "pacifist"—and the President's overall
foreign policy which, TR was convinced, "meant the aban-
donment of the interest and honor of America."[4]

The Senate quickly backed off. In 1921, however, the
State Department reopened negotiations in order to smooth
the way for North American oil companies which sought
concessions in Colombia. The apologies were implicit, but
$25 million did change hands. This time the Senate ratified
the treaty. Theodore Roosevelt had died two years before.

Oligarchs—and Others

The country surrounding the new Canal held about
400,000 people in its seven provinces. The racial composition was complex and potentially dangerous. At the top of
the socio-political-economic ladder stood approximately
51,000 "whites" whose largely Spanish ancestry made
them whiter than most other Panamanians. The leaders of
this group came from several dozen, often interrelated families that comprised the oligarchy. They not only traced
their lineage to the 1903 revolutionary leadership, but to
the early Colombian and Spanish eras. Sometimes this required mighty efforts. One family even tried to claim Pedrarias the Cruel as an ancestor. Such genealogical detec-
tive work was necessary since Panamanian sensitivity to
skin color helped determine the power hierarchy. Accord-

---

4. Harbaugh, *Power and Responsibility*, pp. 464–465; Henry F. Pringle,
Theodore Roosevelt, a Biography (New York, 1931, 1956), p. 407; Arciniegas, *Caribbean*, p. 444.

ing to popular sayings, the rule was that "White is right," and "Blacks go to the back." Although the mass of Panamanians sarcastically referred to the leading families as *rabiblancos,* or white-tails, the oligarchy made white, Spanish-speaking ancestry the key to social acceptance, and what it termed "kinky hair" the sign of the outcast. In reality few Panamanians could legitimately claim pure white bloodlines. The oligarchy could not profit from living at the world's crossroads without coming in close contact with many races.

Panamanian social status consequently became determined not only by bloodlines (real or supposed), but by economic power. The oligarchy remained relatively small, but it was open to new members who possessed wealth. Among the oligarchs the ubiquitous Chiari family grew rich from sugar growing; the Boyds from cattle, dairy, and import businesses. Arnulfo and Harmodio Arias came from a poorer family, yet Arnulfo's coffee plantations and Harmodio's legal and publishing businesses ultimately gave them social status.

Not accidentally, the same names dominated political life. Wealth was a prerequisite for political power. Panamanian politics have never organized around parties or issues, but around charismatic, rich men. Without a party apparatus, candidates were forced to pay political expenses themselves, and given the rampant corruption expenses ran high. But politics, in turn, became the key to preserving wealth against competitors and expanding landholdings or concessions. Few Panamanians left high office without having piled up large bank accounts to cushion the pain of retirement.

More than 200,000, or well over a majority of the population, were mestizo (Spanish and Indian blood) or mulatto (black and Spanish blood). The vagueness of the figures indicates the racism of the society, for while outside experts could estimate mulattos outnumbering mestizos two to one, the ratio was reversed when the Panamanians themselves were asked about their racial background. Few claimed black blood if they could pass for mestizo. It remains difficult to challenge them since mestizos and mulattos have married the whiter Panamanians and each other ever since Spanish soldiers first impreganted Indian and black women some four centuries ago.

Panamanian racial discrimination thus cuts fine. Just how fine has been demonstrated by the experience of the blacks. In 1914 about 50,000 of them occupied the bottom of the socio-political scale, but some were more unequal than others. Those who entered as slaves during the Spanish era learned the native language and became more easily assimilated than later arrivals. Several of the Spanish-speaking blacks later became Vice-Presidents of Panama. The late arrivals were brought from the British West Indies by de Lesseps or the American engineers to do the back-breaking work on the Canal. Since they spoke English, immigrants won preferred status in the Zone at the expense of Panamanians who wanted those jobs. For seventy-five years, the English-speaking blacks, or *chombos* as they are called, have been the most visible targets of racial discrimination in Panama.

Several thousand Asians and Jews congregated in urban areas. The Jews prospered and generally became assimilated in the society. Many of the Asians also did well; by the 1960s they were among the most astute of Panamanian businessmen. But their racial differences made them so conspicuous that they were often victimized as scapegoats, particularly during times of economic or political tension. At least 35,000 native Indians lived in such inaccessible areas that census-takers could not find them.

Since political-economic power divided racially, it also tended to divide geographically. The *rabiblancos* dominated urban centers, while the mixed races and Indians peopled the outlying provinces. In 1910 one-third of the population lived in twelve towns. Panama City contained 38,000, and another 18,000 lived at the other end of the Canal in Colon. David, the capital of wealthy Chiriqui Province (site of the United Fruit Company's expanding banana plantations and many oligarchical land holdings), had more than 15,000 population.[5] The urban oligarchy controlled the country for 60 years, and a striking aspect of post-1969 Panama has been the attempt of the Torrijos government to reduce the cities' political power in order to help the impoverished peasants in the interior. The attempt has not been overly successful.

Panama's racial sensitivities needed no honing, but they were sharpened to a fine point by the Canal Zone's policies. The blacks earned twenty cents an hour, and they were bossed by men who had experience with black labor—that is, whites from the Gulf States who in the words of one scholar "were sent to the Canal Zone with instructions to make an inter-racial society work as well as it did in our Deep South."[6]

While the Canal was being built, some 5300 United States citizens and a few Panamanians received wages in gold coin. The remaining 31,000 laborers, including most Panamanians and all the blacks, were paid in lesser silver coin. The gold and silver payroll made the aristocracy instantly recognizable. Soon the labels—and the segregation—spread to drinking fountains, toilet facilities, and nearly every other public service. The discrimination was hardly surprising since Jim Crow laws (segregating whites and blacks on transportation, in schools, etc.) were sweeping through the United States, and as many as a hundred blacks were being lynched annually in the South. But when Jim Crow laws and lynching gradually disappeared in the United States after World War II, the gold and silver distinctions remained entrenched in the Canal Zone (although the terminology officially disappeared). The racially sensitive Panamanians never forgot or forgave the United States, for they had not joined the blacks in the silver lines by choice.

5. This section has in part been drawn from material in Willis J. Abbot, *The Panama Canal: An Illustrated Historical Narrative.* . . . (New York, 1922), pp. 273–274; Thomas E. Weil, *et al.*, *Area Handbook for Panama* (Washington, D.C., 1972), especially pp. 195–200; John and Mavis Biesanz, *The People of Panama* (New York, 1955), pp. 208–210.
6. Mercer D. Tate, "The Panama Canal and Political Partnership," *The Journal of Politics*, XXV (February 1963), 119–120.

The United States Colony, or Nabobs in Panama City

Panamanians have been quick to condemn what they termed the "colonial presence" of the United States in the Canal Zone. But they tended to miss—or, particularly if they were oligarchs, were reluctant to confront—the larger problem: although their country was legally sovereign and independent, in reality it was a United States colony. That colonial relationship helps us understand both the hatreds that developed and why many North Americans and some Panamanians considered Panama unfit to run the Canal in the 1970s. That relationship was also why the Canal could be described as "a body of water entirely surrounded by trouble."[7]

Rupert Emerson, an authority on colonialism, has defined it as "the establishment and maintenance, for an extended time, of rule over an alien people that is separate from and subordinate to the ruling power." The term no longer refers only to colonies formed by settlement abroad of people from a mother country, as it did in eighteenth-century England. Emerson sees colonialism as "white rule over peoples of different race inhabiting lands separated by salt water from the imperial center," and a rule "asserting racial and cultural superiority over a materially inferior native majority." But "more particularly," he concludes, "it signifies direct political control by European states or states settled by Europeans, as the United States . . . over peoples of other races."[8]

7. E. J. Kahn, Jr., "Letter from Panama," *The New Yorker*, Aug. 16, 1976, p. 66.
8. Rupert Emerson, "Colonialism: Political Aspects," in David L. Sills, ed., *International Encyclopedia of the Social Sciences*, Volume III (New York, 1968), pp. 1–5. "Informal colonialism" seems to be a more accurate description of United States-Panamanian relations, particularly through the 1930s but beyond as well, than "dependency." Theotonio Dos Santos has defined dependency as "a situation in which the economy of certain countries is conditioned by the development and expansion of another economy to which the former is subjected. The relation of interdepen-
(Continued)

All of these relationships, and especially the last, have characterized Washington's ties with Panama. The colonial ties were informal; that is, they were not systematically designed as a colonial system to be operated (as it was in London) by a Colonial Office. Panama ostensibly retained independence and sovereignty. Yet the North American control of Panama fit Emerson's criteria, with the relationships developing less formally, less systematically, and handled by the State Department rather than a Colonial

(Continued)
dence between two or more economies, between these and world trade, assumes the form of dependence when some countries (the dominant ones) can expand and can be self-starting, while other countries (the dependent ones) can do this only as a reflection of that expansion, which can have either a positive or a negative effect on their immediate development." This is a widely accepted definition of the term. Dependency has received much attention from Latin American scholars, and several of the elaborations are applicable to U.S.-Panama affairs. C. Richard Bath and Dilmus D. James, for example, note how scholars agree that development and underdevelopment are two components "of one unified system." That approach provides some insight into Panamanian underdevelopment. Dependency is less useful than "informal colonialism" in understanding the Panamanian case, however, because it does not go far enough in describing the extent of United States control. As the Dos Santos definition indicates, dependency revolves around economic factors, but Washington's power in Panama allowed the use of direct political and military intervention. That power, moreover, was legitimized by treaty and did not depend on "free trade imperialism," as does Dos Santos's dependency relationship. The United States integrated Panama into its system not through trade, but through treaties, including an agreement that made the dollar interchangeable with Panamanian currency. If dependency is used to analyze United States relations with large Latin American nations (Chile seems to be a favorite example), it is doubtful it can be used to explain adequately the wholly different type of relationship between Washington and Panama City. The following recent studies have been especially useful in enabling a non-Latin Americanist to understand the dependency concept: Theotonio Dos Santos, "The Structure of Dependence," in K. T. Fann and Donald C. Hodges, eds., Readings in U.S. Imperialism (Boston, 1971), pp. 225–236; Ronald H. Chilcote and Joel C. Edelstein, Latin America: The Struggle with Dependence and Beyond (New York, 1974), especially pages 26–32, 40; and C. Richard Bath and Dilmus D. James, "Dependency Analysis of Latin America:Some Criticisms, Some Suggestions," Latin American Research Review, XI (Number 3), pp. 3–36, particularly their suggestion of considering dependency in terms of "linkage politics." Most valuable have been the continued and often unavailing efforts of Professor Thomas Holloway of Cornell to initiate me into the mysteries of dependency theory.

Office. As a foreign affairs expert observed in 1932, "The relations of the United States with Panama are in many respects similar to those of the British Empire with Egypt and Japan with Manchuria."[9]

The colonial relationship began when the 1903 treaty gave the United States power over Panama's economy, immigration, city services, and foreign policy. In 1904 the Panamanian currency was tied to the dollar (change in Panama still has to be given in North American coins). That same year the U.S. Minister disbanded the Panamanian army, thereby making the government dependent on North American military units for maintaining order. In 1905 the Liberals, whom Taft had carefully kept out of power in 1904, argued that United States policy was contradictory. If Washington guaranteed public order, they claimed, "it is strictly logical and just that it should guarantee the existence of an absolutely lawful system of government."[10] Panamanian opposition groups might have thought such a position logical, but North Americans equivocated. On the one hand they demanded cooperative Panamanian regimes, but on the other they wanted no formal, long-term responsibility for publicly policing Panama's elections.

Washington consequently embarked on a search, still in progress three-quarters of a century later, for a method of shaping isthmian politics without ostentatious interference in Panama's affairs. The search seemed initially successful. In 1908 a United States commission of fourteen members publicly cooperated with Panamanians to ensure that the election would be orderly (if not incorrupt). The Liberals won, but this time Taft and Roosevelt did not mind. The Conservative oligarchs had fought among themselves until the party split. Former Conservatives moved into the Liberal party and it also became factionalized. So began the era of fragmented, personalized political parties that lasted until 1969.

9. R. L. Buell, "Panama and the United States," *Foreign Policy Reports*, VII (Jan. 20, 1932), 409.
10. *FRUS, 1905*, p. 718.

United States participation in the elections profoundly influenced Panamanian politics. In 1908, for example, the acting President, José Domingo Obaldía, could control the election process and, not surprisingly, decided to be a presidential candidate. The opposition hoped the United States would either guarantee a free election by cracking down on Obaldía's manipulation of the voting, or stand aside while the opposition overthrew Obaldía with a coup. Washington naturally rejected both alternatives. The latter could cause a disruption in canal construction, and the former would result in a blatant, bothersome intervention. After all, Taft sighed, one must expect "the use of government aid to secure the fraudulent election of a government candidate." The United States consequently did not intervene directly to ensure a fair election, only indirectly to guarantee order and, not entirely coincidentally, the continuance of a cooperative regime.

Four years later 180 North American election supervisors ineffectively attempted to reduce vote fraud as another Liberal candidate, Belisario Porras, triumphed. In 1916, however, Porras asked Washington to stay out. The opposition pleaded for more United States supervisors to prevent the President from fixing the results. The Woodrow Wilson administration cooperated with Porras and his party easily won.[11] Washington's adherence to the status quo was best demonstrated in the 1918 local elections. Faced with increasing opposition, the government simply cancelled the election. It reversed itself only after the United States moved troops into Panama City and Colon, promised to supervise the balloting, and acted as an arbitral commission to judge disputed results. The North Americans decided that indeed the government's candidates won a majority of the provinces.[12] The Panamanian electoral process had become unrepresentative and a farce. Dedicated above all to

11. Porras's great abilities and personality are described in Ernesto J. Castillero Reyes, *Historia de Panamá* (Panama, 1955), pp. 169–170.
12. Buell, "Panama and the United States," p. 416.

maintaining order and cooperative regimes, the North Americans helped shape that process.

In retrospect, Washington's sensitivity to isthmian politics was amazing. In these elections, as in most others held since, the leading candidates belonged to the oligarchy, showed equal commitment to close ties with the United States, and were prepared to pledge their property, lives, and honor to preservation of the status quo. To tell the top candidates apart required the splitting of political issues with a precision that taxed even Taft's legalistic mind. In reality, Washington cared little about supposed differences between Conservatives and Liberals after 1908. It worried only that the supporters of each candidate might take their cause so seriously that violence could erupt, then spread into the Canal Zone and hinder operations. Efficient functioning of the Canal took precedence over the political development of Panama. Debates over meaningful political issues not only became irrelevant, but dangerous. The waterway consequently flourished, but Panamanian political life became corrupt and stagnant. As in India, where the native nabobs remained in power by working within the rules of the British colonial empire, in Panama the oligarchy retained power by acknowledging the supremacy of the Canal's needs, as Washington defined those needs.

The "Outlying Possession"

In Washington's view, those needs, and its power to fulfill them, were becoming ever larger. Supervising elections constituted one method of protecting United States interests. Military intervention, control of Panamanian foreign policy, and domination of the country's economy were other methods.

Under the 1903 treaty and Article 136 of Panama's Constitution, the United States possessed the right to intervene to "reestablish public peace and constitutional order." In return, the North Americans guaranteed Panama's independence. By World War I, however, the Panamanians were having second thoughts about this arrangement. Their independence was secure. The threat of a Colombian invasion vanished years before. Panamanians began to argue that Washington could intervene only when they asked for help.

The United States nevertheless continued to intervene at will. In 1912 riots occurred in the red light district of Cocoa Grove, which the city fathers had placed, with considerable foresight, between the hospital and cemetery and adjacent to the Canal Zone. Anti-Yankee in origin, the rioters killed a U.S. sailor and wounded nineteen others. Panama City police ended the fracas, but the government stalled when Washington demanded an explanation and assurance of future protection. In 1915 riots again erupted in Cocoa Grove, spreading this time to Colon before they were extinguished.

The State Department dressed down the Panamanian government, warned that such disorders would not be further tolerated, and—to make the point clear—demanded that the Panamanian police surrender their high-powered rifles which, the State Department claimed, threatened unarmed North Americans. Panama angrily told President Woodrow Wilson that such demands infringed upon its sovereignty. Wilson did not push the issue until Panama unwisely threatened to appeal to other Latin American nations for mediation. The State Department then sharply defined Panama's rights: any proposal to have Latin Americans interfere in United States-Panamanian relations was "unworthy of serious consideration."[13] The police were left with pistols. The rifles were taken to the United States for sale.

U.S. troops intervened periodically in Panama during these years. The interventions exemplified a policy being followed throughout the Caribbean and must be understood within that larger context.

The Wilson administration cited the need to defend

13. FRUS, 1915, p. 1236.

the Canal as a justification for many of those interventions, much as Roosevelt had justified his Corollary. Because of the Canal, Secretary of State Robert Lansing wrote the President in late 1915, European political control should be excluded from the region. Since the "small republics of America . . . have been and to an extent still are the prey of revolutionists, of corrupt government, and of predatory foreigners," the United States needed the right to create "stable and honest government, if no other way seems possible to attain that end." Caring little about "our humanitarian purpose" or the "benefit which would result to the peoples of those republics by the adoption of this policy," Lansing urged only the protection of his nation's "national interests."[14]

Wilson and Lansing consequently sent United States troops into Mexico, Santo Domingo, Cuba, Haiti, Nicaragua, and Panama. The motivations were complex, differed from one case to the other, and most—contrary to Lansing's note—bore little relationship to the Canal's defense. The policy usually resulted from the desire to stop or contain revolutions (as in Mexico, Cuba, and Nicaragua), or protect United States investments threatened by either default or European competition (as in Santo Domingo, Haiti, and Nicaragua). Defending the Canal became just one more reason for intervention, not a primary or sole justification. As Lansing's letter illustrated, it was a reason that nicely fit into a policy of creating a Caribbean political system that was non-revolutionary and under United States control. The Canal became a symbol of North American expansionism, but it was by no means the primary cause of the expansion.

In Panama the first major military intervention occurred in Chiriqui Province, site of the banana plantations

14. Lansing to Wilson, Nov. 24, 1915, "Personal and Confidential Letters," Robert Lansing Papers, Library of Congress, Washington, D.C. (Microfilm); Wilson's interventionist policies in Latin America are analyzed by Lloyd Gardner in Gardner, LaFeber, and McCormick, *Creation of the American Empire*, chapter XVI, from which the interpretation in this section is drawn.

owned by the Boston-based United Fruit Company. Chiriqui was also the country's richest agricultural area, although its income was perhaps the most inequitably distributed of any Panamanian province. The intervention was triggered by riots which erupted after a fixed election in 1918. One North American was killed in fighting which the rifleless Panamanian police could not prevent. United States troops moved in and remained for two years. As the weeks, then months, passed, the Panamanian government strongly protested. It argued that, under the 1903 treaty, troops could land only at Panama's request and be used only in Panama City and Colon. Washington flatly rejected that argument.

The troops left Chiriqui by 1921, but the debate continued. If the United States possessed blanket right to intervene "without the authorization of our government," the Panamanians argued, "the guarantee in the treaty [in which the United States promised to protect the country's independence] would not be of independence but of absolute subjection."[15] Washington did not budge an inch. In 1918, without waiting for Panama to ask, it had landed troops in Panama City and Colon to cool election fevers. Three years later, at President Porras's personal request, United States soldiers protected him from mobs besieging the Presidential Palace. Only in 1925 did the Panamanian government use Article 136 to justify calling in North American aid. When rent riots erupted in the capital, Marines with fixed bayonets stopped the uprising. They were also used later in the year to guarantee peace during elections.

Landing the Marines was the most spectacular but not always the most important display of Washington's colonial authority over Panama. Beginning in 1911, the U.S. Navy sought a monopoly of Panamanian wireless stations. The State Department agreed that since radio control was essential to Canal defense, Panama did not even have to be consulted. In 1914 the Wilson administration abruptly de-

15. Quoted in Buell, "Panama and the United States," p. 414.

manded an "immediate monopoly," and after the usual strong and ineffective protest, the Panamanians surrendered "complete and permanent control" over their radio communications.[16]

If they could not control their own communications, or internal order, Panamanians would logically encounter difficulty in controlling their foreign policy. The country developed its own diplomatic corps, belonged to the League of Nations (which the United States refused to join), and proudly became a member of the elite League Council in 1931. All this, however, was window-dressing. Washington had laid down the rules in 1909 when the Taft administration announced that it possessed the "moral right to prevent Panama from getting into a controversy with any government which might eventually require the United States to take a part in the controversy and support Panama."[17]

In 1921 the Panamanians learned the meaning of this rule. They agreed to settle a long-disputed boundary question with Costa Rica by accepting the mediation of a commission headed by a justice of the U.S. Supreme Court. When the justice turned over the disputed land to Costa Rica, however, the Panama police prepared for war. Warren G. Harding's newly installed administration sharply instructed Panama to surrender the land, then sent a battleship and 400 Marines to ensure compliance. That same year Washington reversed a 1905 decision and announced that foreign diplomats acting as consuls in Panama required separate exequaturs to work in the Canal Zone. Panama naturally protested that the Zone was not separate from the surrounding country. The United States rejected the protest. Humiliation followed humiliation. In 1923, at the request of the Canal Zone government and the State Department, Congress suddenly repealed the 1904 Taft agreement. Panamanian merchants again faced competition from Zo-

16. *Ibid,*, p. 418; George W. Baker, Jr., "The Wilson Administration and Panama, 1913–1931," *Journal of Inter-American Studies*, VIII (April 1966), pp. 279–293, especially p. 281.
17. *FRUS*, 1909, pp. 469–70.

nian sellers who bought at prices subsidized by the United States.

Ricardo Alfaro, Minister to Washington, complained to Harding's Secretary of State, Charles Evans Hughes, that Panama understood Washington's need to control the Zone for Canal operations, "but when it comes to commerce and other sovereign rights [as the exequatur] it was a different matter." Hughes's reply was brutal. "This government could not and would not enter into any discussion affecting its full right to deal with the Canal Zone . . . as if it were sovereign of the Canal Zone and to the exclusion of any sovereign rights or authority on the part of Panama. . . . It was absolute futility," Hughes added icily, for Panama "to expect any American Administration, no matter what it was . . . ever to surrender those rights."[18] Hughes's prophecy left much to be desired, but the essential question was: who had the rifles? No one doubted the answer. The U.S. Navy went ahead to establish in the Zone a special squadron capable of quickly landing Marines anywhere in the Caribbean area.[19]

Hughes finally agreed to renew the Taft agreement of 1904, but he would not promise to stop seizing lands adjacent to the Canal Zone or reverse his policies on exequaturs. Washington indeed demanded that Panama hand over part of New Cristobal (a section of the country's second largest city, Colon, and the Atlantic terminal of the Canal). The North Americans also requested further monopoly rights in radio communications, airways, and sanitation policies. To cap the negotiations, Panama, on the initiative of one of its own diplomats, promised to join the United States automatically whenever Washington decided to go to war. When the pact embodying these changes arrived in Panama City, it was attacked so viciously in the legislative Assembly and street rallies that the government refused to consider it.

18. FRUS, 1923, II, 684; Joseph Tulchin, *The Aftermath of War: World War I and U.S. Policy Towards Latin America* (New York, 1971), pp. 95–96.
19. Kenneth J. Grieb, "The United States and the Central American Federation," *The Americas*, XXIV (October 1967), 121.

The refusal was a brave act, but it changed nothing. As was sometimes the case, President Calvin Coolidge was inadvertently accurate in 1928 when he called Panama one of "our outlying possessions." As regards the Zone, Taft had defined the situation when he privately argued that the United States could agree Panama had "titular sovereignty," since the term was a barren scepter "that had a poetic and sentimental appeal to the Latin mind."[20]

"Spiggoties" and "Gringos"

Economically the country had long been an appendage of United States interests.[21] As early as the 1880s Colombia absorbed $14 million of North American investment, much of it in Panama. The United Fruit Company, which started banana plantations in Colombia's western provinces in 1899, owned 23,000 acres of land and 73 miles of railroad worth over $2 million when Panama declared its independence. In 1906 less than one percent of the country's land was cultivated, but one-third of the land under cultivation belonged to United Fruit. Investments flooded in, including the Central and South American Telegraph Company, a tobacco monopoly, large-scale sugar production, saw mills, distilleries, coffee plantations—all controlled by North Americans. They built Panama City's street railways, electric power company (later controlled by General Electric), telephone network, and ice service. By 1913 the total value of Panama's private property was about $33 million, and United Fruit alone owned $7 to $8 million.

The State Department closely watched the financial situation. When Panama went deeply in debt to finance

20. Quoted in Liss, *The Canal*, pp. 33, 35. A Panamanian view is given briefly in Ernesto J. Castillero Reyes, *El Canal de Panama* (Panama, n.d. [1965?]), pp. 137–141.
21. Much of the following is based on the superb account by William D. McCain, *The United States and the Republic of Panama* (Durham, N.C., 1937), pp. 97–104, 106–118.

internal improvements in 1916, Washington insisted that a United States financial adviser be hired. The Panamanians protested, one claiming the demand meant the death of the young republic. In 1918 the first of a series of advisers nevertheless moved in to control the country's fiscal system. When Panama wanted to issue bonds for railways in Chiriqui Province, Secretary of State Lansing agreed in 1917 on the condition that the government cooperate fully with loan demands set down by National City Bank of New York. Panama refused, then, with no choice, finally agreed. But when Panamanians wanted to build feeder rail and wagon roads to tap the lucrative traffic in the Zone, Lansing turned them over to the War Department, which operated the Zone. Nothing was done.[22]

During World War I the United States suddenly became the world's richest nation. Loaning vast amounts to both the Allies and Central Powers, it moved to the center of the globe's money exchanges. Panama was one of several Latin nations targeted by capital-rich North Americans. The Isthmus possessed no regular banking services until 1910, but after the war Chase National and National City, both of New York, moved in. A decade later National City held immense power. It pressured the government, for example, to undertake a thorough survey of the country's resources. The survey would be headed by an executive of the bank. Panamanians loudly objected, but the government again gave in. United Fruit meanwhile built its holding to 250 miles of railways, 26,000 acres of bananas, and more than 20,000 acres of other food products.

This penetration was accompanied, indeed protected, by a 1929 State Department decision that North American airway companies would not be allowed to compete for the rich access routes to Panama. Instead, one company, Pan American, received a monopoly and mail contract subsidies. As the State Department argued, "it is certainly desirable and perhaps essential that the United States should, in so far

22. Baker, "Wilson Administration and Panama," pp. 288–289.

as possible, control aviation in the Caribbean nations."[23] In
some circumstances, marketplace competition was not to be
trusted.

As the country began to slide into the morass of economic depression in 1930, Panama City and Colon were
rapidly growing urban areas of 74,000 and 33,000 people
respectively. The 40,000 people living in the Zone on
United States government salaries seemed a buffer against
economic troubles. In some years the Zone provided as
much as one-third of Panama's national income.

The Zone, however, gave the Panamanian economy a
rosiness that hid a dangerous fever, not good circulation. By
1930, North Americans held nearly $29 million in direct in-
vestments and $18 million in Panamanian bonds. Panama's
foreign trade was a misnomer; it was actually North American trade. In 1930 the United States provided more than two-
thirds of the nation's $19 million of imports and took 94 per-
cent of its $4 million in exports. Panama City depended on
the Zone; so did Colon, whose economic health was at the
mercy of the U.S. government-owned Panama Railroad. The
company not only operated the city's main hotel, but owned
a number of the most valuable land parcels and buildings. It
frequently leased buildings to Panamanians. In this way Colon's red-light district, whose buildings belonged to the
Railroad, paid rent to Panamanians. As a State Department
official later noted, this arrangement put "an end to the in-
congruity of United States authorities collecting rent from
prostitutes."[24] When the world's greatest economic power
began to capsize in 1929, Panama was one of the passengers
onboard. By 1932 United States investments stopped and
Panamanian exports and imports were sliced in half.

23. FRUS, 1929, I, 542–545, esp. 543. The best analysis of United States
economic penetration into Latin America during the "Progressive" era
(1906–29), and the role played by government in aiding that penetration,
is Robert Neal Seidel, Progressve Pan Americanism; Development and
U.S. Policy Toward South America, 1906–1931, Cornell University Latin
American Studies Program Dissertation Series, Ithaca, 1973.
24. Laurence Duggan, The Americas: The Search for Hemisphere Security
(New York, 1949), pp. 32–33.

As unemployment grew, race relations worsened between the Zone's inhabitants and the people of Colon and
the capital city. The relationship had long been uneasy. In
1914 when the Canal opened, Panamanians believed the
North Americans and black West Indians would shortly
leave so the Zone's jobs would be open for them. The
builders instead isolated the Zone and gave job preference
to the English-speaking blacks who would accept low
"silver" wages. Panamanian intolerance toward the blacks
heightened along with a hatred of North American economic discrimination.

A United States visitor in the early 1920s observed
that Panamanians thought the Canal brought them little but
sanitation, and this convenience they had done nicely without before the Yankees appeared. Panamanians disliked
North Americans, the visitor wrote, because of "their resentment at our hardly concealed contempt for them." The
whiter, Spanish elite did not share these feelings, at least in
such intensity, but "as for the casual clerk or mechanic we
Americans call him 'spiggoty' with frank contempt for his
undersize, his lack of education, and for his large proportion of Negro blood." He responds by calling North Americans " 'gringos' and hating [us] with a deep, malevolent
rancor that needs only a fit occasion to blaze forth in riot
and in massacre."[25]

The "Revolution" of 1931

Such simmering hatred would have been less dangerous if Panama had not been, as Coolidge described it, an
outlying possession of the United States. By 1930 many
Panamanians easily blamed their problems on Washington.
Given the imbalance of fire power in the area, they seemed
to have little chance of breaking the colonial ties. In 1931,
however, Panamanians overthrew their elected government

25. Abbot, *The Panama Canal*, pp. 233–236. Abbot speculates that "spiggoty" came from the attempts of hackmen to lure fares by shouting
"Speaka-da-English."

for the first time, and when this act led them into a dead-end, they focused their discontent on the Canal Zone.

The events that led to the 1931 coup began in the mid-1920s. One dominant family, the Chiaris, controlled the presidency, and since President Rudolfo Chiari could not run for a second term in 1928, he transferred the office to a close associate, Florencio H. Arosemena. The triumph of the Chiari-Arosemena scheme angered the wealthy and politically ambitious Arias Madird family. The Arias's determination to drive Arosemena from power received unexpected help from two sources. The first was the growing economic depression which sharpened political frustrations. The second was a new political organization, *Acción Communal*, which United States Minister Roy T. Davis first suspected of links with the international Communist movement. Investigation soon revealed that it was an indigenous group whose program, in the Minister's words, seemed "semi-radical," and whose real concern was to become a player in the game of trying to evict Arosemena from office.[26]

Acción Communal actually marked a milestone in Panamanian history. Formed in 1926 to fight the treaty made with the United States, it soon attracted members of a small, new Panamanian middle class who were searching for a political home that the oligarchy had no intention of providing. Its members were predominantly mestizo; included teachers, government employees, small businessmen, and some urban workers; and many had migrated from the provinces to find their fortune in Panama City and Colon. On racial, functional, and geographic grounds, therefore, the oligarchy perceived the new arrivals as an enemy. That perception was accurate, especially since the middle class was extremely ambitious (its members often used the verb *luchar*, to struggle, in describing themselves),[27] and saw the

26. This important story is best revealed in the dispatches and instructions in *FRUS*, 1931, II, 890–904, and especially Davis to Department of State, Jan. 6, 1931, pp. 894–902.
27. Biesanz, *People of Panama*, pp. 210–215.

oligarchy's control as oppressive. For these same reasons the new class was also highly nationalistic and anti-Yankee. In its view the United States-subsidized commissaries in the Zone robbed merchants of sales, discriminated against Panamanian workers, and humiliated their country's government. The teachers carried that message into the schools which, in turn, spawned the anti-oligarchical and anti-North American movements of the next half-century.

Harmodio and Arnulfo Arias moved naturally into the leadership of the movement. The brothers were mestizo, made their fortunes in the provinces (where they built a large political following, especially among peasants), and were intially disliked by the oligarchy. In 1911 while a student at the London School of Economics, Harmodio published a widely noticed book arguing that the United States had issued the Monroe Doctrine not for purposes of self-defense, but as the first step of an imperialistic policy. From this premise, as well as numerous legal arguments, he concluded that Washington's expansion must be checked at the Isthmus and the Canal neutralized by international agreement.[28] By the late 1920s the brothers were fighting a two-front war against the United States and oligarchical control. The new middle class appeared to be their natural ally.

For the next four decades Arnulfo was a perennial candidate for the presidency and Harmodio the most accomplished political schemer in Panama. The latter's first move to gain power wonderfully displayed his talents. On the night of January 2, 1931, *Acción Communal* seized the Panama City telephone company and the Presidential Palace. However, it wisely allowed Davis, the U.S. Minister, to pass its guard around the Palace to talk with Arosemena. The President hoped Marines would be sent to restore order, but, according to Davis, "did not insist on it." The Minister decided not to employ troops since news of their landing might lead the opposition to kill Arosemena. The

28. Harmodio Arias, *The Panama Canal: A Study in International Law and Diplomacy* (London, 1911).

ensuing battle could then spread into the Zone. Most important, Davis discovered the Arias group to be quite cooperative, perhaps in part because Davis carefully refused to indicate whether or not Marines would be summoned.

Arosemena resigned and Harmodio Arias became Acting President until Arosemena's Vice-President, Ricardo Alfaro, returned from Washington to assume the top office. By working with those whom he termed the "responsible and representative" opposition members, Davis preserved the semblance of constitutional procedure. Of equal significance, he resolved the crisis before troops had to be landed. Throughout, Harmodio Arias appeared responsible and cooperative.

Washington deeply appreciated such moderation. During 1930–31, a half-dozen revolutions in depression-ridden Latin America threatened the area with political chaos. Secretary of State Henry Stimson declared himself "very blue" over the upheavals, particularly since he and President Herbert Hoover were sharply turning United States policy away from Roosevelt's and Wilson's gunboat diplomacy toward a more peaceful, cooperative policy. Although it started down the uncharted path, Panama, at least, had turned back. The oligarchy, Arias, even the "younger element" of "semi-radical tendencies," to use Davis's phrases, proved to be "responsible." After luncheon with Davis in Washington, Stimson happily recorded in his diary that "what he had done . . . was really very fine, for he had virtually stopped the revolution there."[29]

But of course the sores of economic depression and political frustration continued to fester. Alfaro could do little to remedy them during his two years in office. In the 1932 election Harmodio Arias returned as a Liberal candidate to win the presidency on his own. During the electioneering he encountered no difficulty whipping up support for his commitment to create a new relationship with the

29. Diaries of Henry L. Stimson, Vol. XIX, Nov. 6, 1931, pp. 15–16, Papers of Henry L. Stimson, Yale University (microfilm).

North Americans. All three of the leading candidates indeed joined Harmodio in attacking the United States. The 1932 campaign marked perhaps the first time none of the parties considered asking the United States to supervise the elections.[30].

Roosevelt Revises Roosevelt

Economic conditions worsened in 1933 until 50,000, or about a quarter of the workforce, were unemployed. President Arias tried a range of remedies, including a reduction in civil service salaries and a moratorium on the national debt. He focused relief efforts on the rural provinces where two-thirds of all Panamanians lived, most at subsistence levels. Arias was the first President to extend such state help to the impoverished countryside.[31] To finance the spending, Arias tried to increase governmental bond issues, but credit sources dried up. By 1934 governmental issues totalled $18.7 million, $14.5 million of those were in default because interest could not be paid.[32] When the country's national bank defaulted, bankruptcy seemed near.

Arias's only hope was to draw more revenue and employment from the Canal Zone. It became not merely the country's greatest, but apparently its only resource. Yet Panama had no control whatever over the Canal. As a foreign policy expert drily remarked in 1932, the relationship between the Zone and Panama "would have been simplified had Panama been annexed to the United States."[33] Panamanian sensitivity to the Zone's affairs was illustrated by the uproar that resulted when the United States began

30. McCain, *United States and Republic of Panama*, p. 77.
31. Castillero Reyes, *Historia de Panamá*, p. 188.
32. J. Fred Rippy, *Globe and Hemisphere; Latin America's Place in Postwar Foreign Relations of the United States* (Chicago, 1958), p. 62.
33. Buell, "Panama and the United States," p. 409; McCain, *United States and Republic of Panama*, p. 245 contains the material relating to the Panama City newspaper warning.

selling beer along the Canal. Panamanian merchants had profited since 1920 from the peculiar North American refusal to make or sell beer, but to drink large amounts of it. After Prohibition ended in November 1933, the merchants lost one of their few remaining sources of profit. Several months before, a Panama City newspaper warned that the nation might cut diplomatic relations with Washington if the Zone became "wet." Arias denied the threat, but speeded plans for a direct talk with the new United States President, Franklin D. Roosevelt.

As a guest at the White House for a week in October 1933, Arias got along well with Roosevelt. Noting that "misunderstandings" between the two nations "had become intensified by the continued economic depression," FDR smoothly agreed that two of the provisions Panamanians found most obnoxious in the 1903 treaty should be terminated: the explicit right of the United States to intervene in Colon and Panama City, and the implicit right of freewheeling merchants in the Zone to compete with Panamanians in selling to tourists or in Panama itself.

Roosevelt further understood that the black, English-speaking West Indians could serve as a lightning-rod for Panamanian unrest. (Perhaps that understanding occurred when, as FDR recalled years later, Arias warned "that the Jamaicans in Panama were dangerous; that each Jamaican man slept with three women every week.")[34] The President consequently urged Congress to appropriate funds for repatriating "some of the aliens," who "constitute a serious unemployment problem for Panama," to their home islands.[35]

The famous phrase of the 1903 treaty—that the United States could act "as if it were sovereign"—was not restated. The joint statement issued by Arias and FDR declared only that "the provisions of the Treaty of 1903 . . .

---

34. "Top-secret Memorandum, Annex to Memorandum of March 15, 1945," FDR-Taussig conversation, Box 52, Papers of Charles Taussig, Franklin D. Roosevelt Library, Hyde Park, N.Y.
35. Samuel I. Rosenman, ed., *The Public Papers and Addresses of Franklin D. Roosevelt*, 13 vols. (New York, 1938–1950), II, 407–410.

contemplate the use, occupation and control by the United States of the Canal Zone."[36] Nor did the statement repeat the 1903 clause that the United States could hold its rights "in perpetuity." Roosevelt, however, left no doubt about his feelings when he visited Panama in July 1934. He noted proudly that his "interest in Panama may be said to be of a historical character" since his great-uncle, William H. Aspinwall, built the Panama Railroad in the 1850s. "It was this railroad which began to restore the Isthmus" as the "crossroads of the Americas," Roosevelt announced, and the United States would continue to act as "a trustee for all the world" in maintaining the Canal.[37] while revising part of his cousin Theodore's work in Panama, FDR retained full power over the Zone so the United States could charitably protect "civilization," as TR called it.

Arias and Roosevelt turned the detailed negotiations over to their diplomats. The talks did not go smoothly. Between 1934 and the signing of the treaty on March 2, 1936, 110 conferences were convened. In Panama, Arias was pressured to obtain a more explicit repudiation of the 1903 sovereignty clause. In the United States the War Department took the lead in demanding that FDR reiterate "all rights of sovereignty" granted in 1903, that control over Panama's ports at the Canal terminals be retained, and the Marines be allowed to maintain public order in the ports.[38] The War Department won support for its demands from a powerful group of Senators led by William Borah (Rep., Idaho), Hiram Johnson (Rep., Calif.), and Claude Pepper (Dem., Fla.). Perhaps not coincidentally, Borah and Johnson fondly remembered campaigning for Progressivism in 1912 with Theodore Roosevelt.[39]

Roosevelt fortunately rejected the War Department's

36. Ibid.
37. Ibid., III, 348–349.
38. Secretary of War George Dern to Roosevelt, Jan. 11, 1935, in Edgar B. Nixon, ed., Franklin D. Roosevelt and Foreign Affairs, 3 vols. (Cambridge, Mass., 1969), II, 351–352.
39. Lester D. Langley, "World Crisis and the Good Neighbor Policy in Panama, 1936–1941," Americas, XXIV (October 1967), 140–142.

proposals. He understood, as the military did not, that the political and economic concessions made the Canal more secure, not less. They could also be granted because recent Panamanian presidential campaigns demonstrated that foreign troops were not necessary to assure victory for the "responsible" element. A concern for order underlay the rising nationalism. Such concern could be encouraged, the nationalism contained, the Canal's security therefore enhanced, by overruling the more blatant, less sophisticated policy of the War Department.

FDR's position paralleled his highly publicized "Good Neighbor" approach toward all Latin America. The blunt tool of military intervention, used by TR, Wilson, Harding, and Coolidge, was replaced by political friendship and economic leverage. Roosevelt's Secretary of State, Cordell Hull, launched a massive economic offensive southward, attempting to tie together the Hemisphere through reciprocal trade agreements rather than the irritants of military occupation. As the last United States occupation troops left Central American countries, Hull moved to integrate the area peacefully and economically: Latin American raw materials received favored position in the United States, while U.S. manufactured products and some farm exports benefited from preferred treatment in southern markets.

The Panamanian-United States economic relationship again served as a case study. Events in the Isthmus between 1934 and 1936 demonstrated why those relations had to be tightened. In early 1934 Hull told FDR an unusual number of Japanese had recently arrived in Panama, some of whom had been evicted as spies from the Philippines. Both the Nazis and Japanese initiated trade offensives in Latin America, including Panama. As Hull recalled in his memoirs, he was shocked during a visit to Latin America in 1936 to see how "Axis penetration had made rapid, alarming headway under various guises."[40]

40. Nixon, ed., FDR and Foreign Affairs, II, 33–34; Wallace to FDR, June 5, 1936, ibid.; Cordell Hull, Memoirs of Cordell Hull, 2 vols. (New York, 1948), I, 495.

With Axis pressure intensifying, in March 1936 the two sides finally signed the Hull-Alfaro treaty that marked a significant, if short step toward recognizing Panamanian rights. The treaty's first sentence abrogated Washington's guarantee of Panamanian independence. The isthmian nation was no longer to be a legal protectorate under the United States. The North Americans next renounced the right to seize additional lands or waters without Panama's consent.(Within five years that issue threatened again to rip apart relations between the two countries.) A number of economic concessions lessened competition between the Zone and Panama's businessmen, theoretically allowed the latter to bid on supply contracts in the Zone, and gave the Panamanian government the right to tax many of its own citizens who worked on the Canal. After thirty-three years Panama regained control over most of its immigration by being able to prevent aliens from entering Panama through the Zone.

Contrary to the War Department's wishes, the right of United States intervention for the maintenance of order in Colon and Panama City was terminated. Finally, the United States agreed to increase the annual annuity from $250,000 to $430,000. The increase was illusory. In 1934 Roosevelt had devalued the dollar, cutting deeply into the worth of the payment which Panama received. The new 1936 figure merely restored what FDR had earlier taken away unilaterally.

Panama's National Assembly immediately ratified the treaty 27−4. The United States Senate, however, refused to accept it for three years. Panamanian anger grew, but the Senate continued to stall. If Roosevelt's overriding of the War Department was far-sighted policy, it was also dangerous politics. The military's friends in Congress shared its concerns about surrendering any rights. The anti-treaty forces were especially apoplectic over FDR's promise to include Panama when making plans (such as the timing for seizing additional Panamanian lands), to protect the Canal "in case of an international conflagration." Actually no one should have doubted that in an emergency the United

States would move first and consult Panama later, particularly since Panama had no army, navy, or air force. Yet the War Department continued to be unhappy, and FDR finally issued sharp orders to the military leaders regarding what to say and not say when the Senate called them to testify. He warned them that ties with Panama must be examined in proper context: "It is highly important to the relations of this Government with all the other American republics that this treaty be ratified."[41]

Roosevelt's prompting did not work. The Senate and the War Department finally accepted the pact in 1939 when intimations of a Second World War forced Washington to put western hemispheric affairs in order. Even then FDR was forced to mollify the Senate through a further exchange of notes with Panama that gave the United States the right to react without consulting Panama if a military emergency occurred.[42] On the urging of military officers, moreover, the Senate refused to act on another agreement that gave Panamanians jurisdiction over two radio stations, even though the pact provided that Washington would retain ultimate control of the stations. Panama remained without its own radio frequencies.

Obviously the Senate did not display undue sensitivity for Panamanian concerns. Any doubt about the Senate's feelings disappeared when it dealt with FDR's promise, expressed in a note of March 2, 1936, which accompanied the treaty, to provide equal opportunities for Panamanians who sought jobs in the Zone. At the request of Canal Zone authorities, Congress passed a measure in 1939 directly contradicting Roosevelt's promise. The bill placed high-paying jobs at the disposal of United States citizens only. The President protested, but he signed the legislation since its proponents had the foresight to attach it to legislation pro-

---

41. FDR to Hull, March 29, 1936, in Nixon, ed., *FDR and Foreign Affairs*, III, 276.
42. A. R. Wright, "Defense Sites Negotiations Between the United States and Panama, 1936–1948," *U.S. Department of State Bulletin*, XXVII (Aug. 11, 1952), 213.

viding for enlarging the Canal through a third set of locks. The third-lock system was never completed. A few approach channels dug during the World War became swamp homes for alligators. Panamanians remained excluded from the better jobs along the Canal far into the future. The Zone commissaries, moreover, refused to carry through in good faith the economic concessions promised to Panamanian merchants.

As the two nations prepared for world war, Panamanians were embittered that they had received less than had been promised in 1936. Their hopes for the treaty were finally reduced to the belief that at least the United States recognized their sovereignty over the entire Isthmus. Article III contained the magic words: "The Canal Zone is territory of the Republic of Panama under the jurisdiction of the United States." A Panamanian historian later justifiably claimed that this provision, along with two other parts of the agreement, "confirmed" his country's sovereignty over the Zone.[43] The North Americans meanwhile simply assumed they held total control; Article III was of little significance in their debates between 1936 and 1939.

The United States view of the pact's importance suddenly appeared in 1940 when it was used not to improve relations, but as a lever to seize more Panamanian territory. Another crisis resulted and another government was overthrown—but this time by legitimately armed Panamanian police. A new era was beginning.

43. Castillero Reyes, *El Canal de Panamá*, p. 157.

4 Arias, Remón, and Eisenhower

With war approaching from both east and west in 1938, Roosevelt and Hull desperately sought Latin American support. But despite the Axis threat, six years of the Good Neighbor, the Panama Treaty of 1936, and several successful Inter-American conferences, the southern neighbors remained suspicious. When Hull attempted to create a collective security agreement, the Latin American delegations at the Lima Conference pointedly amended his motion so that it condemned intervention by either a "continental or extracontinental power." Memories of Wilson and the earlier Roosevelt remained fresh. At the 1939 Panama City Conference, however, Hull finally obtained a security zone around the hemisphere which was declared out-of bounds for any belligerent. The Americas also pledged to follow strict neutrality, denying, for example, bases to warring powers.

Panama fully supported the United States. Not that the Panamanians had much choice; on matters of peace and war they were bound to Washington by geography and treaty. Relations between the two nations nevertheless

seemed improved. Roosevelt raised the United States legation in Panama City to embassy level, pleasing status-
conscious Panamanians while signifying the importance
FDR placed on the area.

Underneath the diplomatic protocol, however, tensions were building, tensions that became noticeable even
after Hitler suddenly brought the Low Countries and France
to their knees in June 1940. For regardless of Nazi triumphs, the same inexorable problems divided Panama and
the United States. The isthmian economy, for example, remained unhealthy and unbalanced. With only primitive
communications linking east and west Panama (and the
Zone posing the greatest barrier), no national market existed. Populous urban areas suffered from high unemployment and the poor farmers were isolated in the provinces.
With little incentive and less responsibility, the oligarchical families invested much of their capital overseas. To
make matters worse, Washington not only refused to grant
Panamanian demands that the black, English-speaking
West Indians be sent home, but as planning began on the
new third-lock system in 1939, the United States shocked
the Panamanians by bringing in more Jamaican labor.[1] The
1936 treaty seemed little more than a deception.

In late 1939 the War Department leased a huge area
from private citizens for building the Rio Hato air base.
Washington next demanded ten one-acre base-sites for air
tracking facilities. The leases would run 999 years. That
seemed an inordinately long time to most Panamanians,
and they further objected that these "little Canal Zones," as
they called them, would pockmark their country. Refusing
to agree to the demands, they nevertheless watched pas-
sively as the United States moved into some of the sites.
Washington argued that possession was justified by the
1936 treaty. Legally the action was questionable; politically
it was irresponsible. In October 1940 the United States ap-

1. A. R. Wright, "Defense Sites Negotiations Between the United States
and Panama, 1936–1948," *Department of State Bulletin*, XXVII (Aug. 11,
1952), 217.

proached the newly elected Panamanian President to legalize the occupation and obtain as many as one hundred more sites. The new President was Arnulfo Arias.

The Rise and Temporary Fall of Panameñismo

Arias was a phenomenon in Panamanian politics. In 1940–41 he disrupted a political process caked with tradition and corruption. Since Taft's intervention in 1904 a small group of oligarchs had controlled affairs, with the possible exception of 1932 to 1936 when Harmodio Arias ran the country. But even he proved to be "responsible." Although the governmental structure resembled the three-branch North American system, the President actually dominated a rubber-stamp legislature (the National Assembly), and used his powers of appointment and patronage to control the Supreme Court. The presidency had carefully been kept within the club, in this case the posh Union Club of Panama City which commanded a magnificent view of the Pacific. Within the Union Club gentlemen made deals ensuring that no political faction would be burdened with either suspicious foreign ideologies or simple promises to distribute wealth more equitably. Factions formed, but along personal and kinship lines. Since party programs were meaningless, a member was known less as a Liberal or Conservative or one of the many other formal titles, than as a follower of "The Fox," "The Rifle," or "The Cripple." Party labels carried less clout than nicknames.

Doubly ensuring stability, oligarchical leaders devised voting procedures that tended to guarantee electoral triumphs. Ballots, for example, were counted by an election board under the President's control. The government was so democratic in distributing *cedulas* (or identity cards needed for voting), that even friendly aliens received them. The President obtained support from remote provinces by working with the *cacique*, or provincial political boss, who used methods not unfamiliar to the ward machines in Memphis, Chicago, or Kansas City.[2]

In light of his cooperation between 1931 and 1936, Arnulfo Arias (or "El Hombre"—"The Man"—as he was better known on the streets), apparently posed no danger to the Union Club's grandes. Quite unlike the oligarchy's leaders, Arnulfo came from a poor family living in the interior. It was not related to the rich, aristocratic Arias clan that had been influential throughout the nineteenth century (and was again in the 1950s). Through luck and skill Arnulfo received training as a physician at the University of Chicago and Harvard. Returning to Panama he gained a reputation for ministering to the poor and quickly turned it to advantage, for his real talent lay in politics.

In 1940 United States Intelligence reported that Arnulfo had remained "friendly to Americans" until he became Minister to Italy in 1934; there he served intermittently until 1938. When he returned home he led campaigns against United States- and Canadian-owned businesses in Panama, forcing National City Bank and Chase National, among others, to move their offices into the Canal Zone. Some observers linked his change to an audience with Hitler in 1937. "Those who have known him for years can offer no explanation to the change of sentiment towards the United States," the Intelligence report concluded, "other than that he has reached some understanding with the Berlin and Rome Chancellories."[3]

Returning to economically devastated Panama, the charismatic "El Hombre" pieced together a political coalition, including some oligarchs with fascistic tendencies and the growing, nationalistic middle class. He swept into power by a vote of 107,750 to 3,022. The supporters of his opponent, the distinguished diplomat Ricardo Alfaro, decided to protest Arias's certain victory by boycotting the

2. John Biesanz and L. M. Smith, "Panamanian Politics," *Journal of Politics*, XIV (August 1952), 394.

3. Memorandum by Military Intelligence Division, Oct. 7, 1940, 819.00/ 2106, Box 3728, NA, RG 59.

polls. So began a political career that ended only after two more short but dramatic terms as President. Arias made it an interesting quarter-century.

His political genius lay partly in his ability to tap the country's centuries-old nationalism and its more recent anti-Gringo feelings. Breaking with oligarchical tradition, he advanced a highly ideological program called *panameñismo* meaning, in the words of a sympathetic Panamanian historian, "government by Panamanians for the happiness of the Panamanian people."[4] The United States Embassy's report of his Inaugural speech, however, presented another side to *panameñismo*. Arias, in the Embassy's words, rejected "as biologically without justification the 'demogogic concept' that 'all men are born free and equal,' " then "referred to the desirability of improving the nation's racial strains by selected immigration and criticized the entrance of large numbers of negroes." Arias reiterated the need for friendship with the United States, but he also advocated constitutional reform.[5] The last point appeared ominous, given Arias's racial views.

The new President moved quickly to implement his program. English signs were replaced by Spanish, English newspapers could only be supplements inside Spanish journals, government officials talked only Spanish to North Americans, West Indians faced deportation, and in the provinces Arias confiscated Chinese and Hindu businesses, turning them over to political cronies (who, in most instances, soon lost or sold them). Beginning his own New Deal, Arias planned a social security system and initiated some agricultural reforms. Meanwhile the Axis presence grew in Panama until it influenced newspapers; Germans and Italians obtained quick citizenship rights through easy provisional naturalization. By July 1941, Harmodio complained to the American Ambassador that his brother was

4. Ernesto J. Castillero Reyes, *Historia de Panama* (Panama, 1955), p. 201.
5. Memorandum by Willard F. Barber, Oct. 9, 1940, attached to 819.001/ Arias, Arnulfo/42, Box 3729, NA, RG 59. This memorandum noted the dangerous aspects of Arias's program.

using racketeering methods to gain control of his newspaper so it could be used for totalitarian purposes. Harmodio begged the United States to make no agreements with
Arnulfo's administration that would "increase its prestige."[6] The story doubtless lost little in the telling. Jealous
and fearful of his younger brother, Harmodio, in one of his
typical political schemes, plotted to have the embassy act
as front-man in bringing down Arnulfo.

Harmodio spoke to a receptive audience. Washington
tempers were growing short. At a Cabinet meeting Secretary of War Henry Stimson detailed Arias's refusal to cooperate with United States defense preparations. Roosevelt,
Stimson wrote in his diary, "appreciated this fully—told
me of his troubles with Arias and told Hull to try some
strong arm methods on him."[7] Nor were the State Department's fears lessened when the popular journalist, John
Gunther, returned to inform North American foreign policy
experts that "Panama has the closest thing to a totalitarian
government—Paraguay excepted—that is to be found in
the Western Hemisphere. It is ruled by a Harvard-trained
neurotic." In 1967 a careful scholar offered an assessment
at least equally accurate: "Arias was a logical product of the
decades of anti-American antagonism on the isthmus."[8]

In retrospect, 1940–41 marked a radical turn in Panama's politics. A fascistic charismatic leader of middle-
class background appealed across class lines to confront the
oligarchs and United States officials with an explosive political program; indeed to their eyes it appeared doubly
dangerous since it appealed to so many Panamanians. For
the first time, demands for radical social change linked up
with Panamanian nationalism. That nationalism, particu-

6. Edwin C. Wilson to Sumner Welles, Personal, July 2, 1941, 819.00/2134
1/2, Box 3729, NA, RG 59.

7. Diaries of Stimson, Stimson Papers, XXXII, 9 Jan. 1941, p. 94.

8. "Study Group Reports," John Gunther, March 13, 1941, *Records of
Meetings*, VI, Council on Foreign Relations, New York City; Langley,
"World Crisis and the Good Neighbor policy in Panama, 1936–1941," pp.
147, 152.

larly its anti-Gringoism, had ironic aspects, for it came
mainly from a middle class created by North American dollars and jobs. The economic impact of the Canal Zone
turned the small, pre-1903 middle class into a large, and
vocal group of office workers, professionals, and teachers
whom Harmodio and Arnulfo Arias first utilized to gain
power in the early 1930s. Arnulfo received strong support
in Panama City and Colon, where most of the middle class
lived, when he attacked blacks. The new class was the most
anti-black of all Panamanian groups, due partly to fears of
economic competition, partly to a proud nationalism that
feared outsiders might mistake their country for a "Black
republic." The very success of the Canal Zone, and its thousands of West Indian laborers, had created a middle class
whose anti-Yankeeism and dislike of blacks formed the basis of Arnulfo's burgeoning power.[9]

Not surprisingly, negotiations involving the 100 new
military sites did not progress. Arias refused to agree until
the United States dropped the 999-year lease demand, promised $25 million of economic aid, and built a bridge over
the Canal to connect eastern and western Panama. He also
required that the West Indians be returned to their island
homes, the Panama City and Colon water and sewer systems be given to Panama, and rent on Rio Hato be raised to
$30 million a year (the annual lease was then $2400). Roosevelt refused to meet most of the demands, threatening
instead to occupy the bases. Arias then approved leasing
one small site. When Winston Churchill and FDR announced the Atlantic Charter's promise of freedom and self-
determination in August 1941, Arias announced his delight
that Roosevelt finally recognized "the right of all people to

9. The Panamanian middle class was thoroughly studied during the
1940s, especially in essays by John Biesanz, Georgina Jiménez de López,
and Carolyn Campbell and Ofelia Hooper published in Theo R. Crevenna,
Materials para el estudio de la clase media en la America Latina, Volume
IV (Washington, D.C., 1950); see especially pp. 8–10, 20, 66–68; also for
general background, Eric Wolf and Edward C. Hansen, *The Human Condition in Latin America* (New York, 1972), p. 196.

adopt that government which is most in accord with their idiosyncrasies and their needs, and with the desire of their own people."[10]

A month before, United States Ambassador Edwin C. Wilson had reported rumors of a coup, although he discounted them since Arias supposedly controlled the police. On October 7, however, Wilson received "reliable information" that Arias's attempt to curb the Guard's powers was making it restless. That morning Arias suddenly left for Cuba, ostensibly for medical reasons, actually to spend a few days in Havana with his mistress. On October 9 a dissident Cabinet member and the second-in-command of the Guard asked Wilson how the United States would regard the overthrow of Arias. Could they count on immediate recognition? Wilson replied he could give no "indication whatsoever on these points," since under the Good Neighbor the United States did not involve itself in the internal affairs of other nations.[11] Wilson thus signaled that Washington would not try to stop the coup, but also would not directly encourage it. The anti-Arias group, however, did not need further encouragement, only a sign of United States intention to abstain benignly when the coup occurred. This they received.

National Guard officers announced that Arias was deposed and First Vice-President Ernesto de la Guardia was the new President. The Panamanian Supreme Court gave the proper constitutional blessing to the overthrow by declaring that de la Guardia's ascension was legal since Arias had "abandoned" the presidency.[12] The new President quickly rescinded many of Arias's policies: newspapers were again delivered with the English language sections outside, the National Bank recalled newly issued Panama-

---

10. Donald Marquand Dozer, *Are We Good Neighbors?* (Gainesville, Fla., 1959), pp. 102–103.
11. Wilson to Secretary of State, Oct. 9, 1941, 819.001/Arias, Arnulfo/90, Box 3729, NA, RG 59.
12. Wilson to Secretary of State, Oct. 14, 1941, 819.001/Arias, Arnulfo/98, Box 3729, NA, RG 59.

nian paper money which Arias had hoped would break the
country's tie to the dollar, and the government confiscated
games of chance, especially slot machines, which were a
highly profitable racket for the Arias faction. When the
"traganiqueles," or nickel swallowers, were hauled away,
the U.S. Ambassador reported, supposedly with a straight
face, that crowds cheered.

Reports circulated widely that the United States en-
gineered the overthrow of Arias. Hull denied any involvement "clearly and uncategorically." Stimson nevertheless
observed the coup was "a great relief to us, because Arias
has been very troublesome and very pro-Nazi."[13] Adolf
Berle, a top State Department official and FDR "brain-
truster," believed the United States "had absolutely nothing to do with" the coup, yet welcomed it since Arias was
"pro-Nazi" and "a nuisance." Berle then defined a dilemma
which increasingly confronted Washington policy-makers:
"I don't like revolutions on principle," but this one was
"probably all to the good."[14] Significantly, this marked the
first time U.S. officials faced such a problem in Panama. It
would not be the last.

Washington's leverage in Panamanian affairs remained strong. In 1944 the U.S. Chargé in Panama candidly
discussed his nation's domination of isthmian politics. "As
a matter of fact," John Muccio told the State Department,
"there has never been a successful change of government in
Panama but that American authorities have been 'consulted'
beforehand—remember 1931 and 1941!"[15]

Another First: The Riots of 1947

A former student at Dartmouth, de la Guardia was
warmly disposed toward North American interests. He ac-

13. Diaries of Stimson, Stimson Papers, XXXV, 9 Oct. 1941, p. 123
14. "Memorandum," Oct. 10, 1941, Diary, Papers of Adolf Berle, Franklin
D. Roosevelt Library, Hyde Park, N. Y.
15. John J. Muccio to Phillip W. Bonsal, June 6, 1944, 819.00/6–644, Box
3729, NA, RG 59.

ceded to most of Washington's demands for 134 base sites, although he limited the lease-duration to the war plus one year after the signing of a peace treaty. For its part the United States turned the sewer and water systems of the two major cities over to Panama and granted new economic assistance, but refused to deport the West Indians or pay high rents for the sites. Panama, moreover, was one of only two Latin American nations that received no Lend-lease help from the United States. (The other country was Argentina, which Hull considered pro-Nazi, an outcast, and a personal obsession.) The State Department sent no Lend-lease since it wished no large arms supplies given to the National Guard.[16] The United States remained not just the largest, but the only important military force on the Isthmus.

As an economic stimulus, Lend-lease would not have been important. The Panamanian economy boomed as military traffic tested the Canal's capacity. With its usual North American imports going to European or Pacific war theaters, Panama's domestic production rose rapidly. Production of milk, sugar, electricity, and slaughtered cattle nearly doubled between 1939 and 1946. The government accelerated the take-off by increasing its expenditures fourfold, but the real catalyst was the influx of dollars: wartime savings drove up bank deposits nine times and bank loans rose four times.

Dollars poured in also through direct investments. Between 1930 and 1943 United States capital investments dropped sharply in every Latin American country except Venezuela (where oil was found) and Panama. The latter enjoyed the higher percentage increase of the two as investment multiplied three times to $154 million, mostly in banking and utilities. Controlling twenty-two enterprises in Panama in 1929, by 1943 United States corporations owned át least seventy-nine. This influx was part of a massive invasion by North American businessmen; between

16. "Memorandum" by Emilio Collado, July 21, 1941, *FRUS, 1941*, VI, 142.

1940 and 1943 they nearly doubled the number of their enterprises in Latin America.[17]

The United States thus fueled hemispheric prosperity, but also made itself an obvious target if the economy deteriorated in peacetime. Growth did decline in Panama during 1946–47, and nowhere was the United States presence more obvious, or, because of the base agreement, more exposed to a new type of nationalism.

In 1946 Washington asked to renew the leases on base sites occupied since 1940–41. President Enrique A. Jiménez, flatly refused. The United States returned over 100 installations, but asked to retain Rio Hato airbase and thirteen of the one-acre sites. The State and War Departments fought bitterly over the terms. The military insisted on leases of thirty or more years and refused to consider any joint control with Panama. The State Department, considerably more sensitive to (and, as it turned out, more realistic about) Panamanian nationalism, wanted a shorter lease period. It also was willing to meet Jiménez's demand for economic aid, but only after he delivered the leases.[18] Finally in December 1947 an agreement appeared on the fourteen sites. Rio Hato's lease would run ten years with an option for another ten, and leases on the thirteen remaining sites would last for five years. The United States would enjoy total control. Jiménez sent the pact to the National Assembly for ratification.

Between December 11 and 17 the streets of Panama City erupted in violence. On the 11th Ricardo Alfaro, the distinguished Panamanian who negotiated the 1936 treaty and the early portions of the 1947 agreement, suddenly resigned to organize opposition to the new pact. Jiménez had refused to listen to Alfaro's warning that if the Presi-

17. United Nations Economic Commission for Latin America, "The Economic Development of Panama," Economic Bulletin for Latin America, IV (October 1959), 48–49; Rippy, Globe and Hemisphere, pp. 43–45. The mass of Panamanians made real sacrifices for the war effort; see Laurence O. Ealy, The Republic of Panama in World Affairs (Philadelphia, 1951), pp. 116–118.
18. FRUS, 1947, VIII, 887, 905.

dent did not obtain a concrete United States promise of economic assistance *before* signing the agreement, "he could whistle for it after."[19] With the government split and the treaty's terms public, students started to riot against the agreement. In clashes with the National Guard, one student was killed, dozens hurt, and at least seventeen police sent to hospitals. On December 16, 10,000 women and children staged anti-Yankee demonstrations outside the Assembly. Professors and students went on strike.

Not only the treaty was in danger. On December 18 the Embassy cabled the State Department that the "Amazing development is actual physical fear which had seized most deputies. President of Assembly spoke of '10,000 boys with knives' which might await them." Several Colon deputies had promised Jiménez their votes, but reneged since they did not promise "to allow themselves to be shot at."[20] In Colon a U.S. soldier was stabbed. At the last minute the State Department tried to salvage the situation by offering to discuss specific economic aid.[21] The message arrived too late. On December 22, surrounded by screaming galleries, a motion rejecting the treaty passed 51-0. Three months later the North Americans evacuated all the sites occupied after 1940.

The 1947 upheaval marked a number of firsts. It was the first time a massive nationalist movement successfully thwarted United States policies in Panama. It was also the first time students were pivotal in the protests. While President, Harmodio Arias founded the National University in 1935. It quickly became what he no doubt intended it to be, an institution of learning for middle-class Panamanians. (Most oligarchs sent their children abroad for education.) In this sense the students' nationalism directly descended from events set in motion by the Arias brothers in the 1931 coup. In 1944 the highly politicized Federation of Panamanian Students was organized at the university. The uni-

19. *Ibid.*, 942.
20. For a description of the rioting see *ibid.*, 943–946.
21. Wright, "Defense Sites Negotiations," p. 219.

versity, and especially the Federation, became ladders for middle- and lower-class students who determined to succeed economically, were willing to challenge the government in the streets, and advocated a political program that was to the left. The oligarchy's politics followed kinship lines, but the students based theirs on reform programs, institutional ties, and a multi-class base.[22] When, for example, they protested the 1947 agreement, lower-class Panamanians gave visible support.

The oligarchy appreciated none of this. Its political power had been severely shaken. Nor did the National Guard welcome student rioting. Since the overthrow of Arias in 1941, if not since the 1931 upheaval, the Guard had acted as the arbiter of Panamanian politics. When the students challenged the Guard's power, the 1947 clashes marked another first that was portentous for United States-Panamanian relations. By the 1960s and 1970s those relations had to be worked out in a Panamanian political context shaped by Guard-student animosity.

Guard strongman José Remón blamed Communist and Socialist leaders for the rioting. Celso Selano, Secretary General of the Communist People's Party (the Partido del Pueblo), indeed directed some of the student activity. The Communist involvement, however, was minute compared with the students' role. Communism held little attraction for the students, at least as long as they could hope for some security within the present system. Harmodio Arias understood this. After the clashes, his influential newspaper vigorously attacked Remón's police for embarrassing Panama internationally by beating up students. (Since the police suffered more casualties than the students, Harmodio's sympathies seemed misplaced.[23]) Arias, with some help from Arnulfo, was trying to group the students and lower classes in a political coalition against Remón and the Guard. Out of the 1947 treaty protests, therefore, emerged the two main pro-

22. Biesanz and Smith, "Panamanian Politics," pp. 401–402.
23. Larry LaRae Pippin, *The Remón Era: An Analysis of a Decade of Events in Panama 1947–1957* (Stanford, 1964), pp. 17–19.

tagonists—the students and Guard—who would shape the nation's politics as oligarchical power declined.

The intensity of the hatred between the Guard and students hinted at a deeper problem. The National Guard recruited many blacks and mestizos from the interior provinces. The students were mainly urban and included whiter Panamanians as well as mestizos. Not only a political conflict impended, but class, ideological, and perhaps racial struggles. The dimensions of this confrontation could not be forgotten in the future, not even when National Guard leaders tried to coopt the students by calling them natural allies in opposing United States policy. Underneath any pretended alliance lurked political divisions and personal hatreds rooted deep in history.

Depression Amidst Gold and Silver

The 1947 riots were also significant because the United States played no direct role in restoring public order. One part of its colonial rule, Theodore Roosevelt's "big stick," was apparently in discard. But the other part of its control remained, for its economic leverage— indeed its dominance—increased. As Washington's wartime spending sharply declined, Panamanians entered a depression that sharpened their nationalism and shaped future clashes with the United States.

Panama again served as a case study of broader hemispheric relations. During the war the Latin Americans sacrificed for the Allies' war effort by sending more than 50 percent of their exports to United States war industries. In some cases entire production of a raw material moved north, despite shortages and growing inflation in the producing countries. After the war ended, the Latins possessed some dollar reserves for developmental purposes, but they needed, and believed they richly deserved, United States help. They particularly wanted access to financial sources and the limited number of North American manufactured goods. Washington turned down both requests, bluntly announcing that Western European reconstruction enjoyed first preference. Latin America, it turned out, was far down the list. As the price of manufactured goods skyrocketed in the late 1940s, raw material prices slumped. Latin American economies entered a crisis period. The United States offered no systematic response, only advice that the Latins ask private investors for help. Those financiers doubled United States investments in Latin America between 1946 and 1955 from $3 million to $6.6 million. Most went into raw material production, especially Venezuelan oil.[24]

In 1947 the Rio Treaty brought South America and Central America into a military alliance with the United States. The following year these nations upgraded the old Pan American movement by forming the Organization of American States. The Rio pact and the OAS, however, rested on sand. No economic foundation existed. With appropriate symbolism, the OAS was born at Bogotá, Colombia, as rioters besieged the city demanding employment and food.

The Good Neighbor seemed to have deserted the neighborhood. Poverty and dictatorship threatened to fill the void, but the United States appeared undisturbed. At a Council of Foreign Relations meeting in 1949, men experienced in hemispheric affairs, including Nelson Rockefeller and Adolf Berle, gathered to discuss the problem privately. The chairman of the group, investment banker Franklin Adams Truslow, outlined a central assumption that henceforth shaped United States policy toward Latin Amerca:

> A distinction should be made between totalitarianism and dictatorship. A dictatorship involves autocratic rule. But totalitarianism is autocratic rule plus total, absolute control of economic life, as for, example, communism.... Totali-

24. Duggan, *The Americas*, pp. 123–126; Rippy, *Globe and Hemisphere*, p. 72. The best discussion is David Green, *The Containment of Latin America* (Chicago, 1971), chapters 7–11.

tarianism we refuse to cooperate with . . .; with dictatorship we will.[25]

When the Korean War broke out, however, and Washington asked for help, not even many of the "dictators"
responded as the United States hoped. The continent was
moving to a "third force" position between the United
States and Russia. As Panama's leading newspaper explained in early 1950, North Americans should not expect
help against Communism "from those [in Latin America]
who have not yet learned the exact significance of the benefits of liberty and democracy which involve their very
existence."[26]

Panama's only alternative was to work with the
United States during the Korean War. The cooperative efforts did not go smoothly, however, nor did they stop the
Panamanian depression. As Canal Zone spending dropped
sharply after 1946, Panama searched for help. The nation
could not manipulate its money supply because the balboa
was tied to the dollar. Tax sources proved inadequate, for
revenues dropped as imports declined. The wealthy oligarchy refused to tax itself for national development; many
members invested in real estate or kept accounts in the
United States and Switzerland. Canal Zone revenues were
held tightly by the United States.

A fourfold increase in public spending between 1946
and 1950 kept the economy from collapse. The only tangi-
ble benefits were a huge Panama City tourist hotel and
Tocumen Airport which soon became, like the Canal, an
international crossroads. Otherwise unemployment and
governmental deficits rose to dangerous levels. Between
1945 and 1955 per capita income actually dropped 2 per-

25. "Study Group Reports, Inter-American Affairs," Feb. 7, 1949, *Records
of Groups*, XVI-D, Council on Foreign Relations, New York City. Truslow
graduated from Yale in 1928, attended Harvard Law School, and formed
his own Wall Street law firm before working during World War II in Peru
as Special Representative from the U.S. Government's Rubber Reserve
agency. In 1947 he became president of the New York Curb Exchange.
26. Quoted in Dozer, *Are We Good Neighbors?* pp. 322–325.

cent as capital investments barely rose and the population increase accelerated. It was one of the worst of a bad lot of economic records in Latin America.[27]

The Zone provided less help than Panama needed. A high United States official explained in 1947, "The heart of the problem is the Gold and Silver rolls," through which "discrimination is practiced administratively." North Americans on the gold roll enjoyed a $1.07 per hour minimum wage, but the silver roll averaged 44¢ to 66¢. Gold teachers received three times the salary of silver teachers, and the silver teachers did the better jobs.[28] The United States continued breaking its 1936 promise to equalize opportunity. The former chief of the State Department's Latin American desk blamed the American Federation of Labor. In order to protect North American workers, he argued, the AFL "browbeat the War Department into setting up two scales of pay, one for United States citizens and one for 'foreigners.' "[29] By the 1940s, most of the "foreigners" were Panamanians.

Conditions were worsened by urban housing—or lack of it. By 1950 one of every four of the 800,000 Panamanians lived in Panama City. Another 100,000 lived in Colon or David. The two Canal cities, Panama City and Colon, contained slums of unbelievable squalor, where the unemployed and underpaid existed in *barriadas brujas,* or "witch quarters." Since the "witch quarters" and the Zone were separated only by a roadway, the situation was highly combustible.

Arnulfo's Return

The economic chaos was mirrored in the political chaos. A power struggle between Presidents and the National Assembly prevented regular elections in 1944 and

27. Pedro C. M. Teichert, *Economic Policy Revolution and Industrialization in Latin America* (Oxford, Miss., 1959), p. 31.
28. *FRUS, 1947,* VIII, 950—956.
29. Duggan, *The Americas,* p. 171.

resulted in a new constitution of 1946. The document proved once again that by themselves, and when surrounded by economic crisis, written constitutions can be irrelevant.

For the 1948 campaign the reigning Liberal Party chose seventy-three-year-old Domingo Diáz as its candidate. Arnulfo Arias rose from the political dead, dusted off his *panameñismo* nationalism, and in an initial count by the National Elections Board apparently won the presidency by 1500 votes. Diáz supporters thereupon attacked the Board, wounding two members. Arias's backers prepared to move into the streets to ensure his election.

At this point José Remón, head of the National Guard, took charge. Under his protection the Elections Board magically made enough of Arias's votes disappear so Diáz became President. (Remón watched approvingly; in 1941 Arias had tried to emasculate the Guard's power and send one of its young officers, José Remón, out of the country.) The Guard then smashed a pro-Arias student rally. When Arias tried to start an uprising, Remón disgustedly threw both Harmodio and Arnulfo Arias in jail. During the next four years Panamanian presidential politics resembled a game of musical chairs, with Remón and the National Guard stopping and starting the music. The political system, the constitutional order, and the oligarchy's power would never be the same.

The country was in transition from the solid oligarchical control of the pre-1931 years to the hard-fisted National Guard domination of post-1968. During the 1947 riots student power and a new, aggressive anti-United States nationalism symbolized by Alfaro had challenged the oligarchy. In early 1949 the United States Ambassador pointed to deeper fissures that threatened a political earthquake unless they were somehow checked. "All too frequently the [political] cleavage comes along racial and class lines," Monnet B. Davis warned the State Department, "a tendency that the subversive elements are at some pains to augment by constant propaganda designed not only to arouse race and class hatred," but to associate the United States "with the now distrusted and hated upper governing class in Panama."[30] For nearly a half-century Washington and the oligarchy had worked hand-in-hand, so both were threatened by the rip-tide of changes. Panama was no longer the obedient, ma-nipulated-from-the-top country of 1903 or 1930.

Díaz faced an additional problem since he was also fighting a losing battle against senility. To buttress his power he devised a new system for cattle slaughtering, one of the most lucrative businesses in the country still under Panamanian control. Díaz granted a monopoly over the slaughter-houses to his son, Temistocles ("Temi"), and Remón. That seemed to ensure a long honeymoon with the National Guard and keep "subversive elements," as Ambas-sador Davis called them, in their place. When, for example, Harmodio Arias plotted a coup, the police smashed it and Díaz suspended constitutional guarantees so Harmodio could be jailed until evidence was collected. Remón's force worked with special effectiveness on this occasion because the U.S. Army's G-2 Intelligence had uncovered the Arias scheme and given the information to the National Guard. Relations between the Army and the Guard, the U.S. Em-bassy told Washington, "have never been better."[31] It might also have been one reason why, as Davis later noted, Pana-manians associated the United States with the "now dis-trusted and hated upper governing class in Panama."

Unfortunately for this cozy arrangement, Díaz sud-denly died in August 1949. First Vice-President Daniel Chanís assumed power, but he was hardly settled in the Presidential Palace before the Panama Supreme Court, in a fit of legality, declared the Díaz-Remón cattle monopoly un-constitutional. With a sure sense for self-destruction, Chanís decided to uphold the ruling. When Díaz and Remón accom-panied their cattle to the slaughter-houses (with pistols cocked so their property would enjoy special consideration),

30. FRUS, 1949, II, 706–707.
31. E. W. Clark to Secretary of State, April 28, 1949, 819.00/4–2849, NA, RG 59.

Chanís summoned Remón to dismiss the Guard's chief and break up the clique. The National Guard promptly surrounded the Palace and rescued their leader. Chanís resigned.

Again, the United States appeared to be an accomplice to the coup. Diáz's body was still warm when "Temi" Diáz, his close and incredibly corrupt friend "Baby" Jiménez, and Remón began plotting against Chanís. They ostentatiously associated with North Americans so it would appear the Embassy and military were on their side.[32] The North Americans happily cooperated in order to gain information. Although they played no active role in Chanís's overthrow, United States citizens were again perceived by Panamanians to be working with the most corrupt elements, this time to destroy a Supreme Court decision through the use of the National Guard.

The Embassy, moreover, was present at the kill. When the National Guard surrounded the Palace, Chanís entertained the idea of resisting. The foreign diplomatic corps immediately warned both the President and the Guard it wanted no bloodshed. Ambassador Davis insisted upon what he called, with perhaps unconscious humor, "our traditional policy observance [of] constitutional and democratic procedures."[33] Chanís graciously upheld such procedures by abdicating power at the point of National Guard rifles. In reality, Davis followed the traditional Roosevelt-Taft approach of choosing order over potential chaos, even if order meant the destruction of whatever small amount of constitutional legality remained in Panama.

But the game of musical chairs was not finished. Chanís was replaced by the Second Vice-President, Roberto Chiari, a wealthy oligarch who also happened to be Remón's cousin. The new President lasted a week. Chanís materialized before the National Assembly, delivered a blistering attack on Remón, and with Harmodio Arias pulling the

32. Memorandum by Sowash, Nov. 22, 1949, 810.00/11–2249, NA, RG 59; Hall to Secretary of State, Aug. 31, 1949, 810.00/8-3149, NA, RG 59.
33. Davis to Secretary of State, Nov. 20, 1949, 819.00/11-2049, NA, RG 59.

strings, the Assembly supported Chanís, condemned Chiari's usurpation of power, and prepared to move into the streets against the police. Having no stomach for such a confrontation, Chairi was about to call for Chanís's reinstatement as President when Remón learned of his cousin's betrayal. The Guard chief gave the new President ten minutes to pack his belongings and leave the Palace. Remón then stunned everyone by putting Arnulfo Arias into power.

Davis and the State Department could not believe it. That Panama, with direct United States help, endured three Presidents within a week in November 1949 was of less concern to the Ambassador than Arnulfo ending the game with the only remaining chair. "What had happened," Davis phoned Washington, "was a complete challenge of democracy and represented extraordinary double-crossing in every respect." Davis was furious that he had stressed the need for "democratic processes," and ended with Arias, "Remón[,] and his gangster associates." He was convinced that Arias would remove Remón "by fair means or foul. His dictatorship can be expected to be absolute and I am confident he will cooperate with our enemies to our embarrassment." Davis even called it "a misuse of force which should be challenged."[34] No longer, however, could U.S. Ambassadors so easily correct their errors by calling in the Marines.

Davis bravely suggested that Washington should continue to recognize Chanís as President. Washington equivocated, however, finally settling on a watch-and-wait non-recognition policy. Strikes spread in Panama, gasoline was in short supply, and a key State Department official, perhaps hoping that economic chaos would lead to Arias's overthrow, announced that "the best policy was for Americans not to interfere in any way with strikes."[35]

The non-recognition policy did not work. Remón

34. Phone call from Davis to Wise, Nov. 24, 1949, 819.00/11-2449, NA, RG 59; Davis to Secretary of State, Nov. 25, 1949, 819.00/11-2549, NA, RG 59.
35. Memorandum of phone conversations between Davis and E. G. Miller, Jr., Nov. 26, 1949, 819.00/11-2449, NA, RG 59.

consolidated Arias's power, even calling in the Elections Board to recount the 1948 results so Arnulfo would win officially. In hours the Board found pro-Arias votes it had been unable to find in weeks after the 1948 balloting. The National Guard successfully moved to end the strikes and restore order. Ambassador Davis could not understand why such bitter enemies as Remón and Arias were suddenly allies. "Everyone very much confused," Davis told Washington. But he had already provided one explanation by noting that Arias, unlike Chanís, willingly accepted the cattle slaughtering racket of Remón, "Temi" Diáz, and "Baby" Jimenez, all of whom duly closed ranks around the President. Remón believed he could handle Arnulfo. Since the new President could not constitutionally succeed himself, moreover, Remón was in perfect position to win the presidency himself in 1952.

Remón and the State Department believed Arias had mellowed since 1941. After watching him for nearly a week, an impressed State Department official observed that he was "saying all the right things and influential sections [of] American business community now favor early recognition." Arias especially reassured Jewish merchants who worried about his fascism of 1940–41.[36] Arnulfo, Panama desk officer Murray Wise concluded, had seen the light:

> [Arias] may have been pro-Nazi earlier because he was convinced Germany would win the war. . . . In any event I believe Arnulfo was more fascist or totalitarian than Nazi. Arnulfo is intelligent and shrewd and can make himself one of Panama's strongest Presidents. It would not be too risky to predict if he can firmly establish himself . . . he might decide to cooperate rapidly and effectively with the United States and take an aggressive initiative in endeavoring to settle many pending problems successfully.[37]

In the context of a Cold War abroad and an increas-

36. Davis to Secretary of State, Dec. 1, 1949, 819.00/11-2849, NA, RG 59.
37. Memorandum by Wise, Nov. 28, 1949, 819.00/11-2849, NA, RG 59.

ingly fragmented political system in Panama, the pro-fascist of 1940–41 looked appealing. The appeal grew in December when, as the British Ambassador to Panama observed, Arias was even winning over the safe and solid members of the oligarchy, "the notoriously fickle, greedy and unscrupulous petit bourgeois who control the commerce and industry of this country."[38] Appeal led to seduction. The United States recognized Arias in December, convinced that "all indications are that he has completely changed his position."

Neither the State Department nor Remón knew their man. The chief characteristic of Arnulfo's story-book career has been his uncanny ability to posture and persuade when out of power, and, once in power, his equally uncanny inability to control his ambitions. Whether dealing with Roosevelt in 1941, Remón in 1950, the National Guard in 1968, or Ronald Reagan in 1976, Arias seemed more interested in a game of political manipulation than retaining and effectively using political power.

Having obtained United States support in late 1949, Arias spent public funds lavishly to build a supposedly impregnable political base. The budget deficit reached $7 million. The Arias family naturally received its share. The President forced owners of choice coffee lands to sell out to him, then built a twenty-seven-mile highway and a bridge on the lands at taxpayers' expense. He put a similar squeeze on Panamanian bankers. A huge narcotics and gold-smuggling operation developed under the alleged leadership of his favorite nephew, Antonio "The Druggist" Arias. "The Druggist" died in 1956 in a mysterious plane accident.

Opposition that could not be bought or coerced was jailed, and Arnulfo established his own secret police independently of the National Guard. In 1951, he went too far. After suspending the 1946 constitution, Arias tried to de-

38. Enclosed in LaRue to Secretary of State, Dec. 23, 1949, 819.00/12-2349, NA, RG. 59. For Arias's unsuccessful attempt to weaken U.S. claims to the Zone bases during the Korean War, see Ealy, *Republic of Panama*, pp. 160–161.

stroy the National Assembly and Supreme Court. The Assembly retaliated by impeaching him and electing Alcibiádes Arosemena as President. Arias asked Remón for protection. Concluding that Arias could no longer be trusted, Remón sided with the Assembly. But when Remón's two top aides served the eviction notice on the President, Arias's supporters killed both in cold blood. A shoot-out followed in which sixteen died before the President was captured. The Assembly brought Arnulfo to trial, stripped him of all political rights, and sent him off into exile. (Within a decade he returned with rights restored, ready for another go-round with Remón's successors.)

An interim President served while Remón and Chiari fought the 1952 presidential campaign. Aided by his politically astute wife, Cecilia, who organized the newly granted vote to women and tramped provincial jungles to gather support, Remón won an overwhelming victory.[39] Another reason for the triumph was the Guard's unremitting efforts in beating down student demonstrations.

Remón

José "Chichi" Remón resembled Arnulfo in at least one respect: he added a new dimension to Panamanian politics. Remón represented the force that replaced United States troops as the guardian of order—if not always law— in Panama, for he used the National Guard as the stepping-stone to ultimate power. And as the authority of the Guard (and Remón) rose, the oligarchy's power became more shaky. Remón thus set precedents followed by General Omar Torrijos in the 1970s.

Remón, like Torrijos, was a self-made man, rising out of a lower income family by joining the police ranks, gaining military education in Mexico and the United States, then nimbly avoiding the traps of Panama City politics until he

39. A fascinating illustrated story on her efforts is in *Life*, May 5, 1952 entitled "A Woman's Place Is . . . On the Stump."

headed the Guard in 1947. As a young officer "Chichi" upgraded police prestige through higher salaries and fringe benefits. After becoming President, Remón turned part of the Guard, then wholly a police force, into the Panamanian army.[40] He cared about prestige (in his travels "Chichi" noted that army officers received greater deference than police), but the change also allowed the force to receive large amounts of United States military supplies. Personally sensitive and politically astute, Remón repaired two splits within the Guard: a division between those schooled overseas and those unschooled, and differences between black and those of mixed blood.[41] Since the Remón years, race relations within the Guard have been much better than within the whole of Panamanian society.

The oligarchy was declining, the small middle class (except for the students) unorganized, and the lower classes effectively disenfranchised or manipulated. Remón's Guard became the instrument for maintaining order and gaining power. No serious rival existed. The Guard maintained close watch on the students; Remón never forgot the humiliation suffered by his men during the 1947 riots. A 1000-member Communist Party appeared in the late 1940s, but when it tried to gain control of unions the American Federation of Labor dealt with it ruthlessly. So had Arias, who used the Communists as scapegoats to excuse the excesses of his presidency.

Nor did Remón have to be concerned with the unions. The AFL only cared about protecting its members from the dual threats of communism and Panamanian demands for equal job opportunities. The only other important union worked closely with the United Fruit Company on the banana plantations. Splits between blacks and mestizos, English-speaking and Spanish-speaking laborers, Jamaicans and Panamanians, paralyzed union organizers.

---

40. "National Guard" has been used through the book instead of "police." The Guard developed directly out of the police, and the police now form part of the Guard.
41. Pippin, *Remón Era*, pp. 1–7, is the definitive treatment.

High unemployment undercut bargaining attempts. Remón and his National Guard reigned unchallenged.

Eisenhower and the 1955 Treaty

Not surprisingly, "Chichi's" personal fortunes followed his political good luck. He accumulated several million dollars by monopolizing cattle slaughtering, selling the gasoline used in police cars, auctioning city bus routes to the highest bidder, and allegedly owning part of Panama City's most renowned brothel. He also collected farms, apartment houses, and race horses, while supposedly profiting from the South American narcotics traffic that moved through Panama on its way to United States street corners.[42]

Remón, however, was more than an Arias with a badge. He committed his administration to social reform and economic development, particularly in the agricultural provinces where his wife had developed strong political ties. Remón moved to equalize the tax structure; more important, to the oligarchy's amazement he began collecting taxes. Following up his success within the Guard, the new President sought to raise the status of blacks, especially for jobs in the Canal Zone.[43] The 2½ years of Remón's presidency initiated the most important reform program in Panama's history. The changes, moreover, were supported by a political coalition that drew its strength from the National Guard and the lower classes. The oligarchy and students were isolated, or, in individual instances, brought into the government on the President's terms.

Remón knew his reforms would be written on the wind unless they could be anchored to a strong national economy. Through public spending programs he accelerated agricultural and industrial production. Panama's eco-

---

42. *Ibid.*, p. 8.
43. Daniel Goldrich, "Panama," in Martin C. Needler, ed., *Political Systems of Latin America* (Princeton, 1964), pp. 137–138.

nomic dependence on the Zone actually decreased temporarily. Those trends, nevertheless, proved misleading. The country lacked the internal market, investment capital, and governmental lending powers to lift itself by its own bootstraps. The only important growth industry was the Canal.

Remón's attention inevitably swung toward Washington. His economic needs, concern for equal job opportunities in the Zone, and personal political future demanded a reordering of relations with the United States. So did an ever-louder Panamanian nationalism. In 1953 a new voice appeared. Ernesto Castillero Pimental was the son of Panama's most productive historian. As Remón assumed power, Castillero Pimental published an historical analysis of Panama-United States relations which scathingly attacked the 1903 treaty and urged that the national holiday be moved from the treaty date of November 3 to November 10 or 18, when the 1821 uprisings began against Spain.[44]

Remón asked the newly elected United States President, Dwight D. Eisenhower, to discuss a new treaty. Eisenhower had spent three years on the Isthmus as a young army officer during the 1920s. He liked the Panamanians and doubted Zonian arguments that only North Americans possessed the talents needed to operate the Canal.[45] Eisenhower was open to Remón's suggestion, but only to a certain point.

That point was the traditional North American determination to maintain control over the Canal Zone. Eisenhower also insisted that any new treaty not be costly to the United States. As talks opened in 1954, he told Remón personally of these conditions. In a long reply, the Panamanian disclaimed any intent to "affect fundamental rights of the United States," but did hope to bring those rights "into harmony with the rights of Panama." As for the money,

44. Castillero Pimental's own views can be found in summary fashion in *Politica Exterior de Panama* (Panama, 1961), especially pp. 50–55 where he lists eighteen United States violations of treaties made with Panama since 1903. A good analysis is Gatell, "Canal in Retrospect," p. 28.
45. Peter Lyon, *Eisenhower, Portrait of the Hero* (Boston, 1974), pp. 56–58, footnote on p. 738.

Remón unsubtly argued that instead of being a request for aid, new financial arrangements would be merely "a means of equitable adjustment of the situation in which Panama was placed by reason of the Canal enterprise." Finally, he claimed that Washington's proposals, contrary to Eisenhower's public statements, "do not provide for equality of opportunity" in the Zone. He was especially incensed that the United States wanted to include a pledge that neither party would ever reopen monetary questions.[46] Panamanians, after all, already had enough trouble with "in perpetuity" clauses; they did not care for what they cynically termed the "perpetual silence" provision.

When Panama asked that the $430,000 annuity be raised to 20 percent of the Canal's gross revenue or $5 million (whichever was larger), the United States counteroffered $1 million annually for ten years to be used specifically for housing. Panama rejected this out-of-hand. The discussions deadlocked. Remón's rallying cry, "Neither Alms nor Millions, We Want Justice," became political dogma, if not an accurate description of his demands. (Twenty years later the Torrijos government placed the slogan on the retaining wall of the National Assembly parking lot, near a striking bas relief mural featuring Torrijos himself. The area, a hang-out for shoeshine boys and vendors, is located only several hundred yards from the Canal Zone.)

The Panamanians were engrossed in the Canal negotiations, but U.S. Secretary of State John Foster Dulles tried to focus Latin American attention on a left-wing government in Guatemala which had seized United Fruit Company holdings. At the Caracas meeting of the OAS in early 1954, Dulles worked mightily to align the Western Hemisphere against Guatemala. Some Latin Americans cooperated, hoping (vainly, as it turned out), that Washington would reward political loyalty with economic preferences. The Panamanian delegation, however, was led by out-

46. Eisenhower to Remón, Aug. 23, 1954; Remón to Eisenhower, Nov. 8, 1954, both in Ann Whitman file, Panama, Dwight D. Eisenhower Library, Abilene, Kansas.

spoken Cecilia Remon who attacked United States policies
in her country, then succeeded in attaching to Dulles's proposals an amendment condemning job discrimination in
the Zone. In May, President Remón nicely followed up his
wife's efforts by declaring that shortsighted United States
policies in Latin America allowed Communist propaganda
to have an "effect it would not have under ordinary circumstances."[47] Dulles stood firm. In June 1954, a United States-
sponsored counter-revolution overthrew the Guatemalan
government, replacing it with a right-wing regime whose
policies satisfied both the United States and United Fruit.
Dulles concluded that the Soviets might have targeted
Guatemala for special attention because it lay only 700
miles from the Canal.[48]

For nearly fifteen years the United States had ignored Latin American problems, many of which were
shaped by unilateral North American economic and political policies. When the Latins were dealt with, it was largely
through military agreements (as the Rio Treaty), or force (as
in Guatemala). The concern of the 1930s with being a Good
Neighbor gave way to a 1950s obsession with global Communism. Order, which to Washington usually meant the
status quo, received highest priority.

In such an environment Panamanians had little
chance of receiving either "millions" or what they considered "justice." In the final 1955 treaty draft they nevertheless received a number of economic concessions. Most
notably, the annual annuity was raised to $1,930,000. The
new figure misled, however, for in real dollars (that is, dis-
counting post-1945 inflation), the rental fee was actually
less than the amount paid by the United States in 1914.[49]

Panama received for the first time the right to tax
Zone employees who were Panamanian, a provision that
could be interpreted as significantly extending Panama's
authority in the Canal area. The United States surrendered

47. Pippin, Remón Era, p. 114.
48. Lyon, Eisenhower, p. 627.
49. New York Times, Jan. 13, 1964, p. 34:2.

the monopoly rights granted in the 1903 treaty over all railroad and highway building (although not canal construction), but no third power could construct future routes without Washington's approval. The North Americans also gave up their authority to control sanitation in Colon and Panama City. Of considerable importance to Panamanian merchants, Zone commissaries were not to sell goods to anyone except United States citizens who worked in the Zone and Panamanian employees (mostly the West Indians) who worked for the Canal and resided in the Zone. The Canal government, moreover, promised to purchase as many supplies as possible in Panama itself—subject, as a carefully written escape clause provided, to the discretion of the Zone's purchasing agents.

The United States handed back some lands outside the Zone. In return, Panama granted a fifteen-year renewable lease for 19 thousand acres in Rio Hato for the exclusive use of North American military forces. The Panamanians received no percentage of the Canal's revenue or any recognition of their sovereignty within the Zone. When the United States Senate considered the pact, a citizens association (representing the North Americans living in the Zone) and some union representatives complained that Eisenhower was surrendering too much. Assistant Secretary of State Henry Holland assured the Senate that Washington still exercised "one hundred percent of the rights of sovereignty in this area."[50]

A "Memorandum of Understandings Reached" was also negotiated. Although it was an informal agreement and not submitted to the Senate for ratification, the Panamanians considered the Memorandum equal in importance to the treaty itself. Eisenhower pledged to create equality of opportunity within the Zone. He also promised to ask Congress for a single wage level for Canal jobs, regardless of whether the worker was Panamanian or North American.

---

50. Lester D. Langley, "U.S.-Panamanian Relations Since 1941," *Journal of Inter-American Studies*, XII (July 1970), 345–346.

(United States citizens, however, would continue to receive a "differential" of 15 percent for serving overseas, as well as leave benefits and income tax allowance.)

The U.S. Senate ratified the treaty 72-14, but only after shippers (who feared that the higher annuity would force a rise in tolls), Zonians (who did not want to share jobs with Panamanians), and the colonialists (who urged that not a comma be changed in the 1903 treaty) bitterly fought the new pact. Unlike those who fought the 1936 treaty, few opponents worried over the Canal's security. The "antis" of the 1950s cared foremost about personal interests which were tied to the status quo. The United States did not return the long-held lands until 1957, and not until 1958 did Congress make an initial, highly ineffective move to create equal job opportunities. Contrary to the agreement, the Zone government continued to purchase food supplies from as far away as Australia when the same product was available from Panamanians.[51]

A Different Panama, A Different World

Remón did not live to see the new treaty. While attending horse races outside the capital on January 2, 1955, two men machine-gunned him to death. The motive remains officially clouded but, to some observers, all too clear. Remón apparently was fighting attempts by the king of organized crime in the United States, Charles "Lucky" Luciano, to take over Panama's vast narcotics traffic. A Cuban crime expert who investigated the killing believed that a Luciano gunman was one of the two killers. The other gunman was apparently Ruben Miró, an eccentric Panama City lawyer. The Luciano henchman was given his freedom immediately after the assassination. Miró was brought to trial.

Then the story grew mysteriously complex. A clique led by Remón's brother and Ricardo Arias (the Second

51. *Ibid.*, p. 349.

Vice-President and no relation to Harmodio and Arnulfo),
implicated the First Vice-President in the killing, took over
the government, began repealing Remón's reform program,
and gathered up large personal fortunes. On the brink of
bankruptcy in late 1954, Ricardo Arias was allegedly worth
$2 million when he left the presidency less than two years
later. Ruben Miró, meanwhile, turned out to be the nephew
of Harmodio Arias, one of Remón's implacable enemies.
The yacht of Harmodio's son, Roberto, was seen stealing
away from Panama City the night of the killing when all
escape routes were supposedly sealed by the National
Guard. This coincidence led some investigators to conclude
that Guard officers worked with Ricardo Arias and Harmodio Arias to kill Remón. These three groups (Ricardo Arias,
the Arias brothers, and the Guard) might have differed
among themselves—and with "Lucky" Luciano—why
Remón had to be removed, but not at all that he should be
removed. With his political connections, Miró was well
protected. A jury found him not guilty. The killers were
never convicted and for some reason the new Panamanian
government did not seem to mind.[52]

    With Remón and his reform program gone, the oli-
garchy moved back into power. The government's apparent
need to hide a political assassination was one of many good
reasons why the 1956 elections were kept under tight control. Ernesto de la Guardia won easily, and the Union Club
members settled back for business-as-usual. But the 1947
student uprisings, the Guard's new role as political arbiter,
and Remón's reform and Canal programs were the seeds of
a new Panama which threatened oligarchical and United
States interests.

    The status quo was indeed growing shaky not only
in Panama but around the globe. In Southeast Asia the
French finally surrendered their colonial empire in 1954.
North Americans replaced France in Vietnam, but their

---

52. The story is well traced out in Pippin's Remón Era, especially pp. 127–
135.

future was not bright. In only five years a series of African independence movements replaced a vast European colonial empire with autonomous, self-governing states. The focus of world attention in mid-1956 was on Suez, where Egypt broke away from British tutelage to gain control of the great canal. Alert to the precedents being set, Panamanians were furious when Secretary of State Dulles specifically excluded them from a twenty-two-nation user's conference called to settle the Suez crisis. With unfailing insensitivity, Dulles humiliated Panamanians, publicly announcing that the United States would represent their interests at the conference. When the Secretary of State suggested internationalizing the Suez, Panama issued a public pronouncement of its own: the United States did not speak for Panama, and under no circumstances would its Canal be placed under international control.[53]

Of course Washington agreed with the latter point. Internationalization could be a substitute for the tottering British authority in Suez, but never for United States power in Panama. That feeling became intense in July 1956 when Egypt took affairs out of Dulles's hands and seized the Suez Canal unilaterally. The British and French, with Israeli cooperation, tried to reclaim their old power through an unbelievably confused invasion of Egypt. Much to their embarrassment, Eisenhower and Dulles had to stop their inept allies before threatened Soviet intervention turned a fiasco into a world crisis.

As the Suez confrontation built to a climax, Dulles appeared inflexible before Panama's demands for a more equitable interpretation of the 1955 pact. Eisenhower approved: "We should be generous in all small administration details," he told his Secretary of State. "Our firmness should be in holding fast to basic principles and purposes of [the] treaty."[54] As Egypt tightened its grip on Suez, a reporter asked Dulles whether the 1955 treaty promises

53. Liss. The Canal, pp. 53–54.
54. Handwritten note on Dulles to Eisenhower, Sept. 28, 1956, Ann Whitman File, Panama, Eisenhower Library.

would be fulfilled. His answer: "I'm not such a Utopian as to think there will never be any problems between us because of the nature of the situation."[55] As global relationships transformed in 1956, Washington clung tightly to the status quo in Panama.

Warning signals were up everywhere. In a private conversation, President Arias tried to make Eisenhower understand United States power in determining Panamanian affairs:

> [Arias] compared the relative positions of the two countries by pointing out that this morning he had been told by Dr. Milton Eisenhower [the President's brother] that the budget for Penn State College is $30 million per year; whereas, the yearly budget for the Republic of Panama is only $50 million.
>
> President Arias stated that despite our recent treaties, thing were not going well and that we are "running into trouble."

President Eisenhower responded by insisting on "justice" for Panama, and blamed the State Department for "not always [keeping] him as closely informed on the problem with Panama." Sitting nearby, Dulles aroused himself enough to say that he "kept up with Panamanian matters but necessarily not as to detail." After all, Dulles was a busy man: "[I am] constantly being confronted with international problems of grave import." Panama obviously did not qualify for his attention. Three months later, newly elected President de la Guardia wrote Eisenhower that he "almost despaired as to the present and future of our relations." Eisenhower privately expressed puzzlement at "what President de la Guardia had in mind."[56]

Puzzlement soon gave way to consternation. While

55. Press conference of Oct. 2, 1956, Papers of John Foster Dulles, Princeton University.
56. "Memorandum of Conversation," July 23, 1956, and Eisenhower to Acting Secretary of State, Oct. 10, 1956, both in Ann Whitman File, Panama, Eisenhower Library.

on a supposed good-will tour through South America in early 1958, Vice-President Richard Nixon encountered a series of violent anti-Yankee demonstrations. In Caracas his car was stoned, spat upon, and nearly turned over. For a moment Eisenhower considered ordering a parachute drop to rescue Nixon.

Eight months later, on New Year's Day 1959, a bearded guerrilla fighter, Fidel Castro, marched into Havana to mark his final victory over the North American-trained and equipped armies of dictator Fulgencio Batista. For sixty-one years United States-Cuban relations were those between a colonizer and a colony, but within six months they were transfigured by Castro's agrarian reform program and the ascendancy of his revolutionary party's left-wing. If the United States could not create a prosperous, stable, and friendly Cuba after six decades of near-total control in an island less than one hundred miles from Florida, it was natural to wonder whether North American overseas interests were safe anywhere.

World history took an important turn between 1956 and 1960. The old bipolar Cold War power structure dominated by the United States and the Soviet Union fragmented into a more pluralistic global order, especially in the southern hemispheres. Whether the United States could navigate this turn remained an open question in 1958–1959. Eisenhower tried to make it, particularly by announcing a massive program of economic cooperation with Latin America. The region would have its own bank, the Inter-American Development Bank (IADB), through which United States and Latin American capital would be funneled into development projects. The IADB initiated what the John F. Kennedy administration would glamorize as the Alliance for Progress.

The 1959 Riots

But Eisenhower's new policies hardly touched Panama. By early 1958 relations with Washington were deteriorating nearly as rapidly as the economy. As Zone employment dropped from 30,000 in 1945 to 12,000 eleven years later, Panamanian unemployment correspondingly rose. Colon became a devastated area, its slums among the world's worst. The city's politics understandably produced Thelma King, the most outspoken nationalist and revolutionary in the National Assembly. King sympathized with Castro, but she denied any Communist affiliations.

Colon represented only an extreme. A United Nations team concluded that Panama's economic expansion was over. Projecting from 1956 to 1966, the UN economists believed the gross national product would barely keep up with population growth; the general living standard would actually drop an incredible 7 percent. Only "dismal prospects of growth" existed. Then came the kind of phrase that haunted Washington policy-makers: "Given the lack of dynamic stimuli for private investment and the demands made by a high investment rate, an increment of about 90 percent would be required in government gross investment. This in itself would imply a radical alteration in the traditional role of the public sector in Panama." If the United States did not like the sound of "radical alteration," the UN team offered one alternative. Since governmental spending and private investment could not revive the economy, only transit traffic and tourism linked to the Canal held out "really dynamic prospects."[57] The United States, in other words, had to choose between two distasteful alternatives: either allow a radically different governmental involvement in Panama's private economy (an involvement that hinted of socialism or fascism), or give Panama much larger economic benefits from the Canal.

Panamanians would not allow Washington to escape that choice. In May 1958, Panama City university students announced "Operation Sovereignty." They entered the Zone peacefully and planted some fifty Panamanian flags at

57. UN Economic Commission for Latin America, "The Economic Development of Panama," pp. 50–56.

strategic points, only to have the Canal police pull up the banners. During other demonstrations that month, several students were shot, supposedly by the Guard although individual snipers might have been responsible. The old hatreds re-emerged between students and the Zone as well as between students and the Guard.

Disturbed by the outbreaks in Washington's backyard, President Eisenhower decided to send his brother, Milton, on a fact-finding trip through Latin America. Panama turned into a most important stop. A Panamanian official explained the situation: "You in the United States inherited vast mineral wealth. . . . Africa was given gold and diamonds. The Middle East is rich in oil. God gave Panama nothing but a waterway. We must make a living from our resources, as others have from theirs." Returning to Washington, Eisenhower recommended carrying out the promises of the 1955 treaty and "Memorandum of Understandings." A few provisions were finally fulfilled, but when he proposed a large program of low-cost housing, his brother's government seemed deaf. And when he urged that the flag controversy be solved by allowing the Panamanian emblem to be flown "in selected locations, at least on ceremonial occasions," Eisenhower ran into a stonewall of Pentagon opposition. The U.S. Army would suffer no gesture that might indicate Panama's "titular sovereignty" along the Canal.[58] The Pentagon decided to fight by standing still.

The strategy seemed appropriate when 1959 began with a comic opera staged by Roberto Arias, Harmodio's playboy son and the husband of British ballerina Margot Fonteyn. Arias led a group of Cubans ashore in northern Panama and straight into the arms of the waiting National Guard. The "Aquatic Ballet," as humorists quickly tagged it, climaxed with Arias fleeing into the Brazilian Embassy and Fidel Castro condemning the whole affair. The Cuban leader apparently was not involved. He publicly announced

58. Milton S. Eisenhower, *The Wine Is Bitter. The United States and Latin America* (New York, 1964), pp. 214, 221–225.

that Panama, unlike Nicaragua, was not a tyranny, then attacked Roberto's raiders for trying to involve Cuba in a conflict with the United States.[59]

The comic interlude was brief. Panamanians directly challenged the Pentagon's standstill strategy. In March 1959 President de la Guardia sharply told President Eisenhower that despite the promises of 1936 and 1955, the Canal's new wage system "perpetuates in essence the old system of discrimination against Panamian workers." De la Guardia threatened to take the question to an international court, then unsubtly ended his message by telling Eisenhower that it was regrettable how the "deterioration in our relations appreciably encourages our common adversaries."[60] By autumn tensions over job discrimination and the possibility of a new flag incident forced the Pentagon to ask Milton Eisenhower what could be done. Once again, the military had waited too long.

On Independence Day, November 3, 1959, a group of Panamanian students moved into the Zone to plant flags. They were led by Ernesto Castillero Reyes, perhaps the nation's best-known historian, and Aquilino Boyd. A former ambassador to Mexico and delegate to the United Nations, Boyd was the descendent of Federico Boyd, a founder of Panama; the son of a former President; a wealthy businessman in his own right; and ambitious for the presidency in 1960. Some observers believed that like others of his class, Boyd hoped to focus the attention of Panamanian malcontents on the Canal and away from the oligarchy's failures. Boyd and his friends, however, thought it righteous nationalism.

As the group departed, several students broke away and tried to re-enter the Zone. The Zone police arrested one. Mobs formed. Fresh attempts were made to rush the police, who were now supported by United States infantry

59. Herbert S. Dinerstein, The Making of a Missile Crisis, October 1962 (Baltimore, 1976), pp. 43, 46, 278.
60. De la Guardia to Eisenhower, March 7, 1959, Ann Whitman File, Panama, Eisenhower Library.

with fixed bayonets. As news of the clash spread, Panamanians moved into the streets. Rioting broke out in Panama City. United States-owned automobiles were burned, buildings operated by North American corporations sacked, windows broken in the U.S. Information Agency, the flag torn down in front of the U.S. Embassy, and North American lives endangered in Colon. At least 120 Panamanians were wounded, 9 by birdshot fired by U.S. troops on students who tried to storm into the Zone. Rioting did not stop until National Guard units deployed to calm the city. This led to another student-Guard clash in which three students were shot.

On November 4, President Eisenhower told a press conference, "In a way it's a little bit puzzling to me," especially since each treaty modification gave "a greater degree or level of rights to the Panamanians." He decided the troubles could be traced to "an excitable group; people that are extremists."[61] Despite his confusion, Eisenhower tried to make changes. His brother's housing proposals were revived. The Governor of the Canal Zone was directed to buy all supplies in Panama or the United States instead of Australia or New Zealand. On December 2 Eisenhower discussed the highly delicate flag question: "I do . . . believe we should have visual evidence that Panama does have titular sovereignty" in the Zone.

That was too much for the champions of the 1903 treaty. They were led, at least rhetorically, by Daniel Flood (Democrat of Pennsylvania), who traced his political lineage back to Theodore Roosevelt. Flood was so outspoken that Panamanians labeled him their "Public Enemy Number One." In February 1960, Congress voted 380–12 against allowing the Panamanian flag to fly in the Zone. The vote was only advisory; it did not tie Eisenhower's hands.

In April the President announced a nine-point program which for the first time opened some skilled jobs to

61. *Public Papers of the Presidents, 1959* (Washington, D.C., 1961), pp. 772–773, 775.

Panamanians. He also dispatched a new ambassador, Joseph S. Farland. The Farland appointment was a masterstroke. The new Ambassador ordered the Embassy staff to stay in touch with all classes of Panamanians. He entertained schools and hospitals with demonstrations of his skill as a magician, proving to be a true magician in quieting anti-Yankee feeling among Panamanian officials.

In September, Eisenhower announced that both flags would be shown in part of the Zone. The statement was historic. The United States flag had not flown in the Zone between 1903 and 1906, but after 1906 the Panamanian flag disappeared. Now it was to return. The announcement was perfectly timed: Congress was in adjournment. Eisenhower, moreover, had removed the possibility of Panamanian riots on the November 3d Independence Day jeopardizing Richard Nixon's chances in the final hours of the United States presidential election.

The 1903 congressional contingent was enraged. Flood called the new policy "Munich in spades" and demanded Eisenhower's impeachment. Of some 180 letters received by the White House, only three agreed with Eisenhower.[62] But the importance of the flag question, while symbolic, was overemphasized. It threatened to take Washington's attention off the fundamental problem of the Panamanian economy.

Some North Americans understood the danger. United States officials in Panama had told Milton Eisenhower that a revival of the Panamanian economy "would relieve the pressures on the Zone and the Canal Company."[63] Congresswoman Leonore Sullivan arrived at the same conclusion. Head of the powerful Subcommittee on the Panama Canal (a part of the House Committee on Merchant Marine and Fisheries), Sullivan blasted Eisenhower for giving away "fundamental American rights." She believed such tactics never worked. As long as slum-ridden

62. Langley, "U.S.-Panamanian Relations Since 1941," p. 353.
63. Eisenhower, Wine Is Bitter, p. 216.

Panamanians lived across the street from air-conditioned Zonians, as long as "economic deprivation . . . generated the political dream of great riches for all if only Panama owned the Canal," no peaceful relations could exist. Only "if Panama were truly prosperous—if it had resources other than this canal," could the Panamanians stop troubling the Zone.[64]

Sullivan's approach would underlie John F. Kennedy's Alliance for Progress program in Panama during the 1960s. But the question was whether enough time remained to test Sullivan's thesis. Nearly two decades of a policy that shunned economic cooperation and emphasized hemispheric military alliances had climaxed in a series of disasters. Panama particularly suffered. Booming in 1945, by 1960 its economy was a disaster area. Massive governmental spending failed to prime the system. Remón's reforms were dead. The economy depended on two stimuli. The first was exports, of which 68 percent were bananas. United Fruit, not Panamanians, controlled banana production.

The second stimulus was the Canal Zone—whose economy, along with Eisenhower's enlightened policies, produced a tragic irony. After some of the 1955 treaty promises were made real, Panamanian workers in the Zone received higher wages; merchants outside the Zone suddenly could sell goods to the North Americans. The Zone provided the major impetus to the country's economy in the late 1950s.[65] Panamanians therefore grew more dependent on the Zone for their own economic survival. Granting Panama concessions accelerated the country's need to break the colonial relationship and control the entire Canal area, or else face economic stagnation.

Meanwhile the political system deteriorated. The Guard reopened its struggle with the students. Oligarchs remained irresponsible. Two North American political sci-

64. *Cong. Record*, Feb., 1960, pp. 1645–1649, Central files, L.B.J. Library.
65. Robert E. Looney, *The Economic Development of Panama: The Impact of World Inflation on an Open Economy* (New York, 1976), p. 19.

entists observed in 1960 that Panama contained "all the conditions for a nationalist revolution which will rival the recent upheavals in Cuba and Egypt."[66] Cuban and Panamanian history contained striking similarities. Castro's emergence raised the question of whether the similarities would continue.

66. Martin B. Travis and James T. Watkins, "Time Bomb in Panama," *The Nation*, CXC (April 30, 1960), 378.

5 Chiari, Johnson, and Robles

In 1903 the oligarchs established themselves in power and a colonial relationship began between Panama and the United States. During the 1960s the oligarchy cracked then fell from power, while the killing of Panamanians and North Americans in the 1964 riots led to a fundamental change in the colonial ties. Washington entered a new, difficult relationship with a different Panama. Sixty years of isthmian history, like a long river kept carefully within its banks, had reached a watershed. Its future course would be less restrained, more unpredictable, and hence more dangerous. But it could no longer be easily dammed up.

The Alliance

Once again Panama was a microcosm. As Castro's triumph illustrated, the whole of Latin America approached an historic watershed. Understanding this in 1961, newly elected President John F. Kennedy set out to control and channel change within the Western Hemisphere. He

wanted Latin American development to move in orderly
evolutionary, not revolutionary, channels. His instrument
was the Alliance for Progress, a projected ten-year, $100
billion program in which North and South, private and
governmental capital, would cooperate to create a dynamic
Latin America immune to Castroism.

Panama received special attention, for as Congresswoman Sullivan had explained, only when Panamanians
enjoyed prosperity would they stop pushing for more control over the Canal revenues. In mid-1961 the first Alliance
grant for Panama was to build 200 rural schoolhouses and
150 miles of farm roads. An agricultural credit system was
planned. The Alliance obviously hoped to create a self-
sufficient agricultural sector which, among other attrac-
tions, would slow the migration from rural to urban areas
and thus stabilize, perhaps even reduce, festering unemployment in city slums which bordered the Zone.

Between 1951 and 1961 the United States had granted Panama only $7 million in economic assistance per year.
From 1961 to 1963 the amount jumped to $41 million. The
Peace Corps, another Kennedy innovation, sent 57 volunteers to help develop schools, health centers, and rural cooperatives. In addition the Canal Zone itself infused at least
$65 million annually through wages, tourism, and pur-
chases into Panama's economic bloodstream.

Panamanians, nevertheless, were not mollified. In
1963 the $100 million gross revenue from Canal operations
produced a net income to the Canal Company of $5 million,
but of that amount Panama received only $1.9 million.
Many Panamanians also disliked the Kennedy administration's use of the Zone for shaping military aspects of the
Alliance. The School of the Americas trained Latin American army and police officers (including Panamanian National Guardsmen) for counterinsurgency warfare. Panama
had no control over the school, nor did its complaints that
the school had nothing to do with Canal operations (and
hence lay outside treaty understandings) have any effect.
Some of the Cuban exiles who waded ashore to be captured

or killed at the Bay of Pigs invasion in 1961 were trained in part in the Zone. By 1963 the United States also used the Canal area for stationing anti-guerrilla paratroop units that on short notice could drop into trouble spots throughout Latin America. As both a test-tube for the Alliance and a base for the military, Panama nicely exemplified the two parts of Kennedy's Latin American policy. Not all Panamanians, however, fully appreciated their role.

The country's new President, Roberto Chiari, was necessarily restrained in cooperating with the Alliance. After winning a 1960 election that was relatively open and not determined by the Guard, Chiari emphasized the need for rapid but not over-extensive change. Without it, he warned his fellow oligarchs, he might be the last official elected from their select circle. The oligarchy's problem was to determine how much reform it could tolerate without losing power. Many in the ruling class refused to believe that slow strangulation through change was preferable to standing still. For example, when the government attempted to build low-cost housing for slum dwellers in the capital, wealthy owners of slum housing fought back with some success through anonymous letter-writing campaigns. Chiari displayed keen sensitivity to such feelings, for his family monopolized milk distribution in Panama City and nearly monopolized sugar. Unsurprisingly he moved slowly to implement reform laws that were to accompany the Alliance's dollars.[1]

The oligarchy also encountered a second trap. For several decades it had focused nationalist rage away from itself by directing it toward the Canal Zone. The 1959 riots, however, were a red flag signaling that such games could get out of hand. The oligarchy and the United States nev-

1. Daniel Goldrich, "Panama," Martin C. Needler, ed., *Political Systems of Latin America* (Princeton, 1964), pp. 143–144; Louis Harris, "Panama," in Ben G. Burnett and K. F. Johnson, eds., *Political Forces in Latin America* (Belmont, Calif., 1968), p. 180; the best detailed analysis of the Alliance for Progress is Jerome Levinson and Juan de Onís, *The Alliance That Lost Its Way* (Chicago, 1970).

ertheless fully agreed on the need to fight Communism. Chiari cut relations with Cuba in late 1961, launched an attack to quiet the 500 to 1000 members of the outlawed Panamanian Communist Party, and—acting more royally than the king—threatened to quit the Organization of American States unless Cuba was expelled.

Hatred, Destruction and Death

Flagellating Communists was easy sport. Other problems seemed intractable, and time was running out for the oligarchy. Surveys revealed that students, who comprised the most effective political opposition, placed considerable hope in Chiari, especially after he promised housing and tax reforms. Above all, however, the students wanted an open system in which they could use their education to gain economic security. They were overwhelmingly anti-Communist, yet a sizable minority considered themselves "extremists." Wanting middle-class respectability and income, the students, Professor Daniel Goldrich believed, threatened Panama with "an increasing possibility of violence and repression, at least during a transitional period,"[2] unless the oligarchy expanded employment rapidly enough to accommodate the well trained (and Panama had one of the top seven literacy rates in Latin America.)

The oligarchy was singularly unresponsive. Political factions continued to be organized around the charismatic and the rich, not reform programs. The exceptions to the rule were the illegal Communists and a moderate Christian Democratic Party organized by highly respected professional men whom the oligarchy's leaders ignored. One percent of the landowners controlled half the privately owned land (while more than half the farmers subsisted on annual

2. Daniel Goldrich, "Requisites for Political Legitimacy in Panama," Public Opinion Quarterly, XXVI (Winter 1962), 664–668; Daniel Goldrich and Edward Scott, "Developing Political Orientations of Panamanian Students," Journal of Politics, XXIII (February 1961), 103–107.

incomes of less than $100), and oligarchs monopolized Panamanian access to banks, coffee plantations, and sugar refineries. Ownership of newspapers, radio, and television was so centralized that six men enjoyed almost total control over the media. Oligarch families sent their children to universities overseas, away from the ambitious and often rowdy middle- and lower-class students in Panama City who seemed to divide their time between classrooms and street riots. Resembling Dr. Pangloss, the oligarchy lived in the best of all possible worlds. A leading scholar of Panamanian politics, Lester Langley, called the oligarchy "perhaps the most socially irresponsible [elite] in Latin America."[3]

Despite, or because of, Chiari's attacks on the Communists, a *Fidelista* movement appeared in Veraguas Province during late 1962. The United Fruit Company, which controlled the province's affairs, was an attractive target. The company's operations, according to one North American visitor, resembled antebellum slave plantations in the South.[4] In other parts of the country peasants seized estates. But the most dangerous outbreak occurred in Panama City, where university students went on strike. The National Assembly went through its ritual of blaming the troubles on the United States and demanding full jurisdiction over the Canal. Chiari visited Kennedy in Washington, and out of the talks emerged a Joint Commission to discuss outstanding issues.

The Commission proved to be a disaster. It started auspiciously by settling several labor disputes in the Zone. Then on January 10, 1963, it announced that Panama's flag would fly with the United States banner at civilian institutions throughout the Zone. North Americans who operated the Canal loudly protested. The Commission appeared paralyzed. In mid-1963 Chiari angrily disbanded it. This was followed by Ambassador Farland's sudden resignation.

3. Lester D. Langley, "The United States and Panama: The Burden of Power," *Current History,* LVI (January 1969), 17; on the media, see Harris, "Panama," p. 184.
4. Liss, *The Canal,* p. 106.

Elected by Panamanians as one of the ten most popular men in the country (an honor no other United States Ambassador had ever received), the Zonians were happy to see Farland leave. So, apparently, was the State Department, which publicly played down his resignation. The Ambassador announced he wanted to return to private life, but actually he had become embittered over the ineffectiveness and limitations of the Alliance, the insensitivity of Washington to the storm signals in Panama, and criticism from the Zonians. Tragically, the State Department tarried in sending a replacement. For the five months before, as well as during the 1964 riots, the United States had no ambassador in Panama.

With Farland's scalp on their belt, the Zonians moved to repeal part of the Commission's accomplishments. Understandably, they liked the pre-1959 status quo. As *Time* magazine noted in 1964, "Few Americans abroad lead a more comfortable life or are more self-consciously American." They live

> in model company towns with look-alike houses, bargain-priced groceries, liquor and clothing from Government commissaries, bowling and Hollywood movies at the service centers. They have their own schools (including a junior college), country clubs and well-kept golf courses; 1600 boats are registered at the yacht basin.[5]

Their average salary was triple the average United States wage.

On the other hand the Zonians believed they fully deserved such benefits. They made the Canal work. Some of them, particularly the ship pilots and tower operators, possessed unique skills from long training and experience. If they suddenly left Panama the Canal would shut down for years before replacements could be adequately trained. They lived far from the mainland in a tropical climate that required "neatly manicured lawns" (as critics delighted in pointing out), not simply for aesthetic reasons but to pre-

5. *Time,* Jan. 24, 1964, p. 18.

vent pools of water in which malaria-causing mosquitoes
could breed. Above all, the Zonians wanted little contact
with the squalor and anti-Gringoism of Panama City and
Colon. Only 20 percent of them spoke Spanish. "There are
some people here," one Zonian remarked, "who haven't
been to Panama for ten or twenty years. And they're proud
of it."

Governor of the Zone was Robert J. Fleming Jr., a
major general in the Corps of Engineers who liked to talk
while pacing about his office, a swagger-stick in hand. In
1963, Fleming later recalled, he told Washington officials
"things had never looked better between the two countries.
We were about to reach the point where you blow the froth
off the beer and get down to essentials." As he later lamented, those "essentials" would not be determined by a
majority of Zonians who were "moderates" and passive,
but by 300 or so who acted as "the radical right. They've
been isolated so long they've developed a reactionary mentality." The Governor added, "It's the perfect situation for
the guy who's 150 percent American—and 50 percent
whiskey."[6]

Seizing upon the flag decision as their cause, parents
and students at the Zone's Balboa High School took matters
into their own hands. They determined that only the
United States flag would fly at the school. On January 9,
1964, several hundred Panamanian University students
marched peacefully into the Zone to protest the absence of
their flag. Zone police finally agreed to allow a half-dozen
Panamanians to exhibit their flag in front of the school.
Four hundred to five hundred North Americans were waiting, and when police sighted them the Panamanians were
asked to retreat. A scuffle broke out, the Panamanian flag
was torn, rocks filled the air, windows and street lights
were smashed. The riot had begun.

Rumors of the clash swept Panama City. As many as

6. The quotations in this and the preceding paragraph are from T. Armbrister, "Panama: Why They Hate Us: More Than One Torn Flag," *Saturday Evening Post*, March 7, 1964, pp. 76–77.

30,000 Panamanians moved into the streets, many swarming down 4th of July Avenue, which bordered the Canal Zone. They were repulsed for a time by Zone police. Finally United States troops took up battle stations in hastily dug foxholes in front of the Tivoli Hotel. Late on January 9 the Tivoli began to receive sniper fire from buildings that bordered the Zone. The U.S. troops first tried to use birdshot to clear out the snipers without killing them, but this proved ineffective. Fire from the Panamanian side increased to 200 rounds an hour. Expert army marksmen moved into the Tivoli with orders to warn snipers first by firing nearby before shooting to kill. According to Washington officials, the sniper fire reached over 500 rounds an hour during the next several days. In response the marksmen in the Tivoli killed several Panamanians.[7]

The rioters demanded that the National Guard attack the troops. The Guard, wisely, not only refused to challenge the U.S. Army, but largely disappeared from sight after telling the demonstrators to go home.[8] Instead of returning home, the mobs roamed through Panama City for 3½ days, burning the U.S. Information Agency building, Pan American and Braniff Airway offices, and the tire plants of Goodyear and Firestone. North American banks were stoned. The U.S. Embassy was beseiged. More than 2000 bullets were later taken from the Tivoli Hotel's walls. (The grand landmark of the Theodore Roosevelt era was later demolished by Zone authorities, partly because of outmoded and decayed facilities, partly because it stood directly across from Panama City's slums as a symbol of the Big Stick era.)

The riots spread to Colon, then deep into the interior. In David the Chase Manhattan Bank and an Esso station were burned. The United Fruit Company prepared to evacuate its North American families. Over $2 million of property was

7. Tondel, ed., *Panama Canal*, p. 54; International Commission of Jurists, *Report on the Events in Panama, January 9–12, 1964* (Geneva, Switzerland, 1964), pp. 16–18, 20–28.

8. Associated Press Dispatch, January 1964, Central Files, Panama, Lyndon B. Johnson Papers, Lyndon B. Johnson Library, Austin, Texas.

destroyed in all. Significantly, Peace Corps volunteers were not harmed, and when several were threatened they were protected by villagers.[9]

By January 13 both sides were worn down by four days of fighting. The National Guard then emerged to clear the streets. Four U.S. soldiers had been killed, 85 North Americans wounded, and several thousand refugees had moved into the Zone, often with the covert but friendly help of National Guard troops. Right-wing groups in the United States alleged that in addition five of their country-men were hanged and another chopped to pieces by Pana-manians; no evidence was ever provided to substantiate these charges. Twenty-four Panamanians lost their lives and more than 200 were wounded. The Chiari government renamed 4th of July Avenue; it became, and remains, Ave-nue of the Martyrs. Nearly 500 demonstrators were arrested, including five Communist leaders who, with their usual sense of timing, arrived at the scene too late to receive credit for the riots but early enough to go to jail because of them.

LBJ: Between "Deformities" and One-Third the Population of Chicago

The shooting erupted as Lyndon Johnson was set-tling into the White House as the successor to the assassi-nated John Kennedy. As a Texan, Johnson believed he knew something about Latin America, particularly Mexico, but his knowledge of Panama went little farther than a de-termination that small countries would not be allowed to harm his chances to become President in his own right in the November elections.

On January 10, the first full day of rioting, Chiari broke relations with Washington and accused the United States of "unjustifiable aggression." A stunned Johnson

9. Minor, "U.S.-Panamanian Relations: 1858–1973," pp. 74–78.

ordered an aide, "Get me the President of Panama—what's his name—on the phone." "Mr. President," the aide implored, "You can't do that. It isn't protocol." "Why in hell can't I," Johnson roared. "Come on now, get him on the phone."[10]

With most of his National Guard in the barracks, Chiari could give LBJ few assurances. Johnson became convinced that "having failed through diplomacy with President Kennedy, Chiari was going to try to exact a new treaty from me by force." He sent Thomas Mann, his chief Latin American adviser, to confer with Chiari. A fellow Texan, Mann had helped plan the Central Intelligence Agency-sponsored invasion of Guatemala in 1954. He tended to summarize policy in such phrases as, "These people need the application of a little muscle and common sense." Mann bluntly told Chiari to restore order immediately. Secretary of the Army Cyrus Vance flew to Panama to announce that the two flags would fly together as the 1963 agreements dictated; he provided the sugar for Mann's salt. But in a news conference Vance indicated that Communist agents trained in Cuba were largely responsible for the riot, an allegation soon supported by Secretary of State Dean Rusk.[11]

Only Washington officials seemed to be able to find Communists who merited such attention. The Panamanian government publicly ridiculed Vance's claim. That some party members were in the streets could not be denied, but as Panama's Second Vice-President observed, "The Communists here are like firemen. They don't run until they hear the bell. But instead of pouring water on the flames, they pour gasoline."[12] An Organization of American States investigation denied that Castro was involved. It reached

10. Eric F. Goldman, *The Tragedy of Lyndon Johnson* (New York, 1968), p. 87.
11. Statement of Jan. 20, 1964, Central Files, Panama, LBJ Papers; Johnson's view of Chiari is in Lyndon Johnson, *The Vantage Point* (New York, 1971), pp. 182–184; Mann's quote is in Goldman, *Tragedy of LBJ*, p. 89.
12. Armbrister, "Panama: Why They Hate Us," p. 78.

this conclusion despite strained relations between the OAS and Cuba. The Commander of the U.S. Army who defended the Zone had a better sense of the situation than either Vance or Rusk. United States views, he believed, were "probably overdominated by the Cuban situation. Too many of us fail to comprehend what lies to the south of us."[13]

An unidentified State Department official was more specific. The "imperialist mentality" of the Zonians, he claimed, played into the hands of the "leftist agitators" who were then able to embarrass such dependable Panamanians as President Chiari.[14] The rioters called Zonians "deformities" and "bastards of the earth," among other things, so the official's perception was doubtlessly accurate, but it was also dangerous policy if carried to a conclusion. For it meant that either the Zonians or Panamanians would have to experience a miraculous transformation in their own attitudes, which was unlikely, or relations could become tranquil only after the Zonians left the country.

The Zonians received vocal support in the United States, support that threatened to trap Johnson politically. Representative Daniel Flood again took the lead, at least rhetorically. The Pennsylvania Democrat scolded Johnson that since the United States enjoyed total sovereignty in the Zone, the President must stop making "accessions to unjustified demands from the mob-dominated Panama government." Appeasement would only lead "to greater blackmail." Flood believed the Panamanian demands for control over the Canal were "part of the audacious, cunning, and far-reaching strategy of the Soviets." He even urged the President to grab additional land from Panama for the defense of the waterway.[15] Former President Harry Truman and a Republican presidential candidate, Senator Barry Goldwater of Arizona, reached rare agreement that the Zo-

13. Minor, "U.S.-Panamanian Relations: 1958–1973," pp. 96–100.
14. Wall Street Journal, Jan. 13, 1964, p. 4:3.
15. Flood to Johnson, Jan. 14, 1964, Central Files, Panama, LBJ Papers.

nian children were correct in raising the lone flag. In the
Senate, Republican Minority Leader Everett Dirksen of Illi-
nois intoned, "We are in the amazing position of having a
country with one-third the population of Chicago kick us
around. If we crumble in Panama, the reverberations of our
actions will be felt around the world."

In the fifteen or so years before and after the 1964
riots, observers often claimed that Panamanian politics prevented cooperation with the United States, even when it
was in Panama's interest to do so. That criticism applied to
both sides, however. As early as 1936, and particularly after
the 1964 riots, United States Presidents frequently developed a conciliatory policy only to discover that their hands
were tied by special Canal interests (shippers, Zonians, labor unions), and vocal groups who loved the Canal Zone as
a symbol of that happier past when Big-Stick diplomacy
kept Panamanians in their place.

In late 1964 these political realities were explained
in detail to Johnson by Richard Scammon, director of the
Commerce Department's Bureau of the Census (and then, as
well as in the 1970s, a well-known political analyst). Although "more than a little concerned with the potential
trouble which Panama could cause us in November," Scammon began, he was not worried about "idiotic kids" or
"Zonians," but something larger. "Given the Castroite base
among the students," the "politnik [sic]" in Panama could
cause "trouble, crises, problems, and difficulties *ad in-
finitum ad nauseum.*" Johnson's support "on the peace issue comes from the [fear of] the atomic question," Scammon continued, "and does not extend to getting pushed
around by a small country about an area which every grade
school history book features with an American flag, a snap-
shot of Teddy Roosevelt, and an image of gallant engineers
overcoming the mosquito." Concessions to Panama, he
warned, would give the Republicans their "first real solid
muscled hit at the Administration." They could exploit a
"ready-made 'wrap-us-in-the-flag' kind of situation." Scammon's warning circulated to Rusk and Vance, among oth-

ers, while Johnson called it excellent and summoned the author for a private talk.[16]

Scammon's analysis was supported by a Gallup Poll indicating that of the 64 percent who knew about the Panama dispute, nearly half urged a "firm policy," and only 9 percent favored concessions.[17] His political antennae quivering, Johnson moved to silence opposition by taking both sides of the question (a tactic he tried to repeat later on the Vietnam issue). In February, for example, he said, "Our school children made a mistake in raising the United States flag without raising the Panamanian flag," then quickly balanced this with, "but that does not warrant or justify shooting our soldiers or invading the Zone."[18]

Johnson offered "to discuss all [sic] problems" with Panama. His bluff was quickly called. After completing hurriedly arranged talks in mid-January, Chiari announced that Washington was offering to renegotiate the 1903 treaty. LBJ heatedly denied this, claiming that only further discussions had been agreed upon. The problem was apparently caused by the use of the Spanish negociar in the agreement; it meant both discuss and negotiate, thus satisfying the two sides at the talks but confusing everyone when it was publicly interpreted.

Although Johnson did not take kindly to Chiari's public pressure, it was the United States President who broke the deadlock with an announcement in mid-March that sounded bland (and thus politically innocuous). He circumvented negociar by declaring he was willing to "review every issue" dividing the two nations. Chiari helped by privately promising Johnson that he would not demand a formal revision of the 1903 pact. Like LBJ, the Panamanian leader was trying to keep the delicate issue out of his

16. Scammon to Ralph A. Dungan, Jan. 17, 1964, and Dungan to Scammon, Jan. 21, 1964, Central File, Panama, LBJ Papers.
17. George H. Gallup, The Gallup Poll: Public Opinion, 1935–1971, three vols. (New York, 1972), III, 1864.
18. The Public Papers of the Presidents. Lyndon B. Johnson. 1963–1964, two vols. (Washington, D.C., 1965). I. 288, 144.

country's upcoming elections. Chiari also had another reason. Johnson announced the United States would begin studies in Central America and Mexico for a new sea-level canal. Faced with the possible loss of their greatest economic resource, Panamanian negotiators were spurred by fear as much as by nationalism.

The canal issue did not affect either presidential campaign. Johnson effectively neutralized the question in the United States. The Panamanian race narrowed to Chiari's choice (and cousin), Marco Robles, and the quadrennial candidate, Arnulfo Arias. This was, however, a different Arias, for although he and Robles agreed on the need for a new Canal treaty, the former Panamañista firebrand had so cooled that he displayed charity toward the North American side of some economic questions. A few United States officials even hoped he would win. In 1964, therefore, the old Arias received nationalist backing and the new Arias won some United States support. But in the end he could not control the ballot boxes. As usual, the government controlled those, and the Panamanian axiom that "He who counts, elects" remained valid. With Chiari's public and private support, Robles won by a small margin.

The Idyllic, Rejected Treaty

A tough banker (whose apt nickname, so necessary for successful Panamanian politicians, was "the Rifle"), Robles displayed his moderation by spending a post-election vacation in New York City talking with leading businessmen, including David Rockefeller of the Chase Manhattan Bank. Robles then demonstrated his toughness by ordering the National Guard to stop student protests, an order which the Guard forcefully carried out twice in 1965 and once in 1966. The President rounded out his balancing act by announcing that Panama's sovereignty over the Zone must be recognized and the "in perpetuity" clause of the 1903 treaty removed.

Lyndon Johnson appreciated Robles's political skills. Re-elected in a smashing victory over Senator Barry Goldwater, the President announced on December 18 that he would seek "an entirely new treaty" with Panama to terminate the 1903 agreement, recognize Panamanian sovereignty, and allow the United States to operate and protect the Canal for a fixed time. It marked an historic turn in United States policy. (Not in the sense, however, that Daniel Flood alleged. To the unreconstructed Rooseveltian Rough Rider, LBJ's policy marked the triumph of the "Bolshevik Revolution of 1917 and the international communist conspiracy.") Johnson's timing was also a political masterstroke. Despite fulminations from a few such as Flood, the President received overwhelming support from the public, particularly from editorials in leading newspapers.

Part of Johnson's political success may have been due to the care with which he had the Central Intelligence Agency track down former President Eisenhower, then on a westbound train out of Chicago, to clear the policy with him, even down to the use of Eisenhower's name at the opening of the public announcement. LBJ also obtained Truman's public support. At the same time he showed Panama his high cards by downplaying the long-run importance of the present Canal. He announced the United States would start negotiations with four governments (Colombia, Nicaragua, Costa Rica, and Panama) for a sea-level route.[19]

A tough United States negotiating policy was outlined by Johnson's National Security Adviser, McGeorge Bundy, in a secret National Security Action Memorandum of December 28, 1964. Bundy observed that until the sea-level canal was built a new pact would have to govern the present waterway. Above all, that treaty must give the United States full power to protect and operate the Panama Canal "until it is replaced." The agreement would also "recognize Panama's sovereignty over the Canal and would pro-

19. Lester D. Langley, "U.S.-Panamanian Relations since 1941," *Journal of Inter-American Studies*, XII (July 1970), 363; Philip Geyelin, *Lyndon B. Johnson and the World* (New York, 1966), p. 274.

vide for a termination date" for North American rights, but that date could only be after the sea-level canal opened. And even after the new canal began operations, the United States would retain a large military presence in Panama by negotiating a "new defense facilities agreement."[20]

Examining these "principles" more than a decade later, they appear idyllic. After 1970 the United States could not realistically hope for such concessions as control of the present Canal through the remainder of its life, or an indefinite military presence in Panama. The military chiefs in the Pentagon obtained all they could have wished. Bundy's paper did recognize the need to acknowledge Panamanian sovereignty in the Zone. This "principle" alone made the memorandum historic. Later another White House aide and State Department legal experts re-examined the question and agreed that officially the United States "has never claimed sovereignty in the Canal Zone" and "We have never had sovereignty."[21] But Bundy's "principles" granted Panama only the shell of sovereignty, while retaining control of the Panama Canal in Washington's hands. The NSC policy did not differ significantly from Theodore Roosevelt's approach when he dismissed the sovereignty issue as less important than ensuring United States control of the Canal.

That point ultimately occurred to the Panamanians. After eighteen months of talks the United States and Panama unveiled three treaty drafts in June 1967. One pact outlined arrangements for a possible sea-level canal. A second provided for the defense and neutrality of the present waterway, while the third set new ground rules for operating it. The United States explicitly recognized Panama's right to exercise sovereignty over the Canal, integrate the

20. "National Security Action Memorandum," Dec. 28, 1964, from Bundy; and "Memorandum for Mr. McGeorge Bundy," by Thomas C. Mann, Dec. 28, 1964; both in Executive File, Panama, LBJ Papers. The Eisenhower story is recounted in John A. McCone to Johnson, Dec. 17, 1964, Executive File, Panama, LBJ Papers.
21. James R. Jones to W. Marvin Watson, Jan. 17, 1967, Executive File, Panama, LBJ Papers.

Zone into Panama, and receive a larger portion of the Canal's revenue. The entire Zone would revert to Panama in 1999. The Panamanians had long demanded those concessions. But in return they provided *quid pro quos*. The Zone would be operated by a commission comprised of five North Americans who could theoretically outvote four Panamanian members. A dual court system of one North American and one Panamanian would be established. United States military bases would remain until 2004 and their leases could be renewed.

Robles immediately came under fire in the National Assembly. The makeup of the Commission and the long-term bases were unacceptable to nearly all factions. The two leading candidates for the 1968 presidential election, David Samudio and the omnipresent Arnulfo Arias, condemned the treaty. Robles desperately sent an emissary to Washington for new concessions, but he returned empty-handed. Johnson would offer nothing more. His resolve was perhaps stiffened by a remark from General Robert W. Porter, commander of the U.S. Southern Command stationed in the Zone. To abandon Panama in this "most critical period in the fight against Communism in Latin America," the General proclaimed, ". . . would be contrary to the best interests of Panama, the United States, and the free world." For good measure Porter indicated that more, not fewer, bases were required, and that fears of an arms race in Latin America were only "a figment of the imagination."[22] Little flexibility remained in the United States position.

The Irony of the Alliance for Progress

Another confrontation over the Zone was developing. As in the 1930s and 1950s, it had to be understood in the context of the Panamanians' belief that only the power to tap the Canal's resources could save them from impending economic disaster.

22. Quoted in *Latin America*, I (Oct. 20, 1967), 206.

The State Department and such powerful members of
Congress as Leonore Sullivan had hoped the Alliance
would strengthen the country's economy so the Zone
would lose its interest to Panamanians. The strategy not
only fizzled, but the results backfired. The failure grew in
part from Johnson's growing disillusionment with the Alliance ("a thorough-going mess," one LBJ aide described it),
his general disenchantment with Latin American officials
("The OAS," the President complained privately, "couldn't
pour piss out of a boot if the instructions were written on
the heel"[23]), a growing reluctance to work in the long
shadow of the Kennedys and their pet ideas ("the touch
football crowd isn't making the decisions around here any-
more," Johnson growled), and his intense preoccupation
with Vietnam.

The Alliance's progress was questioned early. Between 1961 and the Panama riots of January 1964, seven
constitutional governments in Latin America fell to military
coups. Washington's good intentions in such areas as tax
reform were deflated by highly publicized Latin American
cynicism: "You know, Brazil's growth is based in part on
not paying taxes," one South American told Time magazine. "If we paid, the government would spend it on fool-
ishness like the army. . . . Taxation is an Anglo-Saxon fe-
tish."[24] North Americans began to agree with the cynicism.
The Wall Street Journal mourned the 1964 riots, then drew
the conclusion: "This disgraceful business ought to be a
sharp reminder to all the sentimentalists who believe we
can uplift Latin America, and be loved for it, simply by
handing out billions of dollars."[25]

Johnson was moving to that position. Applying with
vigor the "muscle and common sense" approach of his chief
Latin American affairs adviser, Thomas Mann,[26] LBJ landed

23. Goldman, Tragedy of LBJ, p. 89; Geyelin, Johnson, p. 254.
24. Time, Jan. 31, 1964, p. 15.
25. Wall Street Journal, Jan. 13, 1964, p. 14:2.
26. Goldman, Tragedy of LBJ, p. 89.

22,000 troops in Santo Domingo during May 1965 to destroy the prospect (already highly unlikely), that a Castro-type regime would come to power. Such use of force, contrary to United States assurances solemnly made when it signed the OAS charter of 1948, delivered a shattering blow to the staggering Alliance program. Johnson and Congress cut Alliance funds nearly 40 percent over the next two years. Vietnam was swallowing those resources, but LBJ and Mann also agreed that Latin America must depend on private, not governmental, monies. Private United States capital, however, was far from sufficient to reach Alliance goals.

Not all the blame could be laid at Washington's door. In Panama the ruling oligarchy was not known for unselfishness or a dedication to correcting glaring socio-economic inequities. Consequently, although Panama enjoyed a large influx of United States funds and one of the three highest growth rates in Latin America between 1961 and 1969 (a rate that doubled from the 1950s to an 8.1 percent annual average), the foundations of the economy remained weak. And although it boasted the highest per capita rate of economic growth during the 1960s of any Latin American nation, inequality and poverty also continued to grow.[27] The figures revealed deeply rooted economic and social crises.

Item.   Per capita income in 1966 was $531, but 5 percent of the population received more than one-third the income. Half of the employed were farmers, and a large majority of farmers earned less than $100 annually. (Such inequity was not peculiar to Panama. United Nations figures showed that of the $100 per capita increase in Latin American income during the 1960s, only $2 reached the poorest 20 percent of the people.[28])

27. Organization of American States, Inter-American Economic and Social Council, *Latin America's Development and the Alliance for Progress* (Washington, D.C., 1973), pp. 40, 334–335.
28. Commission on U.S.-Latin American Relations, *The United States and Latin America: Next Steps. A Second Report.* . . . (no place of publication, 1976), p. 22.

Item. While experts believed Panama should have been a net exporter of food, the country spent $12 million in 1968 to import staples. Lack of transportation in the interior, inequitable land holdings, and archaic agricultural methods were to blame, and so was the oligarchy's educational system. One scholar compared Panama's farming methods "with those existing in the time of the Pharaohs,"[29] yet of the 6700 students in the National University, one-third studied Liberal Arts and one-fiftieth studied agriculture.

Item. Panama possessed over 2000 manufacturing firms, but only sixty employed 50 or more laborers, and these sixty—owned almost entirely by a few oligarchs and/or foreigners—accounted for 61 percent of the nation's manufactured products in value.

Item. The largest employers were the government (30,000 employees), the Canal Zone (13,000), and the United Fruit Company (11,000). The government provided the most lucrative, if inefficient, employment in the country, but mostly for those of oligarchical or skilled middle-class background who chose the right side in the presidential elections. Canal Zone employment had dropped steadily since 1945. The United Fruit Company had grown so large and powerful (providing the country's leading export by producing three pounds of bananas annually for every person in the United States) that the Panamanian government could not control it.

Item. Although the economic growth rate spiraled upward, unemployment reached 25 percent in 1966. The jobless congregated in the already congested slums of Panama City and Colon. The population meanwhile grew at an incredible 3.3 percent annually nationwide, and over 4 percent in the urban areas.

29. Larry L. Pippin, "Challenge in Panama," *Current History*, L (January 1966), 5.

The picture was grim, and the oligarchy did little to brighten it other than blame the problems on United States control of the Canal Zone.

The oligarchy was careful not to condemn the North Americans for dominating the Panamanian economy itself. The elite was so closely integrated into—or dependent on—United States capital and markets that the oligarchs remained nabobs in an informal North American colony. Panamanians held 48 percent of the nation's investment in terms of value. United States citizens controlled 50 percent, including Panama's electric power and telephone services, oil refineries, and bananas, its leading export.[30] Many large Panamanian-held firms, such as dairy and food processing, depended on markets in the Zone or the United States. These companies certainly could not find sufficient markets in the impoverished cities or peasant-dominated provinces, even if the peasants could have been reached.

As the United Nations investigation of 1956 had prophesied, either radical governmental intervention or an additional large amount of cash from the Canal was needed to pump-prime the economy. Neither was on the horizon. Tourists and markets associated with the Canal accounted for nearly one-third of Panama's gross national product, bridging almost single-handedly the huge gap between the country's large imports, such as food, and its exports. But in North American hands, the Canal's value to Panama remained limited. Despite a fifteenfold increase in traffic since 1914, the United States refused to raise the tolls, set when the passageway first opened, so Panama could receive a larger annuity. After the 1964 riots a number of Zonians who operated the Canal talked of early retirement. For a brief moment Panamanians hoped they might be trained for these jobs. The hope vanished as the Canal Com-

30. Carl R. Jacobsen, "Basic Data on the Economy of the Republic of Panama," *Overseas Business Reports*, June 1968 (Washington, D.C., 1968), pp. 8–14; Xabier Gorostiaga, *Panama y la Zona del Canal* (Buenos Aires, 1975), pp. 52–58.

pany continued to recruit heavily in the United States for
the higher-paying positions.

Out of choices, Chiari and Robles followed the usual
line of least resistance and accelerated government spending. They wrote the budgets in red ink until creditors were
reluctant to allow further borrowing. United States governmental loans helped, and the office that operated the Alliance for Progress, the Agency for International Development (AID), stepped in to take up some of the slack left by
the exhausted Panamanian treasury.

AID worked closely with the "Plan Robles," pumping in over $65 million between 1964 and early 1968 to
boost agricultural production and slow the rural-to-urban
migration. The Alliance, however, demanded in return that
an equitable tax system be created and enforced. Only a
completely revamped system could close the gaping budget
deficits. And only through an enforceable tax structure
could the oligarchy be made more responsible—perhaps
even saved from its own myopia.

It was a classic collision. United States officials, determined to promote evolution before revolution endangered their nation's interests in Panama, opposed a
small oligarchy which wanted nothing to disturb the status
quo. The scene was played out repeatedly in Latin America
during the 1960s, but nowhere did United States prospects
for success appear brighter than in Panama, where Washington's power was overwhelming.

"Plan Robles" began auspiciously. Panamanians in
the lowest income brackets traditionally paid a highly dis-
proportionate share of the taxes, but now they received
cuts. Larger incomes, particularly those in real estate, were
taxed at higher rates. "It is not a new little tax law to patch
up the already over-patched system," Robles warned. Alliance for Progress officials announced that the law was "one
of the outstanding ones under the Alliance so far."[31] No

31. Organization of American States, *Alliance for Progress Weekly Newsletter*, IV (Sept. 19, 1966), 3.

one, however, anticipated what happened next, because apparently no one had thought through the effects a new tax law would have if it were actually enforced.

David Samudio was the Panamanian official responsible for carrying through the reforms. Samudio was a longtime bureaucrat and politician, a close friend of Robles, and the President's heir-apparent in the 1968 election. As expected in a man of his position, Samudio was sensitive to the delicacy of the situation. Washington wanted tax reform in return for its dollars; its dollars determined Panama's economic health; the economy's health would help determine Samudio's own political future; he therefore thought it wise to carry out large parts of the tax reform program. Samudio began to collect taxes from sugar refineries, an industry freed from taxes when established 35 years before, and whose millionaires continued to enjoy that freedom in the 1960s. He also focused on the booming, tax-immune cement industry.

Stunned by the actual imposition of taxes, oligarchs in sugar and cement joined with others in rebellion against the Robles-Samudio-Alliance program.[32] The President's Liberal Party coalition fragmented, but the effects of the reform did not stop there. The oligarchy itself further divided. Its headquarters, the Union Club in Panama City, had bounced back in the 1960s after enduring rough days during Remón's reign. Dedicated to the propositions of no more Remóns and no meaningful socio-economic change, the Club's members refused to remain united behind Robles. Some condescendingly pointed out that the President's own family was less a part of the oligarchy than merely related to it through the Chiari family's beneficence. Watching his political opposition self-destruct, Arnulfo Arias happily commented that Panama was "not yet a country but a tribal affair."[33]

32. *Latin America*, II (March 29, 1968), 97–98.
33. *Wall Street Journal*, Oct. 18, 1968, p. 16:3.

As the fissures within the oligarchy threatened to engulf Robles, the President was left with few friends. The Panamanian leftists were politically impotent and unacceptable to Robles and Alliance officials. As the political situation became tense, the United States added the last straw—and several more for good measure. Congress reduced Alliance funds, then President Johnson announced in early 1968 another massive cut in developmental monies. United States banks simultaneously reduced foreign loans while the Inter-American Development Bank raised its interest rates nearly 2 percent. Deserted by his political supporters in Panama City and, apparently, in Washington, Robles retained power only through the grace of the National Guard.

The Guard was not reluctant to demonstrate its authority. In 1966 students had rioted when one of their leaders, Juan Navos, was mysteriously murdered after his return from a trip to Moscow. The government never managed to find the murderer, but the Guard killed two students in smashing the riots. Two years later, Robles was threatened from the other direction. Working through the National Assembly, oligarchical leaders tried to impeach him on grounds that he was illegally using governmental monies to ensure Samudio's election. Condemning the impeachment proceedings as "a political pantomime," Robles refused to appear before the Assembly and instead appealed to the Guard. The army upheld the President, then paraded its power by raiding opposition party headquarters, arresting nearly 500 people, and keeping the Assembly from further mischief by prohibiting it from convening. The Guard commander, General Bolívar Vallarino, had one overriding aim: prevent Arnulfo Arias from gaining power. The Guard officers vividly remembered Arias's attempts in 1941 and 1950 to destroy their power by creating his own police force. That "coffee planter with the silver tongue," Vallarino declared, would not have a third chance.

But in the May 1968 election the oligarchy remained

badly divided. Important members, including former President Chiari, joined Arias against Samudio. For two hectic weeks the National Election Board desperately tried to find enough votes for Samudio. Pro-Robles forces murdered an *Arnulfista* in an attack on a radio station, one student was killed attacking Samudio's headquarters, a National Guardsman was shot to death, and the Minister of Government and Justice's bodyguard was gunned down.[34] Samudio's supporters meanwhile grew discouraged. "We can do away with 25,000 [pro-Arias votes]," one remarked dejectedly, "but how can we get rid of 50,000?"[35] In the end they could not. Vallarino and the Guard announced they would support the duly-elected President. Why Vallarino switched became apparent when Arias assumed power.

Attempting to reform the oligarchical system, Robles and Samudio undermined it. The Alliance for Progress produced many unexpected and unwanted results during the 1960s, but none more ironic than the help it inadvertently gave in dividing an already tottering oligarchy and enabling Arnulfo Arias to become President once again. But a greater irony followed.

The Coup

Robles became incensed when the United States welcomed Arias's victory. Washington's view was shaped by two factors: its concern for stability and tranquility, rather than bloody haggling over election results; and its perception that Arias had turned pro-North American, particularly in matters relating to the Canal.

Robles responded bitterly with an anti-Yankee campaign in governmental newspapers and broadcasts, even accusing the Central Intelligence Agency of planting agents in the National Guard to push Arias into power. Some United States journalists, also blamed for aiding the CIA

34. Minor, "U.S.-Panamanian Relations: 1958–1973," pp. 214–215.
35. *Christian Science Monitor*, May 21, 1968, p. 2:2.

and Arias, received death threats. Robles went too far in mid-June, however. He decreed that Panamanian flagships could initiate trade with Cuba, China, and North Vietnam— Communist countries with whom United States trade was outlawed. Five days later the government blandly announced it was rescinding the decree "in view of [Panama's] existing international obligations and the incidence of various economic factors."[36] Robles had apparently been reminded that it was not the Communist bloc which controlled his country's economy.

With Washington's blessing, Arias became President on October 1, 1968. He immediately moved to neutralize the National Guard. After all, if its acquiescence allowed him to gain power, its opposition could dismiss him—for the third time. Arias worked out a deal with Vallarino. The Guard commander agreed to step down in return, apparently, for a post in the prestigious Washington Embassy. Arias then elevated trusted friends into command of the Guard while sending other officers into retirement or, as in the case of Colonel Omar Torrijos Herrera, to such foreign posts as El Salvador. The President meanwhile recruited a presidential guard which would be under his personal power.

On October 11, Torrijos and other threatened Guard officers staged a coup. Arias fled into the Canal Zone. The military junta accused the President of plotting a dictatorship and the inclusion of Nazis and Communists in his government. The accusation was window-dressing. The Guard acted because Arias was rapidly reducing its power. The thrice-deposed President searched desperately for help and was embarrassed (as was the United States), when no Latin American nation offered asylum. He finally flew to Washington. While driving in from Dulles Airport he decided to conquer the Panamanian Embassy. After completing that operation Arias suddenly appeared before startled officials of the OAS to demand the ouster of the junta. Wash-

36. *Latin America*, II (June 7 and 28, 1968), 176, 208.

ington, however, can be a cold town to those who have fumbled away power. ("Power corrupts," a United States official once observed, "but being out of power corrupts absolutely.") The dejected Arias finally left for the warmer climes of Miami.

The State Department was nearly alone in its sorrow. Expressing shock that "a constitutionally elected chief of state" might be deposed in Latin America, Secretary of State Dean Rusk cut diplomatic relations with Panama.[37] Given the number of coups that convulsed Latin America during the 1960s (including at least one, in Brazil, which the United States encouraged), it is difficult to believe that State Department principles remained that virginal. More to the point, the coup caught Washington with its storm signals down. The top three United States officials in Panama and the Canal Zone, including Ambassador Charles W. Adair, Jr., were out of the country on October 11. Their advisers had assured them that Arias was firmly in control.[38]

The junta, however, moved quickly to win Washington's friendship. The Guard promised to restore all constitutional rights and hold free elections. Panamanians appeared to accept the new government. The State Department expected street demonstrations, particularly after Arias clandestinely used Canal Zone radio facilities to urge his supporters into the streets. United States Army units went on alert. But nothing happened.

During the November 3d Independence Day celebration, however, an old hatred re-emerged. As nearly a thousand faculty and students protested Guard rule, armed troops attacked. Many students fled into a hospital for safety. The Guard followed, using rifle butts and hauling more than 200 off to jail. Panama University closed down and student leaders were arrested.

Secretary of State Rusk coincidentally announced

---

37. *Department of State Bulletin*, LIX (Nov. 4, 1968), 470.
38. *Christian Science Monitor*, Oct. 15, 1968, p. 4:1.

United States recognition of the junta. An era ended in Panama, an era which began in 1903. Yet the October events marked not a revolution but a coup. The junta finished what began in 1931 when United States military withdrawal made the Guard the keeper of the peace, in 1941 when Guard commanders first overtly determined who would rule, and in the 1950s when Remón transformed the Guard into a tool of reform. The cycle was completed in 1968 when the oligarchy committed political suicide.

It was fitting that Arias provided a brief, chaotic epilogue. The Guard then moved into full control. It now confronted the old vexation of an economy both lopsided and colonialized. The nation's prized resource meanwhile remained not only foreign-controlled, but newly stained with North American and Panamanian blood.

6 Torrijos, Kissinger, and Carter

On October 10, 1968, Omar Torrijos was unknown outside the Panama National Guard. Forty-eight hours later he emerged as a member of the junta governing the country. In a year he personally controlled Panama. Soon no Panamanian, or visitor to Panama, could long escape the General's stare, for as a virtual dictator (albeit a benevolent one compared with some Latin American rulers), his picture hung on a wall in every bar, restaurant, hotel, airline terminal, and store in the country.

Most photos showed Torrijos in full field uniform with a large pistol slung carefully but ostentatiously on his side. The picture perfectly captured unalloyed *machismo*, directly appealing to Panamanian tradition while unsubtly warning potential political opponents. As a North American remarked after looking at the picture, Torrijos appeared to be type-cast by Hollywood to play the role of a Latin American general. He strikingly contrasted with some Panamanian politicians of the pre-1968 era whose photographs made them resemble fast-moving corner necktie salesmen. Appearances count for much in politics, nowhere more than in Panama, and to most Panamanians Torrijos at least appeared to be a radical and welcome change.

Behind the pose was a highly complex man. Torrijos was born in 1929 at Santiago de Veraguas, 115 miles from Panama City. As the son of teachers, he came from the country's small but ultra-nationalistic, ambitious, and anti-foreign middle class, the class that first challenged the oligarchy effectively, if briefly, in 1931. He learned to appreciate romantic poetry and the works of García Marquez, but even his admirers would later disclaim that he was an intellectual. Novelist Graham Greene was nevertheless impressed that in interviews "sometimes a touch of poetry appears unexpectedly and unnoticed by himself when he speaks." Greene's example of Torrijos's "poetry"—"Intellectuals are like fine glass, crystal, which can be cracked by a sound. Panama is rock and earth"[1]—actually demonstrated that the General usually employed "poetry" when it was useful politically.

At seventeen he left Panama to attend a military academy in El Salvador, then by avoiding the political minefields of the National Guard he rose through the ranks. Courses in counterinsurgency warfare at the Canal Zone's School of the Americas helped the young officer distinguish himself in the early 1960s when he fought guerrilla movements in Panama's interior provinces.

Consolidating Power

Young Torrijos did not rise to the top immediately after the 1968 coup. The two senior Guard commanders headed the junta, which included five civilian members as well as military officers. After three months, the civilians accused the Guard of establishing a dictatorship and resigned. By that time it was clear that, with the aid of younger officers, Torrijos—the Guard's Commander-in-chief—and Colonel Boris Martínez—the Chief of Staff—controlled the government.

1. Graham Greene, "The Country with Five Frontiers," *New York Review of Books*, Feb. 17, 1977, pp. 10–11; *New York Times*, March 20, 1973, p. 4:4.

In March 1969 Martínez appeared on television, and
with the General Staff at his side announced a radical
agrarian reform program. He also declared that the Guard
would not halt nationalist anti-Yankee demonstrations.
Torrijos instantly moved against Martínez. Supported by
oligarchical elements, and apparently with United States
encouragement, he exiled the Chief of Staff to a comfortable post in Washington. (Martínez never reached Washington; he angrily joined his erstwhile enemy Arnulfo
Arias in Miami.)

The Martínez episode revealed Torrijos's priorities.
He was by no means another Castro. The Commander refused to antagonize the United States and he did not want
to encourage demonstrations. Martínez's summons to the
streets could have triggered a repetition of the 1964 riots,
pitting Guard against students and, if events got out of
hand, demonstrating that the new government was unable
to maintain order. Torrijos preferred to coopt rather than
arrest students. His nationalist proclamations and reform
program soon allied those longtime enemies, the Student
Federation and the Guard. Rumors in Panama City suggested that the Central Intelligence Agency helped Torrijos
depose Martínez; in any case, the United States shortly
thereafter gave $15 million for improving the capital city's
water supply, the first grant issued since the coup. Torrijos celebrated by promoting himself to brigadier-general.

He celebrated too soon. In December 1969 the new
General was attending horse races in Mexico City when a
group of Guard colonels, led by Amado Sanjur, and right-
wing oligarchs announced that Torrijos had been deposed.
Supported by loyal Guard garrisons in David, and helped
by Nicaraguan dictator Anastasio Somoza—who provided a
private plane—Torrijos returned to Panama City, overthrew Sanjur, exiled the dissident colonels, and reclaimed
his power. A State Department official later speculated that
Torrijos actually invited the Sanjur coup in order to draw
his conservative opponents into the open, where he could
destroy them politically.

Maximum Chief and the Forty Thieves

The General shrewdly appointed a civilian, Demetrio Lakas, as provisional President. An engineer as well as politician, Lakas was highly regarded by some oligarchs and most North American businessmen. In reality, power lay in the upper echelons of the army, now an impressive praetorian guard of 6000 men, comprised mostly of blacks or, like Torrijos himself, middle-class mestizos. The Guard's elite groups, the Tigers and Pumas, were disciplined, well equipped, and intimidating. Since Remón built the Guard it had infiltrated most important facets of Panama's life. In the words of one observer, "its intelligence is said to be omniscient, so that people think twice before telling anecdotes about it."[2] Torrijos consolidated his power by giving the Guard higher salaries. He also transformed the oligarchy's posh Union Club into a recreation center for Guard members and their families. (The old Union Club membership reinstalled itself in luxurious facilities on Paitilla Point, where it again commanded a magnificent view of the Pacific, this time in a safer neighborhood of Panama City. The Union Club's reincarnation was an omen.)

Torrijos declared all political parties illegal. The Communists had been outlawed since 1950; other leftists were singularly ineffective. In late 1969, however, left-wing leader Floyd Britton was assassinated by unknown gunmen; urban guerrilla groups retaliated by forming the National Liberation Movement. After the Movement robbed a number of banks and casinos, the Guard trapped its leaders in 1970, killing two Cuban-trained members. A wave of repression accompanied this campaign.[3] Newspapers were either self-censored or shut-down. The government controlled radio stations, using its communications monopoly to urge that any "suspicious persons" and "important information" be reported instantly to the Guard. Estimates of

2. Morris, "Terminal Case of American Perpetuity," p. 48.
3. Donald C. Hodges, *The Latin American Revolution* (New York, 1974), p. 222.

political prisoners ran as high as 1600, and 200 reportedly remained in jail in mid-1971.[4]

In late 1968 the junta had promised open elections, but in 1971 the pretense was dropped. Torrijos publicly condemned the political processes developed by the oligarchs during the previous seventy years. "They allege that we are illegitimate because we are not born out of one of those things they call elections," the General proclaimed to a large Panama City rally. "This is precisely our greatest pride . . . not acquiring credentials of their kind, because we prefer the clean credentials of your support and not the one hundred credentials of their kind which are rolled in the mud."[5]

Torrijos refused to recognize the legitimacy of the oligarchy-ruled National Assembly. His feelings were best revealed when a close associate called it "Ali Baba and the Forty Thieves." That was probably a reference to the aftermath of the 1968 coup, when 24 of the 53 members of the Assembly joined Arias in fleeing the country.[6] The old Assembly was replaced by a new 505-member Assembly of Municipal Representatives. The delegates are elected at the local level in balloting controlled by the Guard. It meets once a year for one month to report on regional activities and vote on legislation. When the first Assembly convened in 1972 (in a Panama City gymnasium), its main order of business was to make Torrijos "Maximum Chief." Lakas continued in the subordinate role of President.

The Assembly also approved a new constitution to replace the 1946 document. It is required reading, especially between the lines, for an understanding of contemporary Panama. The constitution officially recognized the Guard as a governing body and flatly declared that "The

4. *Wall Street Journal*, June 17, 1971, p. 29:3.
5. Quoted in Steve C. Ropp, "Military Reformism in Panama: New Directions or Old Indications," *Caribbean Studies*, XII (October 1972), p. 62; also Omar Torrijos Herrera, *Una Revolucion Diferente* (Panama City, 1972), pp. 81, 107.
6. *Latin America*, Oct. 18, 1968, p. 329, and Jan. 23, 1970, p. 31.

Government alone may possess arms and implements of war." The "penalty of death, expatriation, or confiscation of property" was disallowed, but otherwise "public officials" enjoyed considerable discretion (to say the least), for they could "impose fines or arrest upon anyone who insults them or who is in contempt of their authority." That clause made mass roundups and arrests constitutional. Torrijos was named and given immense power. The days of oligarchical rule and legislative power were apparently over. An all-powerful executive, his authority resting on the National Guard, ruled Panama constitutionally.

The document allowed the Maximum Chief and his government to extend their reach into the far corners of Panamanian society. "The State" assumed the right to "oversee the rational distribution of land" and not allow "uncultivated, unproductive or idle areas." Although "engaging in economic activities is primarily the function of private persons," the supreme law directed "the State" to "guide, direct, regulate, replace or initiate such activities" as it thought the national economy required. "The State" also acquired the power to protect "marriage, motherhood, and the family," possessed "exclusive competence to organize and direct education," and, for good measure, was instructed to defend "the purity of the Spanish language."

The last proviso hinted that state power would be especially sensitive to North American presence. The constitution did not recognize a United States-controlled Canal Zone. It declared illegal the ceding of national territory to any foreign country; it provided that utility corporations and the Roman Catholic Church hierarchy be controlled by Panamanian citizens, and even set rigid restrictions on foreigners who planned to enter retail businesses.[7]

The old, open, laissez-faire Panamanian economy

7. Organization of American States, *Constitution of Panama 1972* (Washington, D.C., 1974), especially pp. 5–7, 11–12, 15, 38–40, 43–44; for the weakness of Panama's public sector before the mid-1970s, Gorastiaga, *Panama y la Zona*, pp. 52–53.

was to be transformed. The constitution indeed gave the government power to make radical changes throughout the system. Torrijos's far-flung authority raised the fundamental question of what he represented: a Castro-type departure or the surfacing of long-term trends?

In important respects the General seemed to belong to a 150-year tradition of the Latin American *caudillo* who assumed power when his nation began to free itself of the mother country. He usually emerged from army officer ranks, used arms to force civilians into line, and displayed the authoritarian attitudes of the military. The traditional *caudillo*, like Torrijos, often seized authority in a nation whose development had been stifled by excessive legalism, inefficient and corrupt civilian regimes, inequitable income distribution, deep racial antagonisms, and geographical obstacles which made the functioning of a truly national government highly difficult.[8] In such "stateless" societies (which Panama resembled), the weakness of the central government had allowed the rich to become richer and the poor to die young. *Caudillos* filled the political vacuum with military authority and built a popular base by promising the poor a better future. Torrijos thus resembled those numerous Latin American rulers who, far from being ideology-bound and left-wing, created personal, pragmatic, and authoritarian regimes with which the United States profitably cooperated.

Although Arnulfo Arias approximated the civilian version of the stereotype, a *caudillo* had never ruled Panama, but many aspects of *caudillismo* were common in Panamanian political life. Leadership on the Isthmus was traditionally based on personal, charismatic authority rather than on written rules or cohesive party systems. The

8. General characteristics of *caudillismo* are taken from William H. Beezley, "Caudillismo: An Interpretive Note," *Journal of Inter-American Studies*, XI (July 1969), 345–352; Edwin Liewen, *Arms and Politics in Latin America* (New York, 1961), pp. 22–24; Eric R. Wolfe and Edward C. Hansen, *The Human Condition in Latin America* (New York, 1972), pp. 223–224.

President enchanted the masses if he conformed to "the virtuoso standard of masculine behavior" (as two students of Panama phrased it), appeared to be daring, and—at least since the 1930s—opposed United States domination.[9] Torrijos's style and some sources of his authority were therefore rooted in an appeal common to the Arias brothers, or even Porras of sixty years before.

But Torrijos also represented something different, a phenomenon perhaps best called a "new *caudillismo.*" For although his authority rested on the army and personal charisma, he had to deal with masses who were conditioned by new media, urbanization, anti-imperialism, and Fidel Castro's long shadow, problems that did not complicate the lives of the old *caudillos.* The new *caudillismo* therefore assumed populist aspects, as Torrijos perfectly exemplified when he condemned the National Assembly for selling out to the rich, and claiming that his power rested on mass support. His government's monopoly of the media ensured that the masses heard the proper message.

Resting power on the barrel of a gun, as had traditional *caudillos,* was one thing. But basing power on rifles, excitable middle-class university students, and masses suddenly experiencing the twentieth century was playing with fire. Particularly when a new *caudillo's* power ultimately depended on his ability to confer largesse, continually and in considerable amounts, upon those soldiers, students, and masses, his political base could erode quickly. Unless Torrijos could create new wealth internally, his future would depend on his ability to deal with the ultimate power in Panama—the United States and its control of Canal revenues.

School of the Americas Radicalism

Close observers of Panama therefore understood that trying to pigeon-hole Torrijos as a "Marxist" or a "reactionary" was useless exercise. His bases of power and his needs

9. Biesanz and Smith. "Panamanian Politics." pp. 389–393.

were too complicated for such simple categorization. And so was his program that began unfolding in 1969. He announced plans for massive structural reform in agriculture, including large-scale land distribution. Direct governmental interference in other areas of economic life aimed at stimulating both productivity and what was termed "social progress." The plans promised, in the words of a knowledgeable foreign observer, "a thorough-going revolutionary reform that would for the first time create a real nation out of Panama."[10] But to some it all too uncomfortably resembled Fidel Castro's Cuba in early 1959. Tremors were felt in Washington and oligarchical neighborhoods of Panama City. Panamanian businessmen pointedly suggested to North Americans that since they had allowed the General to assume power, they were responsible for deposing him.

The inspiration for Torrijos's reforms, however, was not Cuban. Nothing provided a better key to the General's politics than to understand that his program was inspired by that anti-Castro, counter-insurgency institution in the Canal Zone, the School of the Americas. Founded in 1949, the institution produced 34,000 graduates by the mid-1970s.[11] The Panamanian Guard provided 3500, or the fourth highest number, of these graduates, ranking ahead of Brazil, Colombia, and Venezuela. Of the top 24 Guard officers in 1971, 19 attended the School. Torrijos was a proud graduate. As Maximum Chief he nevertheless demanded its removal since its presence violated United States pledges, made solemnly in the 1903 treaty, that any North American military installation would be for the sole purpose of protecting the Canal. The School of the Americas was for a considerably broader purpose of fighting in-

---

10. *Latin America*, Aug. 15, 1969, pp. 260–261; on the other hand, see the succinct statement by Torrijos in his *Una Revolucion Diferente*, p. 109. 11. The analysis of School of the Americas is based upon Ropp, "Military Reformism in Panama," pp. 45–57; Kahn, "Letter from Panama," p. 74; Joanne Omand in *Washington Post*, April 11, 1977, p. A16:4; Richard Gott in *ibid.*, April 16, 1977, p. A10:5–6; and author's interviews.

surgents throughout the hemisphere. Torrijos described it as "this great colonial encampment." On the other hand, his old school ties were such that he admitted Panama profited from the treaty violation, and he frequently visited the institution, taking students on tours of Panama in his helicopter.

The courses taught military officers to forget the old *caudillismo* and develop their country's immunity to communism, not their own bankrolls. They learned that only military discipline could create the order needed for such development. Civilian politics were too compromising, chaotic, and corrupt. Through such courses as "Interrogation Techniques" and "Urban and Rural Counterinsurgency Concepts," the graduates learned to check both the greed of the right and the revolutionary ardor of the left so the state could benefit.

In the 1970s all of Central and South America was under military rule except Colombia, Venezuela, Costa Rica, and Mexico; nearly all the officers who assumed power were graduates of the School. As students who learned their lessons well, they demanded national discipline regardless of the effect on human rights. (The lessons were so well learned that many Latin American leaders were confused in 1977 when President Jimmy Carter began to emphasize human rights instead of fighting terrorists.)

As a new *caudillo*, Torrijos believed Panamanian development required the destruction of political parties, the National Assembly, freedom of the press, the rights of some private-property holders, and the jobs of perhaps 4000 useless, oligarchy-appointed bureaucrats. Some Panamanians expressed concern about such a tradeoff. A businessman worried in 1971, "For peace and prosperity we are giving up certain intangibles, like freedom of speech and other political rights. How soon we get to the point where the sacrifice of intangibles no longer is equal to the tangibles we have gained is the big question."[12]

12. *Wall Street Journal*, June 17, 1971, p. 25:3–4.

Torrijos provided his own perspective in a remarkable letter to Senator Edward Kennedy in 1970. After Castro, the General wrote, "there was a new orientation. We had more contact with people." "There was a preoccupation with social forces" in officer training. After encountering John F. Kennedy and the Alliance for Progress, Torrijos continued, the military became "well prepared professionals with good intentions, that speak, think, and live the language of development" which Kennedy inspired. Then came a revealing phrase: "[in studying Castro and Kennedy,] we came to the conclusion that there was a direct relationship between social justice and social violence."[13]

To achieve "social justice," Torrijos instituted two innovations that left a profound mark on his country. The first stressed massive governmental intervention in the economy. Multi-year developmental programs dated back to the 1960s, but they so depended on the private sector for leadership that the Chiari-Robles administrations remained out of many areas (such as public utilities), that in market-oriented Western Europe had long since been absorbed into the governmental sector. Panamanians were (and, as Torrijos would discover, continue to be) among the most dedicated of any Latins to private enterprise and laissez-faire capitalism. The relative absence of Spanish feudal traditions, and the fluidity resulting from four centuries of constant population movement across the Isthmus, encouraged individual enterprise.

The new *caudillo*'s use of governmental power was consequently path-breaking and, to some, ominous. His regime sponsored urban housing projects and large apartment and office complexes in downtown Panama City. Fresh legislation increased personal and corporate taxes, especially on corporate dividends, to pay for the construction. For both political and economic reasons, Torrijos

13. Quoted in Ropp, "Military Reformism in Panama," p. 54. Torrijos even referred to his version of the Alliance as an inspiration; *Una Revolucion Diferente*, p. 106.

promulgated a labor law in 1972 that became the symbol of his "revolution." The old marketplace relationship between capital and labor was suddenly replaced by a code, enforced by a strong Ministry of Labor, that regulated job conditions, established minimum wages, protected domestic servants, and made collective bargaining compulsory. Political motives were obviously involved. Torrijos hoped to make a strong labor movement part of his political base, much as Juan Perón used Argentinian labor a quarter-century earlier to establish virtual one-man rule and propel himself into international prominence.

In a second innovation, Torrijos placed top priority on rural rather than urban development. Of all Panamanian Presidents, only Harmodio Arias and the late, unlamented Remón had focused attention on the interior provinces, and the impact of their policies proved to be minute. The oligarchy otherwise pumped money and governmental favors into the cities where its own interests lay. Torrijos's new policies were shaped by a condescending dislike of the oligarchy, as well as his hope that the agrarian sectors, like the labor movement, would form an enthusiastic part of his political base. The Guard, moreover, recruited heavily from the countryside. Its men knew first-hand that most peasants earned less than $100 annually, and that their starchy diet created protein/calorie malnutrition in more than 60 percent of all children under five. Raised in the interior, Torrijos had fought guerrillas with whom he strongly identified. He disliked their terrorism, but, as he later reflected, it was understandable why they hoped to emulate Fidel Castro.

In early 1969 the government announced that within three years it would distribute 700,000 hectares of land among 61,300 families, so that ultimately average holdings would multiply nearly five times per family. The expropriated landowners received "agrarian bonds" paying one percent interest and repayable in 40 years. Farm schools were established; contrary to oligarchical educational policy, half the student's time was devoted to practical lessons of farming. Torrijos's most striking innovation was to establish 270 farm collectives of nearly 35,000 people. The collectives were democratically self-ruled, shared profits, and provided with equipment, technical assistance, capital, and over 300,000 hectares of land by the government. As one reporter observed, the collectives seemed "a cross between an Israeli *kibbutz* and a cooperative." On one successful collective, individual annual income grew from $400 in 1972 to $1400 four years later. Considering the new experiment ready-made for political organizing, Marxists tried to infiltrate some of the collectives. The Guard forcefully stopped such attempts.[14]

More serious was the opposition to Torrijos's plans from the Roman Catholic Church, which for centuries had worked among the peasants. Father Hector Gallego, for example, organized peasant cooperatives in Sante Fe Province, but under the direction of the Church, not the government. Of perhaps equal importance, Gallego's efforts to make his flock more self-sufficient hurt the interests of a local merchant who happened to be Torrijos's cousin. In 1971 government agents visited Gallego. Shortly thereafter he disappeared and has never been found.

Archbishop Marcos McGrath of Panama City condemned the government and excommunicated anyone who might have participated in the abduction. McGrath was not to be trifled with. A tall, imposing figure who headed the only independent socio-political organization of any importance left in Panama, the Archbishop was well known for his ardent nationalism. Long before Torrijos appeared on the scene, McGrath worked to bring the Canal under Panamanian control. He enjoyed important political connections in the United States. Torrijos consequently dispatched President Lakas to explain his side of the story to the Vatican. But the Maximum Chief bent no further, threatening to

14. Edward Schumacher in *Washington Post*, July 18, 1976, p. F3:3; the malnutrition suffered in the interior is analyzed in Looney, *Economic Development of Panama*, p. 39. A hopeful Marxist analysis of the collectives is in B. Gonzalez, "New Trends in Rural Panama," *World Marxist Review*, XVIII (June 1975), 124–129.

retaliate by prohibiting missionaries from entering Panama. The General won the battle. Although Panama is over- whelmingly Roman Catholic, it has a long tradition of Church non-interference in state affairs. Panamanians tend to see the Church as unconcerned with their problems of poverty and disenfranchisement. McGrath has tried to change that image, but he could not rally support against Torrijos in the Gallego case.[15]

The General's two new departures—widespread use of governmental power and emphasis on rural develop- ment—were dramatically illustrated in his handling of the North American gift to radical Latin American nationalism, the United Fruit Company. By 1970 the company was no longer an easy target for Latin anti-imperialists. It was sub- sumed into United Brands Inc., and the company's Pana- manian subsidiary was known as the Chiriqui Land Com- pany (CLC). During the 1960s labor unrest plagued CLC, so much so that the company began selling off land to Pana- manians, while keeping the rights to buy and distribute whatever they produced. CLC also sold or gave over 5000 hectares of land to the government for redistribution. Its banana business meanwhile flourished, accounting for two- thirds of Panama's total exports in the late 1960s. Then Torrijos entered the picture.

In 1973–74 an economic downturn combined with poor planning to create severe problems for the General's programs. In early 1974 he sought involuntary help from United Brands. Under his leadership, the seven leading Latin American banana exporting nations agreed to impose new taxes of 40¢ to $1 on each 42-pound crate of bananas. Torrijos immediately imposed the maximum amount on Pan- ama's exports. The several companies affected bitterly pro- tested and refused to pay the tax. Rumors circulated that they were plotting to overthrow the Honduran, Panama- nian, and Costa Rican governments. These rumors owed

---

15. *Latin America*, Sept. 3, 1971, p. 281; J. Lloyd Mecham, *Church and State in Latin America*, (Chapel Hill, 1966), p. 339.

more to the memories of the 1920s than the realities of the 1970s. CLC, however, did stop production. Several other nations cut back their exports. But the governmental ranks broke when Ecuador, the largest producer, and Nicaragua refused to impose the tax. They gathered in windfall profits by exporting large amounts of bananas. Torrijos was furious, threatening that if Panama lost the "banana war we shall throw our production into the Canal." In acts not unrelated to his anger, the General announced the uncovering of a plot to assassinate him during one of his trips to the interior, and in August 1974 mobs broke eighty windows of the U.S. Embassy.

Panama followed the toughest policy of any Central American producer, but in the end Torrijos was forced to compromise on a 45¢ tax. In 1976, however, the government expropriated CLC lands, leased 37,000 acres back so the company could maintain banana production, and required CLC to pay $2 million annually in rents, 50 percent tax on profits, plus the 45¢ a crate export tax. (In the United States, meanwhile, customers wondered why they suddenly paid 25 to 50 percent more for bananas.) The remainder of the CLC land was to be given by the government to collectives. As for United Brands, the "banana war" helped expose questionable financial dealings within the company, dealings that apparently led its president to jump from the 42nd floor of the Pan American Building in New York City.[16]

From Revolution to Reality

The struggle against CLC revealed a glaring weakness in Torrijos's developmental program. He was forced to wage the "banana war" because funds were short. The problem was hardly new; it had threatened his plans from the beginning. During 1969 he stimulated the economy by

16. *Latin America*, Aug. 23, 1974, pp. 258, 260; *Wall Street Journal*, Jan. 9, 1976, p. 6:3; Thomas P. McCann, *An American Company:The Tragedy of United Fruit* (New York, 1976), pp. 215–219.

pumping in $45 million of public investment, half from international banks. Another $50 million was borrowed from Swiss banks.[17] By 1972 debt service alone swallowed up a quarter of all governmental revenues. As credit sources were exhausted, economic growth shrunk from 8 percent of the 1960s to under 4 percent in 1974. Along with other nations, moreover, Panama suffered from an inflation rate that shot up to 18 percent in 1973.

Panama's integration into the United States economy did not lessen the squeeze. Legally dependent on the dollar as the basis for their own currency, Panamanians had no choice but to buckle themselves up as United States inflation skyrocketed and the dollar value of their imports spiraled upward. They were consequently hit from two sides: North American goods cost more, and a less valuable dollar was used in their other international trade. Panama was so closely tied to the United States that it could control neither its currency nor, in many respects, its trade.[18]

The 1970 tax reforms proved insufficient for capital needs, but when new laws appeared in 1972 they imposed regressive rates on liquor, tobacco, cigarettes—taxes that especially hurt the lower classes. The law actually backfired, for it increased smuggling from the Zone to the point that although the measure doubled the tax on liquor, imported liquor revenues decreased. For Torrijos it was one more reason why Panama needed the Zone.

In formulating the 1972 tax program, Panamanian officials exhibited a necessary sensitivity to bankers in Panama City. Torrijos's dependence on them revealed the limits of his reform program. Only five foreign banks operated in the country in 1963, but 46 were there a decade later, and 74 by 1977. Bank assets tripled in the four years after 1967.

The turning point came with the 1970 banking law

17. Minor, "U.S.-Panamanian Relations, 1958–1973," p. 225.
18. Harry Johnson, "Panama as a Regional Financial Center: A Preliminary Analysis of Development Contribution," *Economic Development and Cultural Change*, XXIV (January 1976), 286.

which made Panama the Switzerland of Latin America.
Banks could be established with minimal requirements and
funds whipped in and out of the country with no questions
asked. The government helpfully imposed a lid on the interest rate paid domestic savings, but allowed other rates
(for example, bank lending) to be determined by the vaga-
ries of the marketplace. The 1970 law, combined with Panama's currency being interchangeable with the dollar, the
country's excellent location, its foreign communications
(which some bankers believed superior to London's), and
its political stability made the Isthmus a banker's paradise.
As the manager of a Dutch bank explained the operation,
"We borrow in Europe, funnel money through Panama, and
then lend it out to our branches in South America. Because
of Panama's laws, the profit we gain is tax-free."[19]

Only indirect benefits for Panamanians peeled off
from the billions which traveled hurriedly through the
country. Panama was at the banks' mercy, for it imposed no
reserve requirements and consequently the institutions depended on policies made far from the Isthmus. If a parent
bank weakened in Paris, or the London government forced
a credit squeeze on British banks, the Torrijos government
would be defenseless against the closing of Panamanian
branches. One student of the system concluded that the
1970 law contributed little to governmental tax revenues.
"All things considered," his study ended, "the evidence
does not lend much impressive quantitative support to the
view that the growth of the financial sector is a powerful
lever for promoting Panamanian economic development."
But if a nationalist regime tried to control the nation's economy by cutting its ties to the dollar, the banks would close
their doors and move elsewhere, while Panama's trade
would be in chaos. The impact of the 1970 law on the
internal economy is measureable: in 1960 local Panamanian

19. *Wall Street Journal*, March 12, 1973, p. 6:2; Looney, *Economic Devel-
opment of Panama*, pp. 96–97; Robin Pringle, "Panama, A Survey," *The
Banker*, CXXV (October 1975), 1201; *Latin American Economic Report*,
May 27, 1977, p. 78.

banks controlled 70 percent of the deposits and 96 percent of loans in the country; in 1976 foreign banks controlled 91 percent of the deposits and 77 percent of the loans. The economy remained colonialized; only the forms were slightly altered.[20]

Torrijos's regime profited in one respect from the law: politically the measure placed the bankers squarely in the General's corner. The acid test occurred in 1973 when the economic downturn raised questions about the Maximum Chief's staying power. Stories circulated that Torrijos was about to share the fate of Chile's recently deposed president, Salvador Allende. At that point the Panamanian subsidiary of New York's First National City Bank created a banking consortium that loaned the regime $115 million to refinance the embarrassing national debt and maintain public investment rates.

The General soon returned the favor. At the bankers' request he rescinded his decree that threatened to impose restrictions on mortgage lending. Panamanian businessmen did not fare as well. When they planned a one-day strike to protest a three-year rent freeze and other discriminatory decrees, Torrijos proclaimed he would exile any protester to Miami, "the valley of the fallen reactionaries of Latin America." There was no strike.[21]

His economic spokesman, Nicholas Barletta, had prophesied in early 1973 that the "excessive dominance of the Canal Zone would be broken" and "the country's dependence on the United States would be lessened."[22] The opposite occurred, and as Torrijos had to negotiate with the bankers, so he was forced to turn his attention to the Canal.

History repeated itself not, as Karl Marx would have it, first as tragedy and then as farce, but repeated itself naturally and inevitably because Torrijos's Panama was ultimately as dependent on the Canal revenues for survival as was the Panama of Harmodio Arias, Remón, and Robles.

20. Johnson, "Panama as a Regional Financial Center," p. 284.
21. *Latin America*, Oct. 26, Nov. 30, 1973, pp. 338, 383.
22. Quoted in Looney, *Economic Development of Panama*, p. 5.

Not only the country's greatest resource, the passageway was Panama's last hope.

Superficially the issue appeared unrelated to Torrijos's concern with the development of interior provinces. On one of his quick helicopter forays into the isolated interior, he supposedly asked a *campesino* what he thought about the Canal. *"Canal"* is Spanish for "channel," and since Panamanians are addicted to television channels two and four, the peasant replied, which *"canal—dos a cuatro?"*[23] The *campesino's* immediate concerns were more closely tied to the waterway than he knew. Was cultivatable land needed for collectives or for orderly expansion of compacted Panama City and Colon? Then Panamanians noted that 51 percent of the Zone, or 250 square miles, was unused. (The United States employed 4 percent of the Zone for operating the Canal and 37 percent for military bases.) Was money needed in ever larger sums for developmental purposes? Panamanians observed that in 1969 the Canal's net income reached $15.6 million, but they received only one-seventh of the amount.

During his first four years in office Torrijos said little publicly about the Canal except in 1970 when, to no one's surprise, he declared the 1967 agreements dead and buried. In the autumn of that year he informed the Nixon administration that the Zone must be incorporated into Panama, a claim that led the *New York Times* to condemn Torrijos for bowing to undisciplined nationalism. Nixon, however, agreed to start discussions in 1971. Progress was agonizingly slow until 1973, when Torrijos, with economic problems closing around him, publicly demanded a radically new arrangement for the Zone. He caught United States foreign policy in the middle of a significant change.

The Third Cold War

Since 1945 the United States has waged a long and often bloody Cold War. Three decades after its beginnings,

23. Kahn, "Letter from Panama," p. 69.

however, the conflict appears to be not one but three different wars. The First, lasting from 1945 until the mid-1950s, pitted the United States against the Soviet Union in a world divided between the two superpowers. In the mid-1950s the Suez crisis, Eastern European revolts, and massive decolonization in Africa and Southeast Asia fragmented that "two-camp" world, ushering in an age of pluralism that provided the context for a major revision of United States-Panamanian relations.[24] After 1956 the United States dealt with many non-Soviet problems, and some of them, e.g., Vietnam and Castro, required close attention. Throughout the Second Cold War, North Americans continued to believe they possessed the military and economic power to solve or at least contain the problems on Washington's terms. Particularly in the economic arena, the United States appeared unchallengeable.

In the early 1970s a Third Cold War began. The Nixon administration continued to confront a host of problems relating to the ambitious, fragmented, developing nations of the southern hemispheres, but it no longer enjoyed overwhelming power to deal with them. The rapid decline of the dollar in 1970–71 and the success of the Arab oil embargo in 1973 revealed unexpected economic vulnerability. North Vietnam's triumph starkly displayed the limits of Washington's military and political power. The Third Cold War is consequently marked by highly complex problems and a growing inability of the United States to dictate solutions.

Richard Nixon understood this shifting balance of power. He hoped to gain time, and an honorable, perhaps triumphant, exit from Vietnam by playing off China against Russia in a delicate game of big power politics. Once the two Communist giants were sufficiently neutralized and the United States freed of the Vietnam morass, the logic of the Nixon policy ran, North Americans could deal with the developing nations to the south. Meanwhile

24. See discussion in Chapter IV.

Latin America would have to await developments in East-West relations.

Nixon accepted Johnson's approach to the Canal question. In the 1971–72 talks, the United States agreed to remove the "in perpetuity" clause and cede jurisdiction over the Canal to Panama at a definite date. The Panamanians would receive a larger share of the revenues. Nixon, however, demanded United States control of the Canal for another fifty years, and, if a sea-level waterway was built on the site of the present Canal, for eighty years. Torrijos refused to allow Washington's control beyond 2003, a number which, for obvious historical reasons, began to have magical properties for Panamanians. Positions tightened, then the discussions halted.

Relations became critical, and in early 1973 *Newsweek* reported that two years before, the White House "plumbers" unit, now famous for the Watergate burglary and various other crimes, was assigned by unnamed top administration officials to kill Torrijos—because of his treaty demands—and other Panamanian officials who trafficked heroin into the United States. The "plumbers" were supposedly traveling through Mexico when the plans were cancelled.[25]

Other than the friendly bankers, Torrijos had little reason to show affection toward North Americans. United States relations with Panama, like those with many third world nations, were at their nadir in 1973 when Washington officials confronted a series of crises that symbolized the new Third Cold War: a growing realization that the Soviets were achieving military parity with the United States, the economic disasters slowly arising from the oil embargo, the final evacuation of Western troops from South Vietnam, and the withering effect Watergate exercised on those executive powers that directed Cold War strategies.[26]

25. *Newsweek*, June 18, 1973, p. 22.
26. Latin American policy is placed in this context in a speech by Assistant Secretary of State William D. Rogers in *Department of State Bulletin*, LXXIV (Jan. 5, 1976), 18.

The United States needed help, preferably from friends who would share their oil and raw materials at low prices. Latin America seemed an obvious candidate for a new partnership, but the Latins, to understate the case, were cool. Three years before, the Nixon administration not only refused to discuss long-term economic relationships, but declared virtual economic war by imposing a 10 percent surcharge on imports and attaching tough conditions on bilateral aid. In late 1973 the United States needed access to markets and raw materials in the south, and Secretary of State Henry Kissinger—who previously had pointedly ignored Latin America—moved to push aside political obstacles that impeded that access. Attempting to unclog diplomatic channels, Nixon and Kissinger asked for a "new dialogue." Few Latin Americans seemed anxious to respond. They were turning away from the United States to open relationships with Japan, Russia, Canada, and Western Europe. As Latins saw themselves as part of the southern third world rather than a partner in the Western Hemisphere, the gap widened between South and North Americans.

Kissinger understood these changes. Noting that carrying on the "new dialogue" through regional diplomacy pitted the United States virtually alone against a Latin America that was acquiring a new identity, he switched to a divide-and-conquer bilateral diplomacy.[27] The United States would deal with one nation at a time. The limitations suddenly imposed upon North American power forced the employment of a rifle rather than the more prodigal shotgun approach. Even in Latin America.

The Seeds of a New Treaty . . .

In Panama, talks on the Canal issue were at a deadend. Many North Americans were pleased. In early 1973

27. Ben S. Stephansky, " 'New Dialogue' on Latin America: The Cost of Policy Neglect," in Ronald G. Hellman and H. Jon Rosenbaum, eds., *Latin America: The Search for a New International Role* (New York, 1975), pp. 153–157.

the House Merchant Marine and Fisheries Committee, which exercised considerable power in Canal policy, announced that the United States must retain "undiluted sovereignty" in the Zone, then recommended that a special radio station be established to instruct Panamanians on the virtues of the status quo. A top State Department official dismissed stories that Torrijos might organize mass demonstrations against the Zone. If this occurred, the official believed, "it might show up the Panamanian authorities as being unable to control their own situation." (He did not dismiss the possibility, however, that spontaneous demonstrations could erupt.[28])

Torrijos shrewdly neutralized the mobs and appeased Panamanian nationalism by inducing the United Nations Security Council to hold a meeting in Panama instead of New York City. In the March 1973 meeting the General successfully focused world opinion on the Canal issue. Entering the Legislative Palace in Panama City, delegates could see on one side the city's steamy slums, on the other the Zone's air-conditioned bungalows and green fairways. (They did not see a restaurant formerly named "La Frontera," which bordered the Zone, for the government had "invited" the owner to change the name since it affronted "the sovereignty of Panama." Nor did the delegates see the nine-foot-high fence in the Zone that had separated these two worlds; it was dismantled by U.S. officials when they learned of the meeting.)

The General did not intend to align himself with Russia or Cuba (he indeed assigned as the Spanish-speaking guide to the Soviet delegation a Hungarian who fought against the USSR during the 1956 uprising). Torrijos hoped instead to organize a broad international consensus against the United States. On March 21, thirteen of the Security

28. Stephen S. Rosenfeld, "The Panama Negotiations—a Close-Run Thing," *Foreign Affairs*, LIV (October 1975), 3–4; U.S. Congress, House, Subcommittee on Inter-American Affairs, Committee on Foreign Affairs, 93d Cong., 1st Sess., *United States Relations with Panama* (Washington, D.C., 1973), p. 15.

Council's fifteen members supported a moderately phrased resolution that accepted Panama's view of the Canal problem. The fourteenth member, Great Britain, abstained. The fifteenth, the United States, killed the resolution by casting only its third veto since 1945. U.S. Ambassador John Scali explained that while his government wanted to continue negotiations, it refused to be "subjected to this kind of outside pressure." The resolution, moreover, ignored Washington's "legitimate interests."[29]

Torrijos made his point. Latin American support was particularly strong. President Carlos Andres Perez, of oil-rich Venezuela, later exemplified that support by asking, "How can the United States, which is a leader of democracy in the world, take a colonial's stance" on the Canal issue? Unless it was settled rapidly, Perez added, "Very bad relations will develop between the two Americas, North and South." Venezuela's emergence as the champion of Panama's case was significant. The Caracas government hoped to combine its surplus oil revenues with Panama's extensive banking facilities to create a launching pad for multinational corporations, under Latin American control, that could be used in the North-South dialogue on behalf of the poorer nations.[30] Kissinger's fear of a potent anti-Yankee bloc in Latin America was not misplaced. Relationships were further soured by Washington's aid to the Chilean army when it overthrew President Salvador Allende in 1973, and the 1974 publication of Philip Agee's Inside the Company, which detailed covert Central Intelligence Agency activities throughout Latin America. Traditional friendships began to chill.

Kissinger's alternatives were few. Plans for a sea-level canal, for example, provided Lyndon Johnson with leverage against Panama in 1967, but by 1974 the $3 to $4 billion cost virtually killed the project. New digging on a third lock system in the Canal itself would be more feasible.

29. Richard P. Stebbins and Elaine P. Adam, eds., American Foreign Relations, 1973. A Documentary Record (New York, 1976), pp. 134–139.
30. Latin American Economic Report, May 27, 1977, p. 78.

The leverage thus passed to Panama. Torrijos talked threat-eningly about the consequences if agreement was not soon reached. If a mob marched on the Zone, he announced, two alternatives would be available, "to smash it or lead it, and I'm not going to smash it."[31]

By 1974 the necessary conditions for fresh negotia-tions were in place. Washington's need for economic coop-eration with Latin America, a growing anti-United States bloc among the southern nations, Torrijos's success in mo-bilizing world opinion, his desire (indeed his need), to co-operate with North American businessmen and bankers if the Canal question could be settled, the absence of the sea-level canal alternative—all of these developments finally resulted in an eight-point agreement between Kissinger and Panamanian Foreign Minister Juan Tack in February 1974. It marked a major step toward a final settlement.

The United States agreed to replace the 1903 treaty with a new agreement having a fixed termination date (in-stead of an "in perpetuity" clause). The Zone would disap-pear, and the area turned over to Panama in stages. The United States would retain specified rights in operating and defending the waterway during the life of the treaty, but Panama was to share in these functions and, at an un-defined date, assume full responsiblity for the Canal. In the interim, the Panamanians were promised a "just and equit-able" (that is, greater) share of the revenues. These princi-ples differed significantly from the Johnson demands of the mid-1960s. Washington retreated on nearly all the key points, starkly revealing the effects of the Third Cold War on United States foreign policy.

A United States negotiating team headed by Ells-worth Bunker began detailed discussions with the Pana-manians. Bunker was nearly eighty years old, but his long international career in the sugar refining business, an al-most equally long career as a top professional diplomat

31. *Latin American Report*, II (November 1973), 6; *Wall Street Journal*, Aug. 21, 1975, p. 1:1.

(who in his late 70s undertook the final negotiations with the North Vietnamese), and his fondness for Central American sun and risqué jokes made him a natural choice for the post.

. . . And the Frost of United States Politics: Snyder, Reagan, Ford

The Secretary of State soon found himself negotiating on two fronts. In March 1975 Bunker and the Panamanians deadlocked on three central issues: (1) The United States, under intense Pentagon pressure, demanded a 40- to 50-year lease, with possible renewal, for military bases to defend the Canal. Panama refused to allow any North American presence after 2003. (2) The two sides could not agree which, and how much, territory United States bases should occupy during the treaty's life. (3) No agreement could be reached on the specific duration of North American control over the Canal.

The first two items were most sticky. Through the summer of 1975 an intense struggle ensued between the State Department and the Pentagon over the 50-year demand. The military won, and when talks resumed in Panama, Bunker renewed the offer of a 50-year lease with option to renew.[32] The talks again deadlocked.

Stymied on one front, Kissinger simultaneously faced an uprising on Capitol Hill. Even pro-treaty Congressmen complained that the State Department made no effort to keep them informed. News of the talks usually came from Panamanian sources. Congressmen who ardently wished to preserve the 1903 principles launched a public attack on Kissinger's policy.

In the Senate, Strom Thurmond (Rep.-S.C.) finally rounded up 38 signatures for a resolution declaring the United States must retain "sovereign rights" and full con-

32. Thomas M. Franck and Edward Weisband, "Panama Paralysis," *Foreign Policy*, no. 21 (Winter 1975–1976), 175–176.

trol in the Zone. Only 34 votes were needed to defeat a treaty, and Thurmond's signatories included chairmen and, or the ranking Republican members of a dozen important committees. The State Department was stunned; it had estimated that no more than 20 Senators would oppose a new treaty. On the Senate floor, Thurmond justified his resolution by arguing that the United States had purchased all the Canal lands "in fee simple." He attached a list showing that Washington paid $163,718,571 "for the land, rights, and titles to the Canal Company and the Canal Zone." His cosponsor, John McClellan (Dem.-Ark.), took another tack, arguing that since Panama "has seen 59 Presidents or different governments in the past 70 years," it was doubtful the country possessed the stability to operate and defend the Canal. McClellan added that the United States bore the burden of defending the Western Hemisphere. "We cannot do that by surrendering the sovereignty and control of the Panama Canal."[33]

In June the House of Representatives directly threatened the negotiations. The body was highly sensitive to the talks, partly because it possessed constitutional responsibility for passing on the sale or transfer of U.S. property in the Zone, partly because it was a hotbed of anti-treaty sentiment. A leading opponent of any new pact was Representative Gene Snyder (Rep.-Ky.) who proclaimed that "our sovereignty over the Canal Zone is as legitimate as our owning New York City." He was convinced that Torrijos formed one arm of a giant pincers movement controlled by Castro and the Quebec Liberation Front in Canada which aimed to snatch back the Canal in the South and the St. Lawrence Seaway in the north.[34] Snyder amended a State Department appropriation bill so no funds could be used for "negotiating the surrender or relinquishment of any U.S. rights" in

33. James P. Lucier, "Another Vietnam?" National Review, Sept. 12, 1975, 989–990; Congressional Record, 93d Cong., 2nd Sess., March 29, 1974, pp. S4729-S4734.
34. Stanley Karnow, "The Politics of Bluster and Ballyhoo," Saturday Review, July 24, 1976, p. 13.

the Zone. Without committee hearings or significant debate, it passed 246–164 on June 26, 1975.

The vote was widely interpreted as an indication that
perhaps a majority of the House staunchly opposed significant concessions in a new treaty. A detailed analysis by
Professor Joel Silbey of this and seven other House votes
that followed made such an interpretation overly simplistic
and revealed significant sources of pro- and anti-treaty feeling. Silbey found that the vote was the high-water mark of
the anti-treaty contingent. Throughout the remainder of
1975 and into 1976, opponents of negotiations melted away
until on June 18, 1976, they could round up only 12 votes
to oppose a measure that took much of the sting out of the
Snyder amendment. That ballot was also misleading, but
Silbey could find only 121 Congressmen consistently supporting the extreme hard-line position on negotiations,
while a near majority 210 solidly and consistently voted in
a way that could be interpreted as favoring Kissinger's efforts. The hard core opposition came mainly from Republicans and some Democrats representing southern, midwes-
tern, and western districts. But the leadership, notably, was
found in the near-majority favoring negotiations. Those
most in favor of a new treaty were mainly Democrats and
tended to come from outside the South. Gene Snyder and
Daniel Flood received media attention because of their
frothy attacks on Kissinger's policy, but neither seemed
able to deliver significant numbers of votes from within
their regional delegations or, in the case of Flood, from his
own Pennsylvania group.

Silbey's analysis was preliminary and necessarily
based on only eight roll-call votes, but it demonstrated that
support for the Snyder-Flood position dwindled as Congressmen informed themselves on the issue (or, more
likely, after they first immunized themselves from conservative attacks at home by voting for the Snyder amendment). The fall-off in the "anti" group was especially notable since it occurred during 1976 when Ronald Reagan
used the Snyder-Flood approach to catapult himself into

contention for the Republican presidential nomination. The analysis did not show, of course, the possible vote on an actual treaty. "Antis" would certainly number more than 12 and perhaps more than 140, but if the 1975–76 votes were indicative, the House contained a strong, near-majority pro-treaty core that solidly rested in the Democratic Party and the leadership of both parties.[35]

Kissinger's problem was less in the House than in the Senate, where he needed help quickly. He found it in Senators Hubert Humphrey (Dem.-Minn.) and Gale McGee (Dem.-Wyo.). In July 1975 Senator Harry Byrd (Ind.-Va.) prepared to introduce the Snyder amendment in the Senate. The Pentagon quietly but effectively tried to support Byrd's efforts. Humphrey and McGee nevertheless rounded up enough opposition votes so that Byrd decided not to push his proposal to a test on the floor. The two Senators' most effective argument, however—that the Senate should not interfere in the Executive's right to conduct negotiations— was hardly a ringing endorsement of Kissinger's policy. In September the Senate finally rejected Snyder's amendment by voice vote, and in conference with the House agreed

35. Silbey's analysis was based on eight roll-call votes that were brought together in a Guttman scalogram, a statistical device that orders legislative responses to an issue on a continuum from one extreme of opinion (in this case absolute intransigence against canal negotiations), to the other, successively marking off the groups of congressmen that fall in the various positions between these extremes. It has the virtue of including all votes in determining a legislator's position on an issue, rather than relying only on intuitively selected, and possibly unrepresentative, "important" votes. The eight votes scaled here concerned the Snyder amendment to a State Department appropriations bill. The votes are listed in the Congressional Quarterly Almanac for 1975 and 1976 (1975: pp. 808–809, 82-H, 126-H, 136-H; 1976 edition: pp. 241–242, 88-H.) The use of the scalogram in legislative analysis is explained and employed in Joel H. Silbey, The Shrine of Party (Pittsburgh, 1967). It should be noted that the Snyder amendment reappeared and was again voted on in the House during early 1977. It lost to a more mildly-worded substitute. The lines of division marked in the 1975–1976 voting had not changed. See Congressional Quarterly Weekly Report, May 7, 1977, pp. 882, 884.

Unfortunately, Senate action on amendments comparable to Snyder's House amendments was by voice vote; individual responses could not be recorded and analyzed.

only to warn the Secretary of State to protect the nation's "vital interests" in the Canal, not prohibit the negotiations. It had been a dangerous and ominous debate.

With his finger to the political wind, presidential elections only fourteen months away, and under severe Pentagon pressure, Kissinger committed a tactical blunder. Responding to a question from Governor George Wallace of Alabama, the Secretary of State declared in early September 1975, "The United States must maintain the right, unilaterally, to defend the Panama Canal for an indefinite future." Until this point he liked to argue that unless a new treaty was quickly completed, mobs would endanger United States interests on the Isthmus. He now made himself a prophet. His use of "indefinite" created a furor in Panama. No doubt on Torrijos's orders, or at least with his permission, 600 students broke 85 windows in the U.S. Embassy and overturned cars parked around the building while the National Guard looked on. Without Kissinger's approval, Torrijos then released records of the three "conceptual accords" reached with Bunker. They showed that the United States had reneged on one of the eight Kissinger-Tack principles by insisting on indefinite control of the military bases.

At home and abroad the State Department's handling of the Canal issue was inept, indeed dangerously so. And unlike the late 1930s, when President Roosevelt intervened to support the State Department against the military, President Nixon's appointed successor, Gerald R. Ford (former Republican Minority leader in the House of Representatives), leaned toward the Pentagon view. While Ford wanted a treaty on the military's terms, Kissinger was willing to work for a more moderate agreement. The Secretary of State understood that military bases could not adequately protect the Canal against either sabotage or missiles. In the larger context he knew that settlement of the Panamanian question was a prerequisite to establishing the vitally needed economic partnership with Latin America.

As the 1976 presidential campaign progressed, negotiations continued in Panama, but on an inconsequential level. Torrijos realized that nothing could be accomplished for a year. Representative David Bowen (Rep.-Miss.) captured the feeling: "There is only one thing . . . that invariably makes [my constituents] cheer: 'I say that if we can keep the striped-pants boys out of it and leave the Canal to the Corps of Engineers, then things will work out fine.' "[36]

That insight was used by former California governor Ronald Reagan, who was fighting Ford for the Republican nomination. After setbacks in several primaries, Reagan listened to advisers who urged an uncompromising position on the Canal. He received a briefing on the issue from the exiled but ever-available Arnulfo Arias, who was searching for help in his campaign to bring down Torrijos. Calling Torrijos a "petty dictator," Reagan told enthusiastic Texas audiences that the Zone "is sovereign United States territory just the same as Alaska is and as the part of Texas that came out of the Gadsden Purchase and the states that were carved out of the Louisiana Purchase." The Zone "is ours and we intend to keep it."[37] Reagan suddenly began to win a string of primaries against an incumbent President. The Canal issue did not singlehandedly provide those successes (they occurred in states which were ideologically close to his domestic policies, and Ford's staff waged muddled, ineffective campaigns), but the waterway appeared to be an issue that catalyzed anti-Ford voters.

Reagan and his campaign staff indeed understood it was "a symbolic issue." "People sense in this issue some way, after Vietnam, and Watergate, and Angola, of reasserting the glory of the country," a top Reagan strategist believed. "People once more see a chance for Americans to stand up as Americans." The candidate himself thought the feelings aroused by Panama made "all the other issues possible."[38] It made little difference, as one high official of the Canal Zone privately remarked, that many North Americans

36. Rosenfeld. "Panama Negotiations," pp. 11–12.
37. Quoted in *Washington Post*, May 3, 1976, p. 11:3.
38. *Ibid..* May 9. 1976. p. A6:5.

were not sure of the Zone's location. Reagan appealed to the heart, not the head.

The challenger benefited politically, but his gains were limited, and the issue befogged, by Ford's tough position on the negotiations. The only difference between the two men seemed to be that Reagan wanted to keep the Canal without a new treaty and Ford planned to keep it through a new treaty. After Reagan won several primaries in April, Ford went so far as to repudiate publicly his own negotiator. Bunker had privately informed Congressmen that Ford, in writing, agreed to give up the Zone and the Canal after a long transition period. The President went on record "emphatically—that the United States will never [sic] give up its defense rights to the Panama Canal and will never give up its operational rights as far as Panama is concerned."[39] These words not only undercut key sections of the Kissinger-Tack principles, but reneged on the agreements already approved by Ford himself in the 1975 conceptual accords.

The President's image was further blurred to his political benefit when conservative Senator Barry Goldwater (Rep.-Ariz.) publicly agreed with Ford's approach and added, "I think Reagan would too if he knew more about it." The Senator thought the basic question was, "Are you willing to go to war over the Panama Canal?" When later asked how far he would actually go to retain the Canal, Reagan replied, "How far would we go to stop someone from taking the state of Alaska?"[40] The former California governor, however, faced problems if he hoped to undercut Barry Goldwater from the right.

The Carter (and Kissinger) Consensus

Ford maneuvered himself into an untenable position that was too uncompromising to win over Torrijos, but too

---

39. Captain Paul Ryan, USR (Ret.) "Canal Diplomacy and United States Interests," *U.S. Naval Institute Proceedings*, CIII (January 1977), 44, contains the Ford quotes.
40. *Washington Post*, May 3, 1976, p. 1:8.

moderate to silence Reagan. He felt compelled to search out a consensus on the issue for domestic rather than diplomatic reasons, and the search continued after he secured the Republican nomination. In seeking that consensus, however, Ford was several steps behind his Democratic opponent. Jimmy Carter of Georgia searched out consensus with the alacrity of a choir director.

In a June speech to the New York Foreign Policy Association, Carter effectively worked both sides of the street. North Americans do not recall, he began, that Theodore Roosevelt's treaty "spelled out that Panama should have sovereignty over the Panama Canal Zone; that we should have control as though we had sovereignty." Then he crossed the road: "I would never give up full [sic] control of the Panama Canal as long as it had any contribution to make to our own national security." He recrossed: "I believe the Panamanians will respond well to open and continual negotiations and the sharing of sovereignty and control, recognizing their rights in that respect. I would certainly look with favor on the possible reduction in the number of bases . . . possibly a reduction in the number of military forces we have there."[41]

In his second televised debate with Ford, Carter reduced his position to a single sentence: "I could never give up complete control or practical control of the Panama Canal Zone, but I would continue to negotiate with the Panamanians." That statement mirrored Ford's views, only Carter, unlike the President, did not bear the political embarrassment of having publicly moved toward Reagan's position while simultaneously agreeing with Panama to share control of the Canal.

Resembling the fate of most foreign policy issues in election campaigns since the mid-nineteenth century, the Canal question played no important part in determining Carter's victory. The President-elect, however, placed it near the top of his diplomatic priorities. His Secretary of

41. *New York Times*, June 24, 1976, p. 22.

State, New York lawyer Cyrus Vance, believed a treaty based on the Kissinger-Tack principles was necessary in 1977. Vance's stout belief was notable, for the 1974 principles directly contradicted candidate Carter's avowal of "never" surrendering "complete control or practical control of the Panama Canal Zone." No doubt Vance's concern was sharpened by memories of his involvement as the Secretary of War who flew to Panama to stop the 1964 bloodshed and had to be protected from mob violence. Carter appointed Ellsworth Bunker and Sol Linowitz, a Washington lawyer and former U.S. Ambassador to the OAS, to lead the negotiating team. Linowitz fully agreed with Vance that the issue was a "high priority, urgent matter with a dangerous potential."

Linowitz advocated both a new, equitable treaty and a Latin American policy that harked back to the Good Neighbor approach. In reality he differed little from the post-1973 Kissinger policy toward the Americas. In 1968 Linowitz defined the United States role in Latin America as preventing conditions "in which despotism of the right can provide the foundation and impetus for a dictatorship of the left."[42] The ideal was apparently regimes which maintained order and whose center of political gravity was somewhere in the middle of the Latin American political spectrum. Torrijos was more complicated than that; his rule was not easily categorized along the "right-left" spectrum used by North American political analysts. But the General did meet Linowitz's general criteria, for despite the Panamanian's censorship, exiling or jailing of political opponents, and refusal to hold general elections, he maintained order and cooperated with the United States, even during such trying times as the 1976 campaign.

To Linowitz and Vance, as to Kissinger, Panama presented a small, if formidable, obstacle to be cleared on the way to the ultimate goal of developing a workable economic relationship with Latin America. President-elect Carter

42. Quoted in *Current History*, LVI (January 1969), p. 6.

sounded the broad theme in an historic public hearing before
the Senate Foreign Relations Committee when he announced,
"The future, I think, of foreign policy might be changing,"
for there is a new "emphasis on economic matters."[43]

A month later a report appeared from the privately
funded Commission on U.S.-Latin American Relations.
Commission members included Linowitz as chairman, W.
Michael Blumenthal, Carter's new Secretary of Treasury,
and Richard N. Gardner, ambassador-designate to Italy. The
report repeated earlier Commission warnings that a fresh
Latin American policy must "above all . . . be set in a consistent pattern of global economic policies" that would "make
more stable and equitable the terms of exchange between the
most industrialized" nations and those, "many of them in
Latin America—which are rapidly expanding their participation in the world economy." The Commission saw clear
sailing to realize "latent opportunities" in the Hemisphere,
"except possibly in Panama." Otherwise, "no imminent
threats to U.S. 'national security,' military or economic, are
likely to be posed or perceived in the Americas."

Panama presented "the most urgent issue . . . in the
Western Hemisphere." A failure at the Isthmus and the
United States would indeed lose a prerequisite for meeting
the complex challenges of the Third Cold War, for Latin
America gave Washington "a good chance to fashion a co-
herent and constructive approach to the fundamental issues
of North-South relations generally." If the Canal problem
was solved, Latin America could again act as the laboratory
for United States policies in the developing nations.

As for the Canal specifically, it was "useful," but no
longer "vital" to North Americans. The Commission further
believed the United States did not need "perpetual control
of the Canal nor exclusive jurisdiction" to protect non-discriminatory access to the waterway: "The best protection of
our interests in Panama is not outmoded [1903] Treaty lan-

43. U.S. Congress, Senate, Committee on Foreign Relations, 94th Cong.,
President-Elect Jimmy Carter's Views Concerning Foreign Policy, Nov. 23,
1976 (Washington, D.C., 1976), p. 8.

guage but rather Panama's own vital interest in preserving
its greatest natural resource."[44]

Top Carter administration officials therefore viewed
the Panama crisis as a key to their entire foreign policy.
With a new treaty they could work out a *rapprochement*, at
least on the economic level, with Latin America. That new
relationship might serve as a doorbell to the remainder of
the developing nations. And with those doors open, the
North Americans would be better able to resolve the problems of the Third Cold War. The chances seemed bright,
not least because of Torrijos's calculated policy shift in
1975–77.

Farewell to Reform

Like a reflex action, Panamanian governments traditionally pushed for a new treaty when their domestic economic programs hit dead ends. The Canal then appeared
less as a waterway than a life raft. Torrijos's regime was
no exception. The General stepped up pressure on the Canal in 1972–73 when the government's resources and the
country's economy went into a parallel slide. The 8 percent annual growth rates of the 1960s declined to less than
2 percent in 1975. World inflation was to blame, but so
were several home-grown problems. Heavy real estate
speculation collapsed, leaving Panama City pockmarked
with unfinished high-rise apartment and office buildings.
Burdened with the highest external debt per capita of any
Latin American government, Panama faced deep financial
retrenchment after overspending during the pre-1972
boom. Rural areas suffered severely as world sugar prices
plummeted.

Government corruption reappeared. During the early
1970s the Guard had cracked down on graft. By 1975 Guard
officers themselves were accused of handling stolen goods

44. Commission on United States-Latin American Relations, *The United
States and Latin America: Next Steps* (No publisher, 1976), pp. 1–6.

in illegally established trading companies. Some officers apparently facilitated the stealing, especially from importers. Accusations of nepotism reached Torrijos himself: his brother became Ambassador to Spain where he allegedly invested the General's money in real estate, including a castle once owned by Cuban dictator Fulgencio Batista; more than 30 members of Torrijos's family prospered in high governmental positions, including such delectable posts as head of the national lottery and director of the government's casinos.[45] The regime's early idealism was apparently no match for the more hallowed aspects of traditional Panamanian politics.

The number of stories about corruption increased with the unemployment rate and prices of milk and bread. During the summer of 1976 the broadly painted slogans on walls in the National University area of Panama City infrequently demanded "Yankee Go Home," and instead roundly condemned the government for high prices and anti-student activities. The composition of the country's population compounded the economic downturn. Its 3.3 percent annual growth rated as one of the world's highest. Forty-four percent of the population was under age 15, and when that group began to bear children "the situation," one economist believed, would "become insupportable."[46]

Teenagers already threatened to flood a labor market in which one-quarter of the urban workers were unemployed. Despite the agricultural reforms, Panama City attracted rural laborers until its population spiraled from 200,000 to 500,000 in 15 years; most of the new arrivals piled up in the already horrendous slums. In 1976 per capita income of $800 ranked as the highest in Central America, but wealth was as maldistributed as during the pre-Torrijos years. Nor had the Maximum Chief solved the chronic un-

45. New York Times, Feb. 17, 1977, p. 2:3–4; Alan Riding, "Is America Giving Away the Panama Canal?" Saturday Review, July 24, 1976, p. 64; Martin C. Needler, "Omar Torrijos, the Panamanian Enigma," Intellect, CV (February 1977), 243.
46. Looney, Economic Development of Panama, p. 37.

favorable balance of trade. The balance even worsened. Panamanians developed expensive tastes for North American products. (On the street a visitor quickly notes these tastes even as he avoids the onrush of old, U.S.-manufactured cars. "Pana-Macs" are dispensed in large numbers beneath Golden Arches, and a bright sign in downtown Panama City proclaims, in Spanish, that the Colonel's chicken is so good "You'll Want To Lick Your Fingers.")

The intractable problems of the 1960s remained. Buffeted by the unfavorable economic winds, and with his reform program exhausted, Torrijos returned to the bankers for help. Citicorp (First National City Bank of New York) again formed a syndicate that gave a five-year, $45 million loan to bolster the governmental treasury. Continental Bank of Chicago led three banks in extending $17.5 million for sugar production.[47]

In 1975 Torrijos invited multinational corporations to bid for rights to develop the Cerro Colorado, possibly the richest undeveloped copper deposit in the world. Texasgulf won, gaining 20 percent equity interest. Panama retained the remainder. With no experience in large-scale mining, the Panamanians held the power to make policy decisions but gave Texasgulf authority to operate the mine during the five-year construction period and the first fifteen years of production. The pay-off promised to be worth the effort for Texasgulf. With at least one billion tons of copper ore in the mine, the multinational hoped to produce 180,000 tons annually by 1982, a year when analysts believed copper could be close to $1 per pound on the world market. Panama's interest in the mine was watched over by Rodrigo (Rory) Gonzalez, president of the State Mining Corporation and an operator of rare talents. His source of power was compelling: frequently living in Gonzalez's house, Torrijos entrusted his private financial affairs to his host. Gonzalez's impressive clout was not often employed for reform pro-

47. Wall Street Journal, Sept. 9, 1975, p. 37:3; Latin America March 28, 1975, pp. 101–102.

grams. One close associate became Ambassador to Washington, and two nephews moved into the government as Foreign Minister and Finance Minister.[48]

Officials associated with left-wing politics lost their jobs. The new colonel in charge of land reform placed less emphasis on redistribution and more on discouraging political activities on the collectives. Labor, that other beneficiary of the early Torrijos programs, received similar treatment. The wide-ranging 1972 labor code was ignored as the government allowed the weakening of seniority rights, the dismissal of workers according to company determination, the two-year freezing of labor contracts, and severe limitations on the right to strike. With little industry, no natural base existed for a strong labor movement. The Panamanian middle class feared the 1972 code would allow lower classes to threaten its privileges. Torrijos's alliance with labor was over, at least for a while.

Businessmen expressed delight with the General's policies, although some continued to protest against the regime's political repression. The National Council of Private Enterprise (CONEP) demanded more rights, especially freedom of the press. Torrijos immediately condemned such demands as "anti-Panamanian" since they could lead to what he called, in an interesting Orwellian phrase, "semi-information" that could "provoke social tempests."[49] The populist side of the new *caudillismo* required the media to remain in the Maximum Chief's hands.

Torrijos decided to quiet rising left-wing protest with a highly publicized junket to Cuba in early 1976. But his heart did not seem to be in it. Just several months before, he felt compelled to tell the Cuban Embassy staff in Panama (the second largest in the capital after the U.S. Embassy staff) to stop propagandizing governmental ministries and inciting Panamanian students. In Havana, Torrijos received what he wanted—a public endorsement of his cautious, pa-

48. *New York Times*, June 15, 1976, p. 51; *Latin America*, May 27, 1977, p. 155.
49. *Latin American Report*, III (January 1975), 6.

tient Canal policy from Castro—then held his own press conference and left the country before he was supposed to join the Cuban leader in a public denunciation of United States foreign policy. When Cuban photographers maneuvered him into a picture whose background was a red sickle, Torrijos demanded that the film be destroyed.

Returning to Panama City, the General continued his balancing act by deporting ten businessmen who, the official explanation alleged, "received support from a U.S. presidential candidate" (obviously Ronald Reagan), in return for "anti-patriotic" statements on the Canal treaty. Torrijos took advantage of this opportunity to deport three outspoken Marxists along with the businessmen.

United States officials were visibly pleased. Torrijos, one State Department expert observed, was hardly "scullian," but he nevertheless got along beautifully with peasants and other rural Panamanians. The General was also trusted by the U.S. military and foreign bankers. The National Guard was disciplined and dependent on the United States for supplies. Its troops were not, in the words of one North American official, "the fat kind who beat up crowds." Like their Maximum Chief, they were "lean and mean." Best of all, in this official's view, members of the old, aristocratic oligarchy were making their peace with Torrijos—or he with them. The oligarchs still controlled important parts of the economy. "This is not an economic revolution, not a 1789 or 1917," he remarked with understatement.

A non-governmental expert on Panama, Professor Martin Needler, saw the same developments from a different perspective. He used the now familiar approach of comparing Panamanian and Cuban history. "It may not be far-fetched," Needler wrote in early 1977, "to compare Torrijos with [Cuban dictator Fulgencio] Batista of the 1930s." Batista was also the "architect of a New Deal program partly out of populist sympathies, but mostly because it gave him a strong political base." The Cuban "ended up on the right wing as greed became his dominant motivation." Castro ultimately overthrew Batista. Needler saw in Torrijos's post-1968 political journey "the lineaments of a classic personalistic Latin American dictatorship not interfering with the social and economic status quo."[50]

Certainly Torrijos responded in the classic manner during September 1976 when he confronted the most serious crisis of his years in power. A severe drought and world-wide inflation forced the government to decree higher prices for milk and rice. Repeating a tactic used by anti-Allende forces in Chile, protesting secondary school students and women banging empty pans swarmed into the street, symbolically on September 11, the third anniversary of Allende's overthrow and assassination. Riots broke out, looting began, and a new Trotskyist student organization moved to take control of the protests. National Guard troops, apparently alerted by CIA agents who infiltrated the student groups, attacked the protesters. Only after intermittent conflict that lasted ten days and resulted in the arrests of over 200 students was order restored.

The September riots opened a critical new chapter of the Torrijos era. Unlike every major outbreak since 1947, they were neither anti-Yankee nor directed against the Zone. One diplomat marveled, "In almost one week of riots here, there wasn't even a mention of 'Yankee go home.'" He believed the economic situation to be so serious that the students considered it more important than the Zone issue.

The role of the students was crucial. As we have seen, the Guard and students have been natural enemies since the mid-1930s, but Torrijos tried to win over the schools in order to focus their ardent nationalism against the United States. The Federation of Panamanian Students faithfully followed the Maximum Chief, but by 1976 the Federation lost ground to the Trotskyist and other left-wing groups. The traditional Guard-student hatreds resurfaced. Watching the police manhandle the students, one old man

50. Needler, "Omar Torrijos," p. 243.

said, "They only want food for their families. I can't understand why the general is responding like this."[51]

The protesters discovered odd political bedfellows, for they were joined by North Americans from the Zone who, for their own reasons, wanted Torrijos to fall. The Guard arrested two civilian employees from the Zone, one U.S. Army private, and a Costa Rican worker from a U.S. military base, all of whom the Panamanians accused of leading looters or haranguing crowds. The government initially accused North Americans of fomenting the riots, but the U.S. Embassy protested the charges, and Torrijos dropped the accusation.

The General's problems were closer to home, and moving closer all the time. The National Guard was described by diplomats as "restive," with younger officers jealous of Torrijos; others complained of lags in promotions and benefits.[52] The chief danger threatened to come from Colonel Manuel Antonio Noriega, a tough, enigmatic figure who from a well-hidden bunker directed the Guard's intelligence and anti-insurgency operations. The State Department publicly discounted such threats. Officials noted that Noriega had long been staunchly pro-Torrijos, that the Maximum Chief enjoyed the personal loyalty of his other top officers, and that he had carefully built a command structure in which they reported directly to him, not to any intermediary. Only Torrijos was in a position to know all critical information. "He is numero uno," one Washington official said in early 1977, "and has it set up to remain that way."

But command structures, no matter how well conceived, have collapsed under pressure. As Guard discontent grew, civilian terrorist cells were discovered just before they set explosives in Panama City neighborhoods. The government linked the cells to right-wing Miami groups. Meanwhile the radical student organizations and anxious labor unions prepared for another confrontation with Torrijos.

51. *Latin America,* Sept. 24. 1976. p. 290; *Washington Post,* Sept. 21, 1976, p. A16:4; the diplomat quoted in *New York Times,* Sept. 18, 1976, p. 26:2.
52. *Christian Science Monitor,* Sept. 22. 1976. p. 3:4.

But the fundamental danger to Torrijos, and indeed all Panamanians, was an economy that produced a zero growth rate in 1976. Exports slumped and the construction industry continued to stagnate. The home market was too small, the inflation rate too high, to attract needed investment. Half the total investment in 1976 was from public sources, financed primarily through foreign loans. As the debt grew, so did Torrijos's dependence on the banks. That dependence could only become greater if the government planned any kind of extensive development program. "The control factor is in the hands of the banks, not the Panamanian government," one expert wrote. Torrijos responded by emphasizing the non-governmental sectors. "This is the hour of private enterprise," his Labor and Social Welfare Minister announced in January 1977. The regime issued laws which encouraged larger personal investment and further shifted tax burdens to the lower classes. An economist once observed that the Panamanian economy of the 1960s "reminds one of a ballgame in which only the stars are allowed to play. One cannot help but wonder how long the other contestants will be content to sit on the bench." That evaluation remained true in the mid-1970s. Only large Canal revenues could rescue the governmental debt and allow other contestants to play the game, and even those revenues could be insufficient.[53]

The Gringo Victory: The Treaty of 1977

The rapidly deteriorating Panamanian economy and Torrijos's increasing dependence on outside private investors set the stage for the climactic negotiations of a new treaty during the summer of 1977. Leverage slowly but perceptibly moved into United States hands. The hesitant, interim government of Gerald Ford was replaced by a Carter

---

53. *Latin American Economic Report*, April 22, 1977, p. 9; *ibid.*, Jan. 14, 1977, p. 5; Pringle, "Panama," pp. 1207–1210; Looney, *Economic Development of Panama*, p. 5.

administration determined to obtain a treaty—a treaty, more-over, that could be sold politically to the United States Senate.

President Carter spelled out his policy in his highly publicized telephone call-in of March 1977. He first per-sonally interpreted the 1903 treaty, then indicated how closely the United States and Panama could cooperate in the future:

> As you may or may not know [the President informed a caller] the treaty signed when President Roosevelt was President gave Panama sovereignty over the Panama Canal itself. It gave us control over the Panama Canal Zone, as though we had sovereignty. So we've always had a legal sharing of responsibility over the Panama Canal Zone. As far as sovereignty is concerned, I don't have any hangup about that.
>
> I would hope that after and expect that after the year 2000 that we would have an assured capacity or capability of our country with Panama guaranteeing that the Panama Canal would be open and of use to our own nation and to other countries.[54]

Carter had moved a considerable distance since the 1976 campaign when he pledged never to surrender "full con-trol" of the Canal "as long as it had any contribution to make to our own national security." On the other hand, his determination to possess the "capacity or capability" of guaranteeing access to the Canal after 2000 revealed the fundamental, and tough, United States position—the same position that, when Kissinger revealed it in 1975, led to anti-Yankee riots in Panama.

Carter was determined to maintain that position, but Washington officials appreciated the need not to push Tor-rijos too far, at least in public. The General, after all, had displayed patience and understanding during the 1976 presidential campaign in the United States. He insisted that North American troops must evacuate the Zone by New

54. *New York Times*, March 6, 1977, p. 33:5.

Year's Day 2000, yet he handled the negotiations carefully so neither side lost hope. Above all, he kept a tight rein on anti-Yankee groups throughout 1976 and—most notably in the September riots—did not hesitate to use force in restoring order. As the North Americans prepared to resume discussions in early 1977, the General dismissed Foreign Minister Aquilino Boyd, famous for an ambitious anti-Yankeeism that included marches into the Canal Zone, and replaced him with 31-year-old Nicolás Gonzalez, Ambassador to Washington, North American educated, and a former employee of First National City Bank and United Brands. The State Department was understandably encouraged.

On August 11, 1977, thirteen years of intermittent crisis and intense negotiations were consummated with a new pact. Reporters were summoned to Panama City's luxurious Holiday Inn to hear the provisions of the two treaties. Four sections were most important.

First, when—or if—the pacts become law (that is, after U.S. Senate ratification and approval by a general Panamanian plebescite), Panama will immediately assume territorial jurisdiction over the Canal and receive part of the Zone's land. Panamanian legal jurisdiction will slowly replace the North American authority over a three-year period. At the end of three years, the Zone will be integrated into Panama. In reality, however, Washington will continue to operate and defend the Canal until midnight, December 31, 1999, for the United States will retain all lands and waters necessary for the passageway's operations and defense, and will have the "primary" responsibility for defending it. During those decades a new nine-member United States governmental agency will operate the Canal. The North Americans will not only have a majority of five in the agency, but possess the power to appoint the four Panamanians from a list submitted by the Panama government. (Torrijos bitterly fought that appointment procedure before acquiescing to Washington's demand.) Throughout the 1980s and 1990s, Panamanian administrators and workers will slowly be phased in to assume present North American responsibilities along the Canal, but until New Year's Day 2000, the United States will operate and defend the waterway as surely as it did before 1977.

Second, the United States citizens in the Zone who work for the North American government and the new agency will retain many of the legal and procedural rights they would enjoy in the United States. Their jobs will have to relate directly to Canal operations, not to the commissaries, bowling alleys, and stores, which Panamanians will take over. The Zonians can remain in the governmental positions as long as they wish, and will be replaced by Panamanians only when they quit or retire.

Third, in a key part of the second treaty, which will govern the Canal after 2000, U.S. forces have the permanent right to defend the Canal's neutrality (and until 2000 have the primary defense responsibilities). These provisions mean that the troops can be used to enforce Panama's guarantee that the United States will have—forever—non-discriminatory access to the Canal for its merchant vessels and warships. This key provision marked Torrijos's major concession in the negotiations and fulfilled Carter's promise made during the March telephone call-in. Although Panamanian forces will assume primary responsibility for defending the waterway after 2000, United States forces can protect North American interests against either an outside or a Panamanian threat. This point was so sensitive that it was written into a second and separate treaty.

Fourth, the United States obtained these sweeping concessions from Torrijos by paying for them—handsomely. Retreating from an earlier position, Washington officials will allow Panama to receive 30¢ per Panama Canal ton on ships and cargo. In addition, the Panamanians will receive at least another $10 million from toll revenue. They will receive an additional $10 million from the revenue if it is available. In all, Panama will receive, instead of the present $2.3 million annuity, $40 to $50 million each year until 2000 when it will control all revenues. In addition, the Carter administration promised to put together a separate package that will give Torrijos (or his successors) $295 million of economic loans and guarantees (not outright grants) over five years, and $50 million in military assistance during a ten-year period. Of course this package will tighten relations between the two countries, especially between the Pentagon and the National Guard.

Given previous Panamanian demands, the exposed North American position in the Zone, and limitations imposed on Washington's power by the Third Cold War, the treaty drafts represented a United States diplomatic triumph. Most important, the United States retained the right to intervene militarily to guarantee access to, and the neutrality of, the Canal. Since no time limits restricted the privilege, left-wing Panamanians condemned Torrijos for accepting another "perpetuity" clause that resembled the hated 1903 treaty provision. Even the fourth category, the economic settlement, gave Washington a kind of victory, for until the last days of negotiations Torrijos demanded that the United States commit itself to pay as much as $1 billion in developmental monies. When the State Department refused to consider such a figure, the General reduced it to $650 million. The North Americans also rejected that out-of-hand. Panama's desperate need for developmental monies could not be doubted. That it could use $1 billion, however (and that all of the funds would go into developmental projects and not into other, more mundane needs of a new *caudillo*), remained questionable. In the end a compromise was worked out, but mostly on Washington's terms. No wonder that United States officials, even in the Pentagon, seemed pleased.

By New Year's Day 2000, Panama will finally make the Canal its own, be free of North American military bases on the Isthmus over which it has no control, and receive a monetary infusion for its anemic economy. Despite these fundamental changes, the treaty provisions incited left-wing groups (especially the Trotskyist students), and right-of-center business organizations to attack the agreements. The critics zeroed in on the long, two-decade transition period in which North American domination will continue, the presence of United States military bases along the Canal until 2000, and—above all—Washington's right to use force after 2000. Panama's chief negotiator admitted the pacts were not all his government had hoped. It is "good for us in some basic aspects, bad in others, and," Romulo Escobar Bethancourt added candidly, "ugly in others." The only alternative, he stressed, was violent confrontation in which "the massacre of the best of our youth would bring more setbacks in the development of our country."[55] Translated, this meant that Torrijos placed top priority on ultimate control of the Canal and immediate access to United States funds.

Constitutionally, the General was in some danger, for he was legally bound to submit the treaties to a national referendum. With criticism growing, Torrijos counterattacked. He quickly moved to consolidate ties with the moderate Panamanian Student Federation so the Trotskyist groups were isolated and vulnerable. Right-wing business criticism was dismissed as emanating from people sitting in comfortable "refrigerated offices" who wanted to send others into a bloody conflict with U.S. troops. Many opponents were not even heard from; they lived in exile in Miami or Latin American cities. The extent of the General's political concerns was perhaps best revealed a week before the new treaties were unveiled, when he quietly asked the leaders of five Latin American nations—including the highly respected nationalist regimes in Mexico and Venezuela—to help him sell the pacts to the Panamanian people. To ensure the success of the sales talk, the General maintained rigid censorship within Panama. Only pro-treaty arguments could be heard on radio and television or read in the newspapers. Torrijos believed he had no choice. If he allowed open debate, critics would launch all-out assaults on both the agreements and his regime. The voters will undoubt-

55. *Ibid.*, August 13, 1977, p. 4:3.

edly strongly endorse the treaties. The methods employed to gather the votes, however, will not be those which North Americans associate with New England town meetings.

Nor will the political pressure on Torrijos abate after the referendum. His personal power could indeed be in greater danger, for he will not have the Zone as a scapegoat to blame for the nation's intractable problems. "It will not be easy once the treaty is signed," he admitted in early 1977. "There will be a vast political vacuum we will have to fill. I am thinking a lot about that. We will no longer have the Gringos to blame then."

The Panamanians had finally received their long-sought authority over the Canal Zone, but under conditions which starkly revealed the extent of their continued dependence on North American power. For both political reasons (that is, to appease nationalist groups with which the National Guard has alternately sympathized and fought in the streets) and economic needs which are limitless, Torrijos had demanded much—and accepted much less. The 75-year treaty arrangements were ending, but the General and his fellow Panamanians were learning the difficulty of snapping 75 years of colonial ties.

Choosing Sides for the Great Debate

The Carter administration also braced for a fight. Polls in mid-August 1977 showed that 78 percent of the North Americans interviewed did not want to give up the Canal. As he happily announced progress in the negotiations, Secretary of State Vance admitted that if the Senate acted immediately on the treaty drafts, "I'm not sure that we'd have the votes."[56]

Opposition was widespread. The Pentagon officially endorsed the pacts, but privately many officers were angry. Those associated with the School of the Americas, for

56. *Ibid.*, June 17, 1977, p. A6:1.

example, had been fighting rearguard actions for years, particularly after some of the School's Latin American graduates returned home to jail and torture political opposition. Led by Michael Harrington (Dem.-Mass.), the House of Representatives outlawed urban counterinsurgency courses at the School. Staging a tactical retreat, the School abolished the courses and continued teaching the same subjects under new names, a substitution made easier since the School lies deep in the Zone and far from Capitol Hill. The location thus had its attractive side, and so did the relatively cheap $5 million annual cost required to operate the School. The treaties allowed it to remain at least five years. It might then move to Florida, whose swamps were admirable for counterinsurgency maneuvers, but whose costs were much higher and the location uncomfortably close to people such as Harrington. A move promised no end of frustrations. As one spokesman for the School complained, most North Americans do not understand people like Harrington; they do know, however, that the politicians, not the military, lost Vietnam.[57]

Other officers, or their spokesmen in Congress, disliked the treaties because they could remove the U.S. Southern Command from the Canal Zone. It too could be relocated elsewhere, but a delightful lifestyle could be cramped. The title was imposing, but as the *Wall Street Journal* reported January 10, 1974, the Southern Command was "the smallest and most rank-heavy of the Defense Department's seven commands that comprise more than one service. Though it numbers only 10,500 military people and can muster little firepower, the command has no fewer than 10 generals . . . plus two admirals and four separate headquarters." The naval unit, "to its embarrassment, doesn't have a single warship here. Its 'fleet' consists of two 45-foot fishing boats used by the brass." The Command served apparently as a rehabilitation center for some officers. A special Defense Department panel in 1970 recommended that it be

57. *Washington Post*, April 16, 1977, p. A10:5–6.

abolished, but President Nixon sided with the Joint Chiefs and the post survived. The Command sometimes performed such tasks as airlifting supplies to earthquake-stricken Nicaragua, but mostly, as one senior officer admitted, "That headquarters is the sleepiest place I've ever seen."

Retired military strategists entered the debate to offer more substantial reasons for retaining the Canal. They argued that if control was surrendered, taxpayers would have to spend massively for a larger two-ocean navy—a navy not presently necessary because the Canal allows rapid passage between oceans. These anti-treaty voices admitted the fleet's thirteen aircraft carriers were too large to use the waterway, but in the words of Admiral David L. McDonald, former Chief of Naval Operations during the Vietnam War, "The fact that carriers cannot transit the Canal is a typical know-nothing State Department view," for the Canal could be used by the other 460 naval vessels, "including the very vital logistic support forces." Hanson Baldwin, former military correspondent for the *New York Times,* resurrected the domino theory: abandoning the Canal would be "renewed evidence that the United Staes is a paper tiger," and would "encourge penny-dictators and minor aggressions everywhere."

One representative article bravely took this argument to its logical conclusion: the United States could justifiably act like the Soviets toward small nations, and Panama would have to submit:

> Panama's lot can be roughly equated with that of Finland, Sweden, Vietnam [sic], Cambodia, and other small nations. It is linked inexorably to that of a major nation, and whether that major nation is a "good" democracy or a "bad" totalitarian state is beside the point. . . . Finlanders, for example, have accepted the truth of impaired sovereignty with resignation, while Panamanians probably do not recognize the sense in which their situation can be compared with Finland's.[58]

58. Ryan, "Canal Diplomacy," p. 52; this essay also contains the McDonald and Baldwin quotations.

Many military privately opposed the treaties. They preferred lobbying quietly within such friendly organizations as the American Legion or by talking with Congressmen. The Army Corps of Engineers could be especially effective. It operated the Canal Zone, and because the Engineers also built politically popular public works in the United States, they enjoyed many close friendships in Congress.

The 10,000 United States civilians in the Zone were less restrained. About 4000 worked in the Zone (the remainder were dependents), but Senator Alan Cranston (Dem.-Calif.) claimed that only 1300 actually operated the Canal; the other 2700 worked in schools, bowling alleys, golf courses, and commissaries, work that Panamanians could perform as well. The elite 1300 employees were vital, particularly the 200 pilots whose incomparable skills were not immediately replaceable. They had seen to that, for despite promises made since the 1950s, in 1976 only two Panamanians belonged to the select group. The 1977 treaty protected the 1300 Canal operators, but not the other 2700 positions, which would now be open to Panamanians. The Panamanians already accounted for 73 percent of the Canal Company's total work force. However, they occupied only 10 percent of the jobs in the eight highest-paying levels.[59]

The Zonians and their unions had protected themselves well, but they could not fend off the new treaties. In 1976 some 290, or twice as many Zonians as in 1975, quit the Canal to look for jobs on the mainland. The number included 14 pilots. They felt defenseless. Some who had committed youthful indiscretions vividly remembered nights in Panamanian jails, and all knew the history of Zone-Panama relationships. As one North American remarked, "If there is a change in the canal, and I have to work for a Panamanian, I don't want to bear the burden of what Joe Redneck did to his dad sometime long ago."[60]

In March 1976 the pilots and 500 other elite person-

59. Cox, "Choices," in Silvert, ed., America in Changing World, p. 146; Riding, "Is America Giving Away the Canal?" p. 9.
60. New York Times, May 8, 1976. p. 6:4.

nel protested by walking off the job. Canal traffic halted, 170 ships tying up at anchor until military personnel moved to reopen the Canal. Under intense pressure, the pilots returned to work. The protest was understandable, but it did not turn out as planned. On Torrijos's orders, Panamanian workers remained on the job, thereby demonstrating—contrary to Zonian mythology—that they could be more committed to the Canal than the North Americans. One influential newspaper roundly condemned the strikes for apparently violating United States law and needlessly tying up international trade.[61]

In April 1977 the Zonians mounted a massive lobbying effort in Congress, presenting an eloquent petition against the pacts to the sympathetic House Subcommittee on the Panama Canal.[62] But the negotiations nevertheless continued. Perhaps their frustration was best demonstrated by the Zonian who took paintbrush in hand, and on a Panama City wall that publicized such student slogans as YANKEE GO HOME, wrote in bold strokes, KISS MY AMERICAN ASS.

Frustration grew even as other groups joined the Zonians. Most vocal were right-wing organizations: the Committee on Latin American Policy (part of the John Birch Society), the Liberty Lobby, the National States Rights Party, the American Legion, and the Veterans of Foreign Wars. The Task Force on the Panama Canal sounded innocuous until it was linked to the American Council for World Freedom, a Washington-based conservative group whose president, Fred Schlafly, said it would spend $100,000 "to stop the surrender of the Panama Canal."[63] Other right-wing groups organized letter-writing campaigns to local newspapers (letters notable for their often accurate if highly selective knowledge about the Canal's

61. *Washington Post*, March 25, 1976, p. A18:1–2.
62. Manuscript copy of "A Position Paper, Presented by the U.S. Civic Councils to the House Subcommittee on the Panamanian Canal, April 12, 1977," in author's possession.
63. Don Oberderfer in *Washington Post*, March 24, 1977, p. A12:3–5.

history) and set up downtown booths to dispense pamphlets about the "sell-out."

Perhaps the most active lobbyist was Phillip Harman, a 55-year-old southern Californian whose Canal Zone Non-Profit Public Information Corporation sent out reams of anti-treaty literature. Harman spent thousands of dollars from his personal fortune. He described himself as not only a "fanatic on anti-communism," but the descendant of a Panamanian Founding Father, José Arango. It was Harman who apparently interested Ronald Reagan in the Canal issue and arranged the original meeting between the candidate and Arias in late 1975.[64]

Debate over the pacts tended to divide the nation along right-left, conservative-liberal lines. Pragmatic politics gave way to ideological rigidities. In the face of Panamanian demands and the constraints of the Third Cold War, a compromise acceptable to the broad spectrum of North Americans seemed impossible. When this rigidity mixed with the post-Watergate congressional skepticism of executive handiwork, the politics of the treaties became highly combustible, particularly since the views of most North Americans were shaped not by historical knowledge of Panama, but by textbooks which often left the impression that if the waterway was miraculous, it must also be North American—forever. Many people, Senator Gale McGee believed, were "still riding up the hill with Teddy Roosevelt."

Pro-treaty forces placed great hope in the few but significant exceptions to the right-left split. Joel Silbey's analysis of congressional voting discovered Congressmen, usually associated with the moderate-to-conservative wing of North American politics, refusing to vote with those who most vigorously opposed the treaty negotiations. William Buckley, a well-known conservative spokesman in his syndicated columns and television programs, returned from a visit to Panama and supported the new agreements. After

64. Richard Hudson, "Storm Over the Canal," New York Times Magazine, May 16, 1976, p. 22.

working out defense procedures, security for the Zonians, and fair tolls, he declared, the United States should "get out—while the initiative is still clearly our own. That is the way great nations should act." As for the arch-enemy of the Zonians, "I give it as my own opinion," Buckley wrote, "that I believe [Torrijos]. In my judgment he is not merely trying to ambush American good nature."[65]

The State Department also warmly welcomed support from influential business groups. Some, especially smaller businesses, contributed to anti-treaty lobbyists, but the U.S. Chamber of Commerce and large multinationals, especially those with much to lose in South America, prepared to fight for the pacts. Direct United States investment in Panama approached $1.8 billion, the fourth largest amount in Latin America and larger than North American investment in such nations as Peru, Argentina, or Colombia. (The Panamanian gross national product only reached approximately $3 billion in 1976.) Banking resources, the hundreds of North American-owned merchant ships registered for reasons of cost under the Panamanian flag, and the multinationals' use of Panama for trade and tax purposes multiplied the country's economic importance. Resembling Buckley, businessmen harbored doubts, but on the whole they found Torrijos cooperative and trustworthy. One executive remarked that if, as the General planned, "You're building an international banking and tourist center, you don't want your downtown burning up."[66]

After the Senate fight over the Snyder-Byrd amendment in late 1975, Senator McGee, with the State Department's full support, asked representatives of more than two dozen multinational corporations to work for the new Canal pacts. They formed the Business and Professional Committee for a New Panama Canal Treaty, complete with a half-

65. William Buckley, "On the Right," *National Review*, Nov. 12 and 26, 1976, pp. 1253, 1306.
66. *Wall Street Journal*, Aug. 21, 1975, p. 19:3; *U.S. News and World Report*, May 24, 1976, p. 29; Penny Lernoux, "American Imperialists," *The Nation*, April 3, 1976, p. 393.

million-dollar budget for propaganda and lobbying. Many executives were appalled at Reagan's jingoism; they considered it foolish to risk losing billions of dollars in Latin America in order to win a Texas primary. By 1977 the Council of the Americas, comprising over 200 United States corporations with holdings in the southern nations, was buttonholing each Senator individually to win support for the treaties.

A highly unlikely volunteer in the pro-treaty forces was the American Institute of Merchant Marine, comprising thirty-five companies which owned and operated over half the ocean-going ships in the United States merchant fleet. James J. Reynolds, president of AIMS, assailed Reagan's comparison of the Zone to the Louisiana Purchase as "sheer nonsense," and denied that the United States ever enjoyed sovereignty in the Zone. He demanded that the Canal be secure and—particularly—the tolls for shipping be kept as low as possible, but he believed the new pacts could provide such assurances. If negotiations broke down, Reynolds declared, the results for "Canal users would be catastrophic. . . . The problem [of rioting and sabotage] is there, and all of the loose talk about shoulder-to-shoulder Marines [defending the Zone] is not going to make it go away."[67]

These business groups were joined by important religious spokesmen. Roman Catholics were in the vanguard. When Senator Byrd threatened to tie up talks by cutting off appropriations, the U.S. Catholic Conference helped organize opposition to the Senator. The Catholics took their lead from Archbishop McGrath: "Morally, the justice of the Panamanian position is unquestionable. Historically [the Canal's] geographical location and configuration are Panama's principal natural resource." McGrath, similarly to the multinationals, Kissinger, and Linowitz, viewed the issue as closely tied to larger Latin American problems. The Church, he believed, had to help solve the Canal question if it hoped to play a positive social role on behalf of human

67. *Panama Star and Herald*, July 25, 1976, p. 2.

rights throughout the Hemisphere.[68] Ironically resembling Hanson Baldwin and the strategists who feared an unfortunate domino effect if the Zone was returned to Panama, the pro-treaty groups feared a domino effect imperiling their own interests if the Zone was not returned.

The Panamanian government meanwhile began a risky and expensive propaganda effort in the United States. For nearly $200,000 it bought the services of a public relations firm headed by F. Clifton White (Barry Goldwater's top strategist in the 1964 presidential campaign), Joseph Napolitan (who headed Hubert Humphrey's media effort in 1968), and Lawrence F. O'Brien (former Democratic Party chairman and presently Commissioner of the National Basketball Association). The firm supposedly did not engage in lobbying on Capitol Hill, but focused on some 6000 opinion-makers in the media and universities who were sent thick, neatly arranged packets of pro-treaty material.[69]

The sides in the great debate were forming. The United States and Panama began coming to terms with three-quarters of a century of common history. How well they accomplished this depended, of course, on how well the two peoples—and particularly the North Americans— understood that history.

68. Marcos G. McGrath, "Ariel or Caliban?" Foreign Affairs, LII (October 1973), especially 91–92.
69. Don Oberderfer in Washington Post, March 24, 1977, p. A12:1–6.

Conclusion: 1903-1977 Five Questions

1. Is Ronald Reagan correct in claiming that the Canal Zone is sovereign United States territory just the same as Alaska?

Articles II and III of the 1903 treaty (analyzed in Chapter II) triggered the never-ending debate on this question. During the first twenty years of the agreement, the United States acted, to use the treaty's words, "as if it were sovereign" in the Zone. A 1907 Supreme Court decision stated that the area was United States territory. A neutrality act of World War I considered the Canal and its environs as part of the United States. In 1920 a congressional act defined Zone ports as "domestic." Other legislation, especially affecting shipping and defense, considered the area as "territory under the jurisdiction of the United States." In 1922–23 conversations with Panamanian officials, Secretary of State Charles Evans Hughes went as far as any North American statesman has gone in claiming full sovereign rights in the Zone (see Chapter III).

Even during these early years, however, the claim

was ambiguous. Theodore Roosevelt, John Hay, and William Howard Taft, the three most important figures in establishing the fundamental United States position, agreed that Panama retained—to use Taft's famous phrase—"titular sovereignty," although all three downplayed its importance. More significant was the testimony from Philippe Bunau-Varilla: "The United States, without becoming sovereign, received the exclusive use of the rights of sovereignty, while respecting the sovereignty itself of the Panama Republic." That judgment remained definitive not only because the Frenchman wrote the 1903 treaty, but tried to give the United States every possible advantage in the pact.

For a half-century the United States admitted in a variety of acts that it did not own the Zone as it "owned" Texas or Alaska. Taft's 1904 agreement (noted in Chapter II), recognized that Zonal boundary authorities were not fully sovereign, for the United States surrendered the right to apply its tariff to goods entering from Panama. Congress enacted a separate Canal Zone Code which expressly excluded United States general law (such as the criminal code), from having force in the area. The United States Constitution never automatically applied; the Zone's governor, for example, could single-handedly deport undesirables. Notably, children born of Panamanians in the Zone remained Panamanian. Born in Louisiana or Alaska, they would be United States citizens. A 1930 Supreme Court decision defined the Zone's ports as "foreign," and a Circuit Court of Appeals explicitly said the area was not "a part of the United States." Finally, a 1948 Supreme Court decision flatly declared that while Congress controlled the Zone, the United States did not possess "sovereignty."[1]

1. These points, pro and con, are discussed in R. R. Baxter, The Laws of International Waterways (Cambridge, Mass., 1964), pp. 84–87; Lawrence O. Ealy, Yanqui Politics and the Isthmian Canal (University Park, Pa., 1971), pp. 106, 172; Charles J. Maechling, "The Panama Canal: A Fresh Start," Orbis, XX(Winter 1977), 1007–1023; Helen C. Low, "Panama Canal Treaty in Perspective," Overseas Development Council Monograph Series #29 (1976).

This historical checkerboard led a distinguished legal scholar to conclude that the debate over sovereignty held "greater interest for the legal metaphysician than for the lawyer. The legal status of the waterway is not to be determined by reference to these abstract concepts," R. R. Baxter wrote, "but by a consideration of the relations established among Panama, the United States, and user nations by treaty and the customary law."[2]

Baxter's point provided the key to answering the question. During the 1970s crisis the 1903 treaty language had to be interpreted in the light of nearly 75 years of United States-Panamanian relations. Examined from this historical perspective, the answer was clear: the United States did not own the Zone or enjoy all sovereign rights in it. The turning point perhaps occurred in the 1936 treaty (examined in Chapter III), which termed the Zone the "territory of the Republic of Panama under the jurisdiction of the United States of America." The U.S. Senate constitutionally ratified that pact. After World War II, Washington officials repeatedly recognized Panama's sovereign powers in the Zone. Every President, starting with Dwight D. Eisenhower, allowed the Panamanian flag to fly with Old Glory in the area, an act not allowed in Alaska or Texas. By 1967 Johnson administration officials searched the record then privately concluded that the United States could not claim full sovereignty in the Zone (see Chapter V). In 1976, Ellsworth Bunker, heading the North American negotiating team, summarized the official consensus of the previous four decades by declaring that Washington did not purchase the Zone in 1903, but paid Panama for certain rights: "We bought Louisiana; we bought Alaska. In Panama, we bought not territory, but rights. . . . It is clear that under law we do not have sovereignty in Panama."

Senator Strom Thurmond was mistaken in his belief that "We own it, title in fee simple."[3] If the United States

2. Baxter, *Laws of International Waterways*, p. 87.
3. *Congressional Record*, 93d Cong., 2nd Sess., March 29, 1974, p. S4730.

"owned" it, no argument over sovereignty could have arisen, just as no major argument over North American sovereign control of, say, Florida, has occurred since it was purchased in 1819. Of equal importance, the title was not in "fee simple." The United States at no time claimed that it purchased the Zone outright. After 1903 it paid annual annuities to Panama, a payment which implicitly recognized less than full ownership of the waterway area. In no territorial transaction involving the mainland or such overseas acquisitions as Hawaii or the Philippines did the United States recognize the continuing rights of the sellers by paying annuities.

The Zone cannot be thought of as comparable to either a state or a territory, but more aptly, as Baxter declared, to a "great government reservation."[4] After the reorganization acts of 1948 and 1950, the Panama Canal Company became a corporation controlled by its sole stockholder, the Secretary of the Army, who acted as agent for the President of the United States. No territory, and certainly no state, was ever so controlled. The Secretary of the Army appointed a nine- to thirteen-member board of directors to manage the corporation. Private property in the Zone was virtually non-existent. The governmental corporation owned and operated everything from homes to stores to bowling alleys, partly because of the belief that the land could one day revert to Panama. The same cannot be said about Texas.

2. Since the Canal has not yet been paid for, should not Panama pay the United States for the original cost and later improvements?

The original cost of building the Canal was about $400 million when wages of the workers and prices of materials were roughly one-tenth to one-twentieth of current levels. Whether the investment has been amortized is an

4. Baxter, *Laws of International Waterways*, p. 86.

unanswerable question. The variables created by time and changed circumstances, as well as the different criteria used by experts who have studied the problem, make it comparable to a thousand-piece jigsaw puzzle which has important pieces missing.

It is unarguable, however, that from the beginning Congressmen cared little about amortizing the investment. They were primarily concerned about subsidizing United States shipping that used the canal. Tolls were set not to recoup expenses, but to help shippers. "Basically," two experts on the question concluded, "the policy of the Panama Canal system is that charges to shippers be set to recover only the actual cost of providing the service." Tolls were never set to pay for the original construction cost.[5] It is too late to ask Panama to do immediately what, for understandable reasons, the United States refused to do over a period of sixty years, even if a figure could be agreed upon.

3. Does the Canal remain a vital interest of the United States?

The importance of the Canal decreased notably after 1974, when military traffic to Vietnam declined and the Suez Canal reopened. The Panama Canal Company made good profits until the early 1970s, but after 1973 losses required the raising of tolls three times in four years. The raises occurred after 59 years in which the tolls were not raised at all.

Two other special reasons might be noted for its declining importance. First, the Canal machinery operates efficiently, but it is a superb antique whose parts date back to

5. Norman J. Padelford and Stephen R. Gibbs, *Maritime Commerce and the Future of the Panama Canal* (Cambridge, Md., 1975); Georgetown University Center for Strategic Studies, *Panama; Canal Issues and Treaty Talks* (Washington, D.C., 1967), p. 12; and see ECLA report in *Latin America*, May 3, 1974, pp. 133–134. A Latin American view of the difficulty in measuring the economic (and social) costs of the Canal is Gorostiaga, *Panama y la Zona del Canal*, pp. 11–15.

1914. The Canal will require expensive modification in the not distant future simply to continue moving its present rate of traffic. Large tankers, which form the arteries of the international oil system, cannot squeeze through the waterway. The need to modernize was one reason the Panamanians demanded billions of dollars from the United States when the 1977 treaty was negotiated.

A second reason why it is slipping in importance is an ongoing revolution in international trade. The Canal accommodates ships carrying no more than 65,000 long tons of cargo. In 1964 no bulk carriers went above 80,000 tons; ten years later more than 100 ships carried more than 125,000 tons, and some approached 300,000 tons. In early 1977 as many as 1000 vessels were too large, either in width or tonnage, to travel the passageway.

Of equal importance, ships that formerly journeyed from Asia through the Canal and on to eastern United States ports now anchor instead at West Coast ports and lift their huge, transferable containers directly on eastbound railway cars. A week of transit time and as much as 10 percent in costs can thereby be saved. One container vessel carries the cargo formerly carried by three to five of the merchant ships using the Canal. The container phenomenon has grown so rapidly that hard-hit eastern port authorities recently joined with International Longshoremen to ask the government that the practice be restricted.[6] Containerization, larger ships, air freight, truck trailer rigs with cargo roll-on, roll-off techniques, and the increased processing of raw materials near their sources—all are reducing the Canal's value.

A Library of Congress study concluded that while the waterway remained important for United States and world commerce, "it is not of overwhelming or critical economic importance." Ten to 17 percent of United States oceangoing

6. *Wall Street Journal*, Nov. 15, 1976, p. 6:1; an excellent summary by Zone officials is in U.S. Congress, House, Subcommittee of the Committee on Appropriations, 94th Cong., 1st Sess., *Department of Transportation and Related Agencies Appropriations for 1976* (Washington, D.C., 1975), especially pp. 4–5.

commerce, representing less than one percent of the gross national product, uses the Canal. It is more important to several Latin American nations (who, under the new treaty, can help guarantee the waterway's security), and to Japan, South Korea, New Zealand, and Taiwan than to the United States. As one economic consultant on the Canal remarked in late 1976, "Now that people are fighting not to give it up, the thing isn't worth fighting about."[7]

Militarily, supporting warships and merchantmen carrying supplies continue to use the Canal. But its strategic value has also rapidly declined. Aircraft carriers cannot use it, and nuclear submarines must surface while going through. In 1903 the waterway was vital for Mahan's famous strategy of keeping the one-ocean U.S. Navy together in force while shifting it from sea to sea. But three-quarters of a century later, the nation has long possessed a two-ocean navy. A former senior officer responsible for overseeing transportation expenditures believed that using routes other than the Canal would not have adversely affected the Vietnam war effort; added costs would have been negligible.[8] In a war the Canal would be defenseless against sabotage or missiles. Perhaps Panamanian diplomat Carlos Lopez Guevara put it best: "If the Canal really were vital to the United States, we would not have a chance" of obtaining a treaty.

4. If Congress refused to accept a new treaty, or the United States later decided not to carry out its provisions, what could Panama do about it, especially since its 10,000-man National Guard is largely supplied by the United States?

The government and most Panamanians are determined to obtain the Canal at a fixed future date, but they

7. *Business Week*, Dec. 6, 1976, pp. 84–86.
8. Cox, "Choices" in Silvert, ed., *Americas in Changing World*, p. 140.

are not foolish enough to believe they can wage a war, even a Vietnam type of conflict, against the United States. (Graham Greene made the interesting observation that "The Panamanians are not romantic."[9] That characterization at least seems to fit the National Guard leaders who rule the country.) Realism could dictate guerrilla attacks or small acts of sabotage which raised tensions in the area without closing down the Canal. Sabotage would be easy. Torrijos once accurately described the Canal "as vulnerable as a newborn baby." The area cannot be defended unless an army in excess of 100,000 men was stationed in the Zone, preferably along a Berlin-type wall. Even that defense would be neither impregnable, nor, needless to add, acceptable to many North Americans and most Latin Americans. General George Brown, chairman of the U.S. Joint Chiefs of Staff, believed the Canal's safety was impossible to guarantee without a new treaty: "It is more efficiently and effectively defended in partnership with Panama."[10]

After conferring on the problem, CIA, Defense Department, and State Department officials agreed with General Brown that the waterway was nearly impossible to protect against sabotage, and if the United States was required to defend it against an internal Panamanian threat under the 1903 treaty, it "could not expect much sympathy from Latin American countries."[11] A United States military officer worried about fighting alone: "For those of us who really care about the Army, [the atrocities committed against Vietnamese civilians at] My Lai was an awful blow. We know what that's done to our reputation. The last thing in the world we want now is to be ordered to start shooting into a crowd of Panamanians."[12]

Panamanians have no reason to want the waterway destroyed or even closed down for a period of time. As this

9. Greene, "Country with Five Frontiers," p. 13.
10. *Latin American Report*, IV (July 1976), p. 6.
11. Enclosure in Robert J. McCloskey to Senator Dick Clark, June 30, 1976, manuscript copy.
12. Franck and Weisband, "Panama," pp. 186–187.

book has emphasized, they fought for control because their economic survival depended on the traffic moving through the waterway. Yet in 1956 when the Egyptians suddenly had to choose between bowing to British power or closing the Suez Canal, they chose the latter. If the same kind of choice faced Panama, no guarantee exists it would not follow the Egyptian precedent.

5. Since the United States operated the Canal so efficiently and Panama made hundreds of millions of dollars annually from the traffic and the annuities, why did the Panamanians insist on assuming total control?

Panamanians wanted the Canal for two principal reasons. Of possibly lesser significance is a nationalism that developed long before 1903; as Chapters I and II emphasized, Panamanian separatism long preceded Theodore Roosevelt's taking of the Canal. That nationalism finally accepted the Bunau-Varilla treaty only because Panama both needed United States protection and feared Washington's power. The nationalism ripened particularly with the appearance of student political organizations and a small but active middle class in the 1930s (Chapters III and IV). North Americans never understood this nationalism, partly because they were ignorant of nineteenth-century Panamanian history, partly because they became enchanted with Theodore Roosevelt's self-propagated myth that he created the country on the third day of November 1903.

Panamanians increasingly resented the division of their country by a Zone which for many years they could cross only with difficulty, and they feared a colonial control to which, rightly or wrongly, they attributed many of their nation's problems. The control was not a figment of their imagination. In 1944, John F. Muccio, the acute chargé of the U.S. Embassy in Panama City, detailed the extent of the domination. United States influence, even if

> we should be able to keep our mouths tightly shut and take no overt action, is inescapable. . . . For instance, any cantina or restaurant can be closed by the Public Health authorities. The Army can completely and thoroughly sabotage Panamanian commercial life through simply declaring either all Panama or specific business enterprises "off limits" to soldiers. . . . Our control over water works and other utilities can completely estop the development of whole sections of the cities of Panama and Colon. . . .
>
> Every realistic Panamanian, just as every realistic American, is fully aware that this influence over the daily life of Panama exists, and there is always a question in the minds of the Panamanians as to how this power will be used.[13]

Muccio wrote during wartime, but most of his statements applied to pre-1941 Panama and many to the post-1945 years. In 1950 a confidential State Department analysis concluded that "the virtual dependence of Panamanian economic life on US activities in the Canal Zone and the inferiority complex inherently felt by a small, undeveloped country having close relations with a large and powerful state" caused Panamanians to feel "a highly nationalistic sensitivity and resentment toward the United States." Despite such "resentment," however, the State Department urged greater private investment in Panama, particularly since "by the Constitution of 1946 American businessmen are in a position of economic equality with Panamanians."[14] The 1972 Constitution changed that equal relationship, but the Constitution and the 1977 pacts affected only the degree, not the fact, of Panamanian dependence. The United States possessed $1.8 billion of investments in the country, and North American banks, multinational corporations, mineral-processing companies, and agribusinesses continued to

13. Muccio to Phillip W. Bonsal, Department of State, June 6, 1944, 819.00/6–644, Box 3729, NA, RG 59.
14. *FRUS, 1950*, II, 974, 977.

dominate the nation's economy. The National Guard depended on Washington for its matériel and much of its officer training. The small oligarchy had long since been integrated into a North American marketing system.

As this long history of cooperation demonstrates, Panamanians have not been anti-North American by nature. They have, however, increasingly opposed United States control of the Zone and the blatant anti-Panamanian discrimination carried on in the Zone. With those issues removed, relations between the two countries should be close and largely on Washington's terms.

Finally, Panama needs the Canal for economic reasons. As this account has repeatedly shown, Panamanian governments tried to solve fundamental economic problems with a variety of programs, but always returned to the area's greatest resource, the Canal. For good reason, Panamanians never believed the United States paid them enough for the use of the Zone. While they received between $1.9 million and $2.3 million in annual rental, the United States paid Spain $20 million to $30 million each year for the use of airbases in Spanish territory.

A United Nations report believed the Canal could produce $2 billion annually in revenue for Panama. In addition, the country could develop such new industries as shipbuilding, repair, and drydocks, while expanding existing warehousing and transshipment operations.[15] The 1977 treaty was by no means a cure-all for either the Panamanian or North American problems on the Isthmus, but it was a long step forward in making relationships between the two nations more equitable. In a sense the agreement was most important because it demonstrated a mutual understanding that was impossible to achieve in the previous relationship between the colonial power and the colony. Such a colonial relationship had begun to be historically outdated in Asia and Africa even in 1903 when it was established between the United States and Panama. Certainly it was a dangerous anachronism by the mid-1970s.

15. *Washington Post*, June 3, 1977, p. A24:4.

Postscript.
Byrd, Baker, and De Concini: The Debate of 1977–1978

As Bastidas and Balboa discovered to their sorrow five centuries ago, dealing with Isthmian affairs can be a bewildering experience. The historic 1977–1978 debate over the two Canal treaties proved no exception. One of the most intensive propaganda campaigns in American history was waged, yet few North Americans changed their minds. The Senate devoted three months to exhaustive debate, yet at the end the sides remained almost exactly what they had been at the start. President Carter captured headlines by labeling treaty ratification essential for presidential power in foreign policy, yet the Senate leadership shaped and won the debate. The Panamanian government remained discreetly silent as the North Americans argued, yet afterwards Omar Torrijos dramatically announced that he had been ready to blow up the Canal's locks rather than enter into new negotiations. Finally, after the treaties returning the Canal to Panama were ratified, Panamanian students promptly took to the streets in protest, and two were killed.

The debate thus comprised another strange chapter in U.S.-Panamanian relations. But it also revealed the role (or non-role) of public opinion in foreign policy, the power of the U.S. Congress in the era of the post-imperial presidency, and the perception held by other countries that even when it officially repudiated old colonialism, the United States continued to practice neo-colonialism. For these reasons, the affair deserves close examination.

Debate began in August 1977 when President Carter urged Senate Majority Leader Robert Byrd (Dem.-W.Va.) to move rapidly on the treaties. Byrd bluntly replied that such strategy would be "a total disaster" since public opinion overwhelmingly opposed the pacts. If Carter hoped to win, Byrd advised, the President must first launch a massive effort to transform that opinion. Hamilton Jordan, who directed the White House campaign for the treaties, agreed in more down-home language: "Some of those bastards [in the Senate] don't have the spine not to vote their mail. If you change their mail, you change their mind."[1]

The War for Public Opinion

On September 6 the campaign to change minds opened when Carter invited all Latin American heads of state to witness the signing ceremony in Washington. Nineteen attended, but several, notably the President of Mexico, did not appear because they did not want to sit at the same table with the military dictators of Chile, Brazil, and Paraguay, among others. Many U.S. Senators refused to attend; some who did asked that they not be photographed. The television spectacular did not dent anti-treaty sentiment, but it proved one point: Carter's emphasis on human rights cut apart his hemispheric policy with a scissors-like effect. If he wanted support from dictators to display inter-American unity, he had to de-emphasize human rights; but if he did that, he lost the sympathy of the remaining Latin American democracies and a vast number of North Americans.

1. Associated Press (AP) Dispatch, March 16, 1978; *New York Times*, Oct. 13, 1977, p.67:6.

More helpful was the strong support expressed in congressional testimony by the Joint Chiefs of Staff and former Secretaries of State Henry Kissinger and Dean Rusk, all of whom had many friends on Capitol Hill. Other groups joined the President's side, including the Sierra Club, the American Friends' Service Committee, and the Committee for Ratification of the Panama Canal Treaties headed by such establishment figures as Averell Harriman, John McCloy, and former Republican Senate Leader Hugh Scott. The Harriman group raised hundreds of thousands of dollars, particularly from such corporations as United Brands and Chase Manhattan Bank which had large Latin American investments.

A White House official later commented that business groups, especially the conservative National Association of Manufacturers (NAM), provided the crucial support. The National Chamber of Commerce, on the other hand, early favored the pacts, but after polling members—many of whom, in contrast to NAM members, are small businessmen—turned increasingly against ratification. The American Federation of Labor helped primarily by keeping disgruntled members in the Canal Zone quiet. More important, the U.S. Catholic Conference (USCC) and the National Council of Churches lobbied intensively for the treaties. They were joined by Episcopal, Presbyterian, and Methodist groups who agreed with the USCC that "the moral imperative exists" to repudiate "the colonial politics of the nineteenth century."[2]

The White House was especially proud of its program to invite opinion leaders from individual states for personal meetings with Carter. This experiment began when dubious editors from Kentucky were brought to Washington in the hope that after some presidential persuasion they would pressure their state's senators to vote for the pacts. (In the end, one senator did and one did not.) Other

---

2. *Time*, Feb. 20, 1978, p.19; *National Catholic Register*, Aug. 28, 1977, p.1; Religious News Service, "The Week in Religion," Sept. 16, 1977.

senators immediately saw such visits as a means of shifting public pressure from themselves to the President. They besieged the White House with requests to invite hundreds of folks from back home. In this program, Carter talked to more than 1700 people. The administration also sent officials across the country to make speeches to virtually any group that extended an invitation. This became known in the State Department as "The PITS"—Panama Information Track Score. By late February 1978 the PITS showed that officials had given more than 800 speeches and interviews on the treaties.[3]

At best the results were mixed. After the debate ended, congressional staff members believed that Carter's public campaign had been ineffectual. Senate mail, for example, continued to be overwhelmingly against the pacts. "After receiving thousands of letters opposing the treaties, we were so happy to receive pro-treaty letters," joked an aide of one key senator, "that we framed both of them." But a White House official countered that to the end senators pleaded with Carter to talk to their constituents—in essence, to act as a lightning rod so the public anger would strike him instead of them. He obliged. An administration spokesman noted that little "linkage" exists between public opinion and specific foreign policy decisions, even in the Senate. But he emphasized that on this issue senators nevertheless begged Carter to shield them. The President's assumption of this role probably contributed to his rapidly declining popularity in early 1978.

At times the comments on Carter's performance were unfair. After numerous requests from the Senate and his own staff, for example, on February 1, 1978, he delivered a nationally televised "fireside chat" to explain the treaties. NBC and ABC television carried the speech live, but CBS ran a Joanne Woodward movie. Columnists immediately decided that listeners would prefer Woodward to Carter, and White House officials blasted the CBS decision. Their

3. *Washington Post*, Feb. 26, 1978, p.4:1.

surprise was therefore measurable when the ratings showed that the President heavily outdrew the movie. The country was listening to the debate, and Carter was working hard. That did not mean, however, he was changing many minds.

For he was opposed by a slick, well-financed media campaign operated by conservatives who hoped to use the Canal issue as a lever for regaining the White House in 1980. Their most effective publicist was Ronald Reagan, although his effectiveness suffered somewhat when John Wayne—who had deep personal ties to leading Panamanian families—publicly argued for the treaty. (This allowed Torrijos to claim that at least the better actor was on his side.) Zonians also lobbied intensively against the treaties, and the dark side of their anxiety appeared when gun sales rose dramatically in the Canal Zone. Fearing the Panamanians would sooner or later try to take over their neighborhoods, Zonian women suddenly began taking target practice. "Everybody I know in the Zone is equipped," said a mother of two children. "We have three guns in the house . . . and we've just ordered a semi-automatic through the gun club." A U.S. official on the Isthmus lamented, "The place is a regular arsenal," and he worried what might occur when Panama, after assuming jurisdiction, tried to outlaw the weapons.[4]

Such fears added impetus to the anti-treaty campaign. The Conservative Caucus sent out two million letters and raised nearly $1 million to fight the pacts. The American Conservative Union helped dispatch "truth squads" to specially targeted states whose senators were wavering. The direct-mail fund-raising was run by Richard Viguerie, who had master-minded earlier conservative efforts that pulled huge sums from the grass roots. Regardless of the vote on the treaties, Viguerie could not lose. He saw it as an issue which "rallied new people to our cause" and gave the right-wing a subject it could use in the future. Personally, he stood to profit handsomely. The new names collected

4. *Ibid.*, Sept. 18, 1977, p.A15:1–2.

through the Panama campaign could later be sold to conservatives running for office in 1978 and 1980.

Viguerie believed the treaties could be killed: "Our strength is in Peoria and Oshkosh ... and that's where we're going. We want to have the Senators ... hear from the folks back home."[5] The same point was made in the January 1978 *Conservative Digest* by syndicated columnist (and former Nixon speech-writer) Patrick J. Buchanan, who asserted that the treaties might sweep the liberal Washington suburb of Georgetown "without a dissenting vote," but "in the nation the reverse is more nearly so."

Viguerie and Buchanan were proved wrong. Their mistake illustrated the misreading of, and misplaced emphasis upon, public opinion that occurred throughout the debate. On April 3, 1978, a Lou Harris poll revealed that a plurality of Americans favored both treaties as amended and—more striking—that after Viguerie and other anti-treaty conservatives had blitzed the Midwest for six months, the pacts received the highest percentage of support not in the East and its Georgetowns, but in the Midwest and its Oshkoshes, which approved the second treaty 46 percent to 37 percent.[6]

The conservatives' ineffectiveness was partly due to Carter's efforts on the other side. It was also due to Torrijos's counterattacks. When the anti-pact forces raised charges of human rights violations, for example, the General promptly modified political censorship, invited international agencies to see conditions for themselves, and circulated a report by Amnesty International (a superb watch-dog for human rights around the globe), that, compared with other Latin American nations, Panama was relatively free of such violations.

But overall, the propaganda campaign on both sides produced sound and fury that changed few minds. As political scientist William Schneider pointed out in the *Wash-*

5. William J. Lanouette, "The Panama Canal Treaties—Playing in Peoria and the Senate," *National Journal*, Oct. 8, 1977, p.1560.
6. *Washington Post*, April 3, 1978, p.A9:3–4.

ington Post on February 12, 1978, North Americans had consistently opposed the original treaties by a large majority, but also consistently favored the pacts when amendments were added giving the United States the permanent right to send troops to keep the Canal open for ships of all nations. As early as October 1977, respondents had favored the treaties with this amendment by 63 percent to 24 percent.

That particular provision, along with another giving U.S. vessels the right to move to the head of the line for passage through the Canal in emergencies, was accepted by Torrijos in October 1977. The Senate added both amendments to the Neutrality Treaty the following March. These additions, not the public relations campaign, made the pacts acceptable to at least a plurality of Americans polled and to the two-thirds of the one hundred senators needed to ratify.

In the end, the Senate accepted the agreements not because Carter's public education efforts succeeded, or because Viguerie and Reagan made glaring mistakes in conducting their campaign. Public opinion had little, if any, effect on the day-to-day Senate debate in February, March, and April 1978.[7] The senators finally ratified the treaties because their party leaders, Democrat Robert Byrd and Republican Howard Baker (a Tennessean), insisted the amendments be inserted in the Neutrality Treaty to spell out U.S. rights after the year 2000, then exerted their considerable power to round up the necessary votes. The decisive battles occurred in rooms off the Senate floor, not in the feverish public struggle over who could change the course of public opinion.

The Baker-Byrd Amendments

When the treaties were written, Carter could not be certain that Byrd would support them. Without the Major-

7. This thesis is argued at greater length in Walter LaFeber, "Covering the Canal, Or, How the Press Missed the Boat," *More, the Media Magazine*, VIII (June 1978), 26–31.

ity Leader's approval they had no chance of being ratified. The outlook was hardly optimistic. Although personal relations between Carter and Byrd were correct but cool, the President's programs in Congress were encountering roadblocks that frustrated the inexperienced White House staff, and the administration suffered a series of foreign policy setbacks. Byrd, moreover, was a cautious conservative Democrat who had no known predilection for surrendering U.S. holdings abroad, and who would never call for a treaty vote until he knew the 67 ballots were in the bag. That certainty seemed remote in the early autumn of 1977.

Byrd's (and Baker's) conversion constituted the administration's major triumph in the ratification struggle. The turn apparently occurred after State Department officials convinced the West Virginian the pacts secured U.S. interests in Central America. Byrd took pride in his self-educated, self-made-man image; he had risen from poverty to power, and during his climb had studied for his law degree by attending classes after meeting his arduous Capitol Hill duties during the day. He now read widely on U.S.-Panamanian relations and concluded that the treaties were necessary. Byrd invited the two top State Department lobbyists, Douglas J. Bennet and Robert Beckel, to brief undecided senators in meetings which he hosted.

A central actor in the drama later argued that Byrd was the pivotal figure for three reasons. As the Majority Leader he held the political plums which could be dispensed to cooperative Democrats. Since, moreover, he had pioneered in moving from opposition to support for the pacts, despite strong anti-treaty sentiment in West Virginia, Byrd made the same voyage seem safer for other senators. Finally, once the debate began, the Majority Leader controlled the floor. This proved crucial, for the anti-treaty forces were led by James Allen (Dem.-Ala.), one of the shrewdest parliamentary strategists in the Senate's history. "As long as Byrd was there," one Senate staffer remarked, "nothing was going to sneak through."

The West Virginian was also pivotal for a fourth reason. He and Baker helped convince Carter the treaties could pass only if certain U.S. rights were spelled out in amendments to the original Neutrality pact. This became imperative after the Panamanians issued interpretations of crucial treaty clauses that conflicted with Washington's interpretations. The two senators helped write a Memorandum of Understanding, which was signed by Carter and Torrijos on October 14, 1977. That document specified both the U.S. right of intervention after 2000 to keep the Canal open, and the right of U.S. ships to have priority passage in crises. Without that Memorandum the pacts would never have been ratified.

Baker's political pilgrimage to the pro-treaty group was more difficult than Byrd's. Facing a reelection campaign in 1978 and working toward his party's presidential nomination in 1980, he heard repeatedly from Republican leaders that open support for the treaties would jeopardize the first ambition and destroy the second. Baker's problem was further complicated since his Senate power was not yet secure (he won the Minority Leadership by a single vote after two earlier losses), and his party bitterly divided on the Canal issue between Ford and Reagan factions. The anti-treaty forces therefore believed they could make Baker squirm "like a worm on a hot brick," in the words of Senator Jesse A. Helms (Rep.-N.C.).[8] To warm the brick, the American Conservative Union ran full-page newspaper ads in Tennessee announcing that "SENATOR BAKER ALONE CAN SAVE THE PANAMA CANAL," targeted Tennessee for its "truth squads," and flew a banner over a crowd of 84,000 (including Baker) at a Tennessee-Memphis State football game that urged fans to write the Senator. Baker's office received more than 60,000 pieces of mail on the treaties, nearly all opposed.

Despite such pressure, Baker decided in December to support the pacts. He believed right-wing opposition had

8. Much of the information on Baker is drawn from Lisa Kremer's unpublished paper, "Senator Baker and the Latin American Ditch," May 1978; and Robert Kaiser's analysis in *Washington Post*, March 19, 1978, p.A8:1–6.

peaked and was receding, particularly after the issuance of the Memorandum in October. Baker's own private poll showed that 60 percent of Tennesseans surveyed actually favored a treaty that protected U.S. security. (That result, and similar polls, led many senators to discount heavily the organized mail campaign waged by anti-treaty groups.) Baker and his family, moreover, have long and successful political careers as Tennesseans. Political columnist A. B. Albritton of the Memphis *Commercial Appeal* speculated on December 9 that "What Baker might do to save his political hide would be to attempt to change the treaties to suit his own convictions and political tastes."

The October Memorandum marked the first step in that direction. An incredible second step occurred in January 1978 when Baker led a Senate delegation to Panama and convinced Torrijos that since the legal significance of the memorandum was unclear (indeed, Panamanian officials, for their own domestic purposes, dismissed it as legally meaningless), the Memorandum should be incorporated into the Neutrality Treaty. Baker's achievement was stunning. Rarely has a senator, especially a member of the minority party, succeeded in acting overseas as if he were Secretary of State. Carter allowed Baker to pull off the trick. But then the President apparently had no alternative if the treaties were to be ratified.

The *Washington Post* was not inaccurate in editorializing on January 10 that Baker's handling of the Panamanians was comparable to Theodore Roosevelt's "high handedness" of 1903. Byrd and Baker moved toward ratification for many of the same reasons, but the West Virginian did so quietly and gracefully, while Baker—trying to survive in a quite different political world—publicly flaunted U.S. imperial power over Panama.

The beleaguered Torrijos bent. In the previous October he had submitted the unamended treaties to a national plebescite as Panama's constitution provided. Under U.S. pressure, the General allowed political debate for the first time in eight years. Political parties reappeared. His opponents, led by left-wing university students and some conservative businessmen, seized the opportunity to attack Torrijos's regime instead of—or along with—the treaties. Critics focused on the long 22-year period before Panama could control the Canal. They also attacked provisions legalizing both U.S. military presence in the area and the Pentagon's cooperation with the National Guard. Such cooperation, many believed, meant U.S. domination of the Guard and hence—since the Guard ruled the country—of them. One survey revealed that many opponents, who apparently had long historical memories, simply assumed "the treaty is a trap of the Gringos."[9]

Such suspicions grew when the Memorandum of Understanding appeared nine days before the plebescite was scheduled. Panamanian officials tried to blunt the Memorandum's impact, and not without a sense of humor. Dr. Romulo Escobar Bethancourt, the head of Panama's negotiating team, told his countrymen the Memorandum only clarified the treaty in Panama's interest. After all, he argued, U.S. ships should be allowed to pass through the Canal rapidly since their presence could lead to an attack on Panama itself—and besides, "a lengthy stay in our country would mean that the sailors would have to come ashore." Anyone familiar with the Yankees in World War II did not have "to imagine the extravagances of sailors on shore."[10]

Despite such imaginative arguments, the government, hoping for 80 percent approval, received a vote of 67 percent for the treaties while 33 percent opposed. This occurred despite Torrijos putting his personal prestige on the line and heavy governmental involvement in the vote counting. "Another month of debate and the treaties would have been rejected," one foreign expert later remarked in Panama City.[11]

---

9. An excellent summary of Panamanian attitudes in October 1977 is in J. P. Morray, editor and translator, The View From Panama (Monmouth, Ore., 1978), especially the Villalobos and Porcell articles.
10. Matutin (Panama), Oct. 19, 1977, p.1.
11. New York Times, Feb. 12, 1978, p.8:1.

Torrijos's situation worsened after he gave Baker his approval for including the Memorandum in the Neutrality Treaty. This incorporation clearly changed the pact itself, but the General adamantly refused to submit it to a second plebescite. He argued that since the Memorandum had been announced before the first vote, Panamanians knew about it when they cast their ballots. On the other hand, he clearly could not afford to suppress the mushrooming political opposition while the Senate debated the treaties. In mid-February 1978, leaders from the four major parties met in Miami (where several, including Arnulfo Arias, had learned to tolerate exile) to announce their opposition to Torrijos and reservations about the pacts.

Baker's use of the October Memorandum might have helped save his political career, but it did little for Torrijos except prove that he was not an absolute dictator; if he were he could have safely submitted the revised treaties to a second vote. Instead, the General found himself in a political pressure cooker with the temperature rising dangerously.

The Debate and DeConcini

For six weeks, in February and March, the Senate debate droned on over the Neutrality Treaty (which stipulated how the Canal would be protected after 2000 when the Panamanians assumed control). Byrd and Senator Frank Church (Dem.-Idaho), the floor leader for the treaties, quickly destroyed opposition attempts to attach crippling amendments by tabling them. The discussion thoroughly examined details of the treaties, but it soon became repetitious and produced no memorable speech-making. Senate debates were broadcast for the first time when National Public Radio, comprising 213 stations, carried the proceedings to as many as 14 million listeners.

The broadcasts' effect on U.S. opinion was not measurable but—as has unfortunately occurred before in relations between the two peoples—Panamanians became incensed by words spoken solely for the ears of North

American voters. The debate was beamed to Panama, and as senators attacked the treaties they accused Torrijos and some of his countrymen of being corrupt and inefficient. Panamanians were stunned. Many had never heard their military leaders so described and were angered, or, if they opposed Torrijos, elated, by the Senate attacks. Byrd later admitted the speeches created "ill will" and "could very well have precipitated some disorder" in Panama.[12] One White House official acidly commented that in view of the often low level of debate and the effects on Panama, "It was not the Senate's finest hour."

The Senate leadership's objective, however, was not memorable speech-making but ending the debate as soon as the members made a record for the folks back home. Byrd and Baker had the necessary 67 votes well in hand at the start of the Senate sessions. This became evident February 22; on the first major test involving a procedural point the pro-treaty forces won 67–30. When the treaties passed in March and April, those who cast ballots on February 22 voted exactly the same way with only one exception (Henry Roth [Rep.-Del.], who switched to the opposition). Byrd and Baker had several votes in reserve to compensate for Roth's defection.

After this point the leadership's problem was not gathering the votes. That had been accomplished by the so-called Baker-Byrd amendments adding the October Memorandum to the Neutrality Treaty. The leadership's problem was to hold those 67 votes—that is, not allow a new issue to undercut treaty support, or permit a political error to alienate key senators. Challenges on issues were swiftly handled by a chain-of-command that began on the Senate floor and ended in the State Department or the Pentagon. When a substantive point arose, a staff member who was always present on the floor to assist Byrd or Church rushed into an office just off the Chamber that was controlled by Vice-President Walter Mondale. There State Department

12. *Ibid.*, April 29, 1978, p.8:4–5.

and Pentagon experts quickly provided the information needed to kill opponents' charges. If the experts did not have the information, they picked up a direct line to task forces in State or Defense which had access to all important information on the treaties or on Panama itself. These task forces quickly telefaxed the information back to the Senate office, and staffers took the material onto the floor for use in the debate. "The State and Defense teams were superb," one Senate staff member remarked later.

"On the other hand," he added, "the White House lobbyists didn't know what they were doing. They were going through on-the-job training. They got in the way more than they helped." That estimate can be somewhat discounted, but it reveals a striking characteristic of the debate. As the weeks went by, the administration began to make mistakes. Doubts arose whether the 67 votes could be retained. Bad feelings erupted between the White House and the Senate. The conflict developed less from issues than from White House over-involvement that came from a determination to win a "victory" for a President who had not enjoyed a "victory" for a year. It turned into an institutional, not an ideological, fight that became especially sharp since it developed in a post-Vietnam, Third Cold War climate. The White House sought to regain some of its pre-1973 prestige in foreign affairs, while the Senate attempted to retain and expand its own newly developed power.

At first the two branches worked well together. Senator Robert Dole (Rep.-Kan.), a staunch treaty opponent and a rival of Baker's for the 1980 Republican presidential nomination, insisted in mid-February 1978 that the Senate meet in secret session to consider charges that Torrijos was involved in narcotics traffic. The administration provided detailed investigative materials. The documents showed that Torrijos was apparently innocent of trafficking, although he knew of the network. Republican Jacob Javits of New York expressed the general Senate feeling: "We don't have to prove that Torrijos is an angel. I don't think he is. . . . What is important is whether the treaties [are in the U.S. interest] . . . and I think they are."[13]

Carter also handled some individual senators well. Richard Stone (Dem.-Fla.) had earlier condemned Torrijos and opposed the pacts, but changed his mind partly because of Florida's close ties to Latin America, especially in the economic area. Many Floridians nevertheless condemned the agreements as another U.S. retreat before the demands of "left-leaning, rickety, tin-horn" dictators (as Stone himself once described Torrijos). Senator Stone understood a most crucial point in the debate: many opponents fought the treaty more from emotion and fear than from a close reading of the documents and the historical context. He therefore asked Carter to issue an announcement pledging opposition against any Soviet efforts to establish bases in the hemisphere. The President wheeled out the 155-year-old Monroe Doctrine, promised to maintain U.S. outposts in the Caribbean, and Stone switched publicly to support the pacts.[14] With Stone and other senators Carter also made the telling point that approval was necessary if the world was to believe that the President of the United States had the power to carry out the nation's foreign policy.

As the vote neared on the Neutrality Treaty, however, the White House showed signs of panic. On March 14, just two days before the scheduled vote, the New York Times reported that Carter was bargaining for the support of key senators by sponsoring bills for farm subsidies and copper purchases which he had earlier condemned as inflationary. One high administration official was quoted as saying, "I hope the Panamanians will get as much out of these treaties as some United States senators." Legislators who had risked their political lives by supporting the pacts from the start were furious. Robert Packwood (Rep.-Ore.) warned that Carter should not act as "master of ceremonies at 'Let's Make a Deal.' " Angry at the White House fumbling, Byrd

13. Time, Feb. 20, 1978, p.19.
14. Tom Fiedler's column in Miami Herald, Feb. 7, 1978, p.24.

tried to calm the situation by commenting to a television interviewer that senators "would spit in your face" if offered "deals in return for votes." He carefully refrained from saying whether any "deals" had been offered.[15]

The crucial, almost fatal, mistake occurred 24 hours before the vote when Carter negotiated with Senator Dennis DeConcini, a 40-year-old freshman Democrat from Arizona. In that state the copper industry was depressed but hatred for the treaties prospered. For the national interest and his party's President the moderate DeConcini wanted to support the pacts. But his brother Dino was running for state attorney-general in Arizona, and one poll revealed that 84 percent of the state opposed the Canal pacts. In December, moreover, DeConcini had taken his family to Panama. Torijos, whose mother had recently died, poured attention on DeConcini's mother and talked about his own until the General began to cry. But when the Senator asked whether the Neutrality Treaty allowed the United States to protect the Canal after 2000 if it was closed due to such internal threats as revolution or labor strikes, Torrijos bluntly said no. Panamanians later recalled DeConcini as "a nice guy, somewhat naïve," who "kept checking with his mother" while "his wife asked more penetrating questions than the man himself."[16]

The Panamanians underestimated their guest. In hectic last-minute bargaining, DeConcini told Carter he could vote for the Neutrality Treaty only if it contained a "condition." (A condition, unlike an amendment, is not legally binding on both parties to a treaty but provides one party's understanding of what a provision means.) DeConcini's condition stipulated that if the Canal was closed for any reason after 2000, the United States or Panama could take unilateral action "including the use of military force *in Panama* to reopen the Canal." [Italics added.] The language contradicted other provisions in which the United States

15. *New York Times,* March 14, 1978, p.1:3; *Washington Post,* March 15, 1978, p.A11:1; AP Wire Dispatch, March 19, 1978.
16. *Washington Post,* April 28, 1978, p.A16:3.

promised not to intervene in Panama's internal affairs, the most sensitive of all points to Panamanians. DeConcini said that only with this condition could he and as many as four other senators vote for ratification. At a last-minute talk with the Senator, Carter asked Deputy Secretary of State Warren Christopher whether Panama could accept the condition. Torrijos will swallow hard, Christopher replied, but will accept it.

Carter sent the condition to Capitol Hill with his blessing. Senate experts were confused. One key aide believed it was nothing more than the Baker-Byrd amendment "in naked form." Other staffers, however, hurriedly asked the White House whether Panama could accept such a provision and were told it could. Despite such assurances, Edward Kennedy (Dem.-Mass.)—who, polls revealed, enjoyed more popular support for the 1980 Democratic presidential nomination than Carter—rose in the Senate to deliver a blistering attack on the condition. He believed the treaty already adequately protected U.S. security interests: "We are asking Panama to accept an amendment which has the ring of military intervention—not just during this century, but for all time."[17]

By now news had spread that Torrijos strongly objected to DeConcini's proposal. The General intended to make a television speech denouncing the condition and, perhaps, thereby kill the treaties. Carter called Torrijos to warn him against such a course, and pleaded that he reserve public judgment until both treaties passed the Senate. Torrijos again bowed under Washington's pressure. Despite its knowledge of the Maximum Chief's bitterness, the Senate passed the DeConcini condition 75–23. Several of the leading anti-treaty legislators voted in favor, and a dozen liberal, pro-pact senators opposed. The Senate then ratified the entire amended Neutrality Treaty 68–32.

White House officials later argued that DeConcini's demand had to be met or the necessary 67 votes could not

17. *Congressional Record*, CLXXIV (March 16, 1978), S3824.

have been held. A deeply involved Senate staffer admitted
he did not know what the vote count would be until it was
finally tallied. But one official close to the fight believed that
Byrd could have pressured two other senators to switch to
supporting the treaty if their votes had been required. Such a
switch would have been politically costly for the two senators (because of vigorous anti-pact sentiment at home), and
for the leadership. Byrd remarked that as it was, some of the
"yes" votes could cost senators their jobs.

But as one Senate staffer emphasized, the crisis
could have been averted by modifying DeConcini's language. Carter and many pro-pact senators thought it should
have been rewritten; no ideological division existed between the White House and the Senate on this score. Carter,
however, could not find the leverage to change DeConcini's
mind. If, the staffer argued, the Arizona Senator had been
left to the leadership, it would have modified the wording
and told him to take it or leave it. If DeConcini fought back,
he would have been reminded that he was 97th on the
seniority list of 100 senators, and that if the modifications
were not made, "You'll never get another bill passed as
long as you're here."

Carter, however, had taken the matter out of the Senate's hands. He also received bad advice from his Deputy
Secretary of State and the head of the State Department's
legal division, both of whom attended the President's decisive talk with DeConcini. Neither of the State Department
officials knew Latin America or understood the explosive-
ness of the DeConcini provision. During the next four
weeks as the Senate debated the second treaty, which
would govern the Canal until 2000, the administration desperately sought wording acceptable to both the determined
freshman senator and the embittered Maximum Chief.

A Single Thread

Torrijos was in trouble. In mid-February the largest
rally in Colon since 1968 protested not the treaties but his
domestic policies. After the Neutrality Treaty passed with

the DeConcini condition, Torrijos told his aides, "This is not a day for celebration. There is nothing to celebrate." A poll of 150 Panamanian businessmen, who were usually staunchly pro-U.S., showed 118 opposed to the amended treaty. A Panamanian, who owned one of the nation's largest breweries and also the Coca-Cola concession, originally voted for the pacts but turned against them after the Senate insisted on specifying "how, when and where the [U.S.] troops would come and rape us." A Panamanian lawyer labelled it "The DeConcini corollary to the Brezhnev doctrine. It says the U.S. can treat Panama the way the Russians treat the Hungarians and Czechs." Students began to move into the streets. On April 7 they burnt an effigy of Carter. Six days later youths destroyed a flag in front of Washington's embassy, and only National Guard forces prevented them from pulling down the embassy flag.[18] The anti-Yankee feelings could easily be turned against Torrijos's own regime.

On April 6 the General countered by sending letters to 115 heads of state implying that Panama would reject the treaties if the DeConcini condition remained.[19] Carter was deeply angered. His closest aide, Hamilton Jordan, called Panama City and demanded that the government issue a statement saying it had not decided to reject the pacts. Torrijos again acquiesced and the statement appeared, but Jordan's marching orders did nothing to lessen the tension in either Panama or the Senate.

Howard Baker lectured "our friends in Panama" that "just a twitch of an eyelid, just the slightest provocation . . . and the whole thing could go down the tube." Perhaps Baker was worried his own presidential hopes were going "down the tube," but no one doubted that the political situation was tightening. In six states—Wisconsin, Louisi-

18. *New York Times*, March 18, 1978, p.7:1; AP Wire Dispatches of April 9, 15, 7, 13 1978; *Washington Post*, April 12, 1978, p. A28:1; *Time*, April 24, 1978, p. 27.
19. Torrijos' letter and important related documents are in *Congressional Record*, CLXXIV (April 7, 1978), S4999–S5001.

ana, Missouri, Montana, DeConcini's Arizona, and Baker's Tennessee—anti-treaty groups organized campaigns to recall senators who had voted for ratification. The groups' chances for success were minute due to lack of time and the well-rooted precedent that only the Senate can remove its own members. But the signs were ominous and threatened to force several wavering senators to switch sides and thus kill the second treaty.

Anti-pact forces in the House of Representatives simultaneously moved to obtain Senate approval of an amendment giving the lower house a voice in the ratification process. The congressmen argued that since they had the constitutional right to dispose of U.S. property, they must have the power to act on a treaty that disposed of such property. The Senate disagreed, replying that many precedents existed for U.S. property being transferred under a treaty process requiring only Senate action. It was a nice constitutional point, but at bottom the Senate simply did not want to share its foreign policy powers with either the President or the House, and so swept away the proposed amendment. Congressmen then took their case to the Supreme Court. The Court denied the request, but postponed deciding whether to consider fully the merits of the case. Senator Edward Brooke (Rep.-Mass.) finally attached an amendment to the second treaty barring Carter from signing the pacts until March 31, 1979, or until Congress enacted implementing legislation, whichever occurred earlier. The Brooke amendment gave the Court and the House time to assert the lower body's authority, cause a small revolution in the conduct of foreign policy, and—because House opposition to them was greater than the Senate's—endanger the pacts.

On April 9, an embattled Carter described the chances of passing the second treaty as "hanging by a thread." The *Cincinnati Enquirer* caught the general feeling when it headlined the comment, "Canal Issue Has Carter on Brink of Calamity."[20] At this point Senator Byrd moved forward. Two

20. *Cincinnati Enquirer*, April 10, 1978, p.A7:1–2.

Senate staffers conducted head counts and agreed that no one had yet changed from the alignment on the first treaty vote. Byrd hoped that everyone would "cool it" and not overreact to Torrijos's efforts at placating angry Panamanians. The Senator then asked the White House to step aside while he used the leadership's power to work out an agreement with DeConcini. The discouraged administration turned the problem over to Byrd.

On Sunday, April 16 (two days before the scheduled vote on the second treaty), Byrd and Church met with Gabriel Lewis, Panama's Ambassador to the United States; William Rogers, former U.S. Assistant Secretary of State for Latin America, who had become a private intermediary between Torrijos and the State Department; Deputy Secretary of State Christopher; and Paul Sarbanes (Dem.-Md.) and Alan Cranston (Dem.-Calif.) who were floor leaders in the ratification struggle. The group began with a compromise draft offered by DeConcini, who was notably excluded from the session, and reworked it to Lewis's and the senators' satisfaction. When attached to the second treaty, the provision modified the DeConcini condition by stating that any United States action in Panama shall not be interpreted as indicating a right of intervention, nor have as its purpose "interference with [Panama's] political independence or sovereign integrity." DeConcini was then informed this constituted the acceptable compromise.

That same day a story appeared in the *Washington Post* that raised the fundamental question about the original DeConcini condition, and, indeed, about the demand of many North Americans that the United States reserve the eternal right to intervene militarily to keep the Canal open. Reporter Marlise Simons asked officials in the Zone whether the U.S. Army could operate the waterway in such an emergency. A spokesman replied that because of the long training required, "It would be ridiculous to say [we] could just take over canal operations." One Canal pilot believed "This place would turn into a ships' graveyard if the military just took over." He estimated that at least three years of practice would be required before outside pilots could guide large ships through. As for the Zonian pilots helping in an emergency, one said flatly, "I wouldn't return to bail out the government."[21] The right of U.S. military intervention seemed a good idea to most people in Washington, but few of them apparently had thought of what the military would be able to do after it intervened.

On April 18 the Senate accepted the modification of the DeConcini reservation by a vote of 73–27, then ratified the treaty 68–32. Every senator voted exactly as he or she did on the first treaty a month before. Carter immediately appeared on national television to underline the post-1973 policy premise that forced the treaties into existence: "These treaties can mark the beginning of a new era in our relations not only with Panama but with all the rest of the world. They symbolize our determination to deal with the developing nations of the world . . . on the basis of mutual respect and partnership." The President recognized another aspect of post-1973 U.S. foreign policy when he warmly congratulated Robert Byrd for his role in the Senate fight: "You're a great man—it was a beautiful vote."

Byrd, Baker, Church, Sarbanes, and Cranston succeeded in ramming the treaties through the Senate while defeating 77 amendments intended to emasculate or kill the agreements. Another pro-treaty hero was Democrat Ernest Hollings from South Carolina, a state in which anti-treaty sentiment was regularly whipped up by its powerful senior senator, Strom Thurmond. Hollings educated himself on the issue, supported the pacts from the start, and personally wrote newsletters to his constituents which included some of the best reasoned and researched material available to the pro-ratification forces. On the final day of voting Hollings spent hours with several wavering colleagues to keep them aboard. Less of a hero to the senators was Carter. They had desperately hoped he could deflect public opinion pressure from Capitol Hill, but he had not done so to

21. *Washington Post,* April 16, 1978, p.A22:1–2.

their satisfaction. His inability in March to force DeConcini to modify his language led to the debate's major crisis. As exhausted senators filed off the floor after the final vote, one was heard to mutter that Carter "couldn't sell [prostitutes] on a troop train."

To Panama—and Beyond

But Carter demonstrated considerable powers of persuasion in negotiating the treaties and then gaining the Senate leadership's agreement to push them after they were amended. He also displayed personal courage in traveling to Panama in June 1978 for a formal signing ceremony. The trip gained few if any votes for Carter at home and only further infuriated anti-pact forces, but one was forced to marvel at his decision to go into the Canal Zone and personally explain to frightened, bitter Zonians why the treaties were in the national interest, if not in their own. He pledged to take a direct role in assuring their personal security.

The visit, however, was aimed primarily at Latin Americans. Picking up the post-1973 arguments of Henry Kissinger and Sol Linowitz, among others, Carter understood that the treaties were critically important as part of a new United States approach to the southern hemispheres. The agreements, he told a huge rally in Panama City, go "far beyond the special concerns of the United States and Panama."[22]

Carter had actually waged the treaty fight on three levels: public opinion, the Senate, and Latin America policy. On the first his impact was minimal, although it perhaps blunted the massive conservative effort to kill the treaties. On the second he was ultimately saved by the Senate leadership. But on the third he won a major policy victory and flaunted it in a trip through Latin America during late March and again at the Panama City ceremonies. The danger was that he assumed too much. The treaties

22. Text of the speech is in *New York Times*, June 17, 1978, p.4:2–3.

removed a cancer in U.S.-Latin American relations, but did
little to resolve such other problems as human rights and
high tariffs which plagued hemispheric diplomats. "We've
warned the White House that the treaties are not very mar-
ketable in Latin America," one State Department official
said, but the President nevertheless "seemed determined to
push them."[23] At the same moment most senators only
wanted their constituents to forget about the pacts, Carter
was dangerously close to overselling them.

If Panamanian politics provided any clue, a rocky
road lay ahead for Washington's Latin American policies.
Although Torrijos proclaimed Carter's visit in June "the
Day of Liberation," the General's enthusiasm was restrained. The radioing of the Senate's insults to Panama,
the imposition of the DeConcini condition, an unshakable
economic depression, intense United States pressure to
ease his political controls, the appearance of a growing opposition movement—all combined to turn what should
have been triumph for Panama into a source of frustration.

The frustration grew in Panama during the debate,
peaked with the DeConcini condition, and did not greatly
subside even after the condition was modified and the
treaties ratified. Within twenty-four hours of the second
Senate vote, Torrijos shocked North Americans by announcing that if the treaties had been rejected he would
have sabotaged the Canal rather than enter into new negotiations. Howard Baker expressed anger and a Panamanian
political opponent duly announced that Torrijos "must be
on drugs." The post-1972 situation in Panama, however,
had developed into a crisis that made the General's outburst understandable. After all, a Western diplomat in Panama City observed, Torrijos "spent months bowing and
kissing the hands of visiting American senators, swallowing abuse. And all along he's had to keep his mouth shut
for fear of losing points."[24] Even as the United States

23. Ibid., June 19, 1978, p.A5:1.
24. Washington Post, April 20, 1978, p.A3:6.

moved to give up a colonial enclave, it could do so only by retaining some neo-colonial habits.

Torrijos had nevertheless played the game to the end. Except for the one outburst, he contained his anger. In late spring he allowed exiled politicians to return, despite an announcement by the four main political groups—the Panamañistas, Liberals, Christian Democrats, and Movement of Independent Lawyers—that after gaining power they would renounce the amended treaties. Only conservative business groups and the impotent Communist (People's) Party supported Torrijos. In return, the conservatives demanded key governmental positions and a further weakening of an already decimated union movement. Some of the oligarchy were positioning themselves to strike. "It's like the hunting season opened," one Panamanian official complained.[25]

In early June the most renowned of all the political head-hunters returned. Seventy-five-year-old Arnulfo Arias stepped off a private plane from Miami to be welcomed by 100,000 people. The political fires naturally heated up. Anti-treaty, radical student groups, led by the Socialist Revolutionary League, moved into the streets to protest Carter's visit. They were met by armed, pro-Torrijos students led by the Federation of Panamanian Students. Two radicals were killed. Only then did the National Guard clear the streets, close the university, and ensure quiet during the President's stay.

But such measures were Band-Aids for an economic infection that debilitated Panama and threatened its political stability. The nation's only hope was a long period of quiet in which it could use the new Canal revenues and outside investments for long overdue developmental projects to stop the rural-to-urban migration and ameliorate conditions in the packed slums of Panama City and Colon.

One careful observer believed the new treaties would improve neither those conditions nor U.S.-Panamanian re-

25. *Ibid.*, April 23, 1978, p.A21:3.

lations. Testifying before the Senate Foreign Relations Committee on the unamended treaties, Richard Falk, professor of International Law at Princeton, called the pacts "regressive and unwise, if not utterly imperial" since they provide for a long-term United States presence in Panama, give Washington a perpetual right of intervention in the Canal area, and thus, instead of calming Panamanian nationalist demands, "will probably make the United States the target of a continuing worldwide anticolonialist campaign." Since a large number of Panamanians oppose the agreements, Falk added, they can be effective only "if the Panamanian government becomes even more repressive than it already is." He urged a more rapid withdrawal from the Canal and the termination of U.S. military rights.[26]

The amended treaties are even more susceptible to Falk's criticism, for they spell out in greater detail the U.S. right of intervention. One "reservation" to the Neutrality Treaty also keeps open the possibility that if Panama agrees, U.S. troops can be stationed with the National Guard forces in the Canal area after 2000. Panamanian generals might accept such an arrangement since it would help keep open their access to Pentagon supply dumps and, more ominously, provide public evidence that the United States welcomed political cooperation with the military government. If this occurs, Falk's warning could come true: Panamanian political opposition will not be able to discriminate between their own regime and the U.S. government.

One hopes such a calamity will be avoided. The treaties opened new opportunities for the United States and Panama by putting their dealings on a more equal and equitable basis, and by giving the Panamanians greater control over their own resources and, consequently, their own political and economic policies. The treaty debate also gave the United States new opportunities, but not the opportunities addressed by the DeConcini condition. For the pri-

26. Falk's testimony is available in his "Panama Treaty Trap," *Foreign Policy*, no. 30 (Spring 1978), 69–82.

mary United States problem in the Third Cold War will not be carrying out military intervention or maintaining neo-colonial enclaves, but creating relationships with Panama and other newly emerging states so such intervention and enclaves are unnecessary.

The treaty debate was shaped by that general problem. Many opponents feared that surrendering the Canal enclave was "the culmination of the pattern of surrender and appeasement that has cost us so much all over the world," to use the words of Senator Orrin Hatch (Rep.-Utah). Hatch wondered aloud, "Is America really going the way of Rome?"[27] Such sentiments were heard in the treaty debate because it occurred in the wake of the searing experience in Vietnam, yet they made sense only if one assumed that the alternatives for the United States were either creating an empire or suffering the loss of the republic. The real opportunity, of course, is to avoid both of these alternatives by constructing policies that preserve republican virtues precisely by renouncing imperial practices. Panama presents one such opportunity. After three-quarters of a century, it is past time to close the chapter of North American colonialism on the Isthmus.

27. A short analysis of this context for the debate is provided by Robert G. Kaiser in *Washington Post,* April 12, 1978, p.A27:1–4.

Appendix

THE 1903 TREATY. THE "HAY-BUNAU-VARILLA" CONVENTION

Between the United States and Panama, Signed at Washington, November 18, 1903

The Treaty was ratified by the President of the United States, February 25, 1904.

Article 1

The United States guarantees and will maintain the independence of the Republic of Panama.

Article 2

The Republic of Panama grants to the United States in perpetuity the use, occupation and control of a zone of land and land under water for the construction, maintenance, operation, sanitation and protection of said Canal of the width of ten miles extending to the distance of five miles on each side of the center line of the route of the Canal to be constructed; the said zone beginning in the Caribbean Sea three marine miles from mean low water mark and extending to and across the Isthmus of Panama into the Pacific ocean to a distance of three marine miles from mean low water mark with the proviso that the cities of Panama and Colon and the harbors adjacent to said cities, which are included within the boundaries of the zone above described, shall not be included within this grant. The Republic of Panama further grants to the United States in perpetuity the use, occupation and control of any other lands and waters outside of the zone above described which may be necessary and convenient for the construction, maintenance, operation, sanitation and protection of the said Canal or of any auxiliary canals or other works necessary and convenient for the construction, maintenance, operation, sanitation and protection of the said enterprise.

The Republic of Panama further grants in like manner to the United States in perpetuity all islands within the limits of the zone above described and in addition thereto the group of small islands in the Bay of Panama, named Perico, Naos, Culebra and Flamenco.

Article 3

The Republic of Panama grants to the United States all the rights, power and authority within the zone mentioned and described in Article 2 of this agreement and within the limits of all auxiliary lands and waters mentioned and described in said Article 2 which the United States would possess and exercise if it were the sovereign of the territory within which said lands and waters are located to the entire exclusion of the exercise by the Republic of Panama of any such sovereign rights, power or authority.

Article 4

As rights subsidiary to the above grants the Republic of Panama grants in perpetuity to the United States the right to use the rivers, streams, lakes and other bodies of water within its limits for navigation, the supply of water or water-power or other purposes, so far as the use of said rivers, streams, lakes and bodies of water and the waters thereof may be necessary and convenient for the construction, maintenance, operation, sanitation and protection of the said Canal.

Article 5

The Republic of Panama grants to the United States in perpetuity a monopoly for the construction, maintenance and operation of any system of communication by means of canal or railroad across its territory between the Caribbean Sea and the Pacific ocean.

Article 6

The grants herein contained shall in no manner invalidate the titles or rights of private land holders or owners of private property in the said zone or in or to any of the lands or waters granted to the United States by the provisions of any Article of this treaty, nor shall they interfere with the rights of way over the public roads passing through the said zone or over any of the said lands or waters unless said rights of way or private rights shall conflict with rights herein granted to the United States in which case the rights of the United States shall be superior. All damages caused to the owners of private lands or private property of any kind by reason of the grants contained in this treaty or by reason of the operations of the United States, its agents or employees, or by reason of the construction, maintenance, operation, sanitation and protection of the said Canal or of the works of sanitation and protection herein provided for, shall be appraised and settled by a joint Commission appointed by the Governments of the United States and the Republic of Panama, whose decisions as to such damages shall be final and whose awards as to such damages shall be paid solely by the United States. No part of the work on said Canal or the Panama railroad or on any auxiliary works relating thereto and authorized by the terms of this treaty shall be prevented, delayed or impeded by or pending such proceedings to ascertain such damages. . . .

Article 7

The Republic of Panama grants to the United States within the limits of the cities of Panama and Colon and their adjacent harbors and within the territory adjacent thereto the right to acquire by purchase or by the exercise of the right of eminent domain, any lands, buildings, water rights or other properties necessary and convenient for the construction, maintenance, operation and protection of the Canal and of any works of sanitation, such as the collection and disposition of sewage and the distribution of water in the said cities of Panama and Colon, which, in the discretion of the United States may be necessary and convenient for the construction, maintenance, operation, sanitation and protection of the said Canal and railroad. . . .

The Republic of Panama agrees that the cities of Panama and Colon shall comply in perpetuity with the sanitary ordinances whether of a preventive or curative character prescribed by the United States and in case the Government of Panama is unable or fails in its duty to enforce this compliance by the cities of Panama and Colon with the sanitary ordinances of the United States the Republic of Panama grants to the United States the right and authority to enforce the same.

The same right and authority are granted to the United States for the maintenance of public order in the cities of Panama and Colon and the territories and harbors adjacent thereto in case the Republic of Panama should not be, in the judgment of the United States, able to maintain such order.

Article 8

The Republic of Panama grants to the United States all rights which it now has or hereafter may acquire to the property of the New Panama Canal Company and the Panama Railroad Company as a result of the transfer of sovereignty from the Republic of Colombia to the Republic of Panama over the Isthmus of Panama and authorizes the New Panama Canal Company to sell and transfer to the United States its rights, privileges, properties and concessions as well as the Panama Railroad and all the shares or part of the shares of that company; but the public lands situated outside of the zone described in Article 2 of this treaty now included in the concessions to both said enterprises and not required in the construction or operation of the Canal shall revert to the Republic of Panama except any property now owned by or in the possession of said companies within Panama or Colon or the ports or terminals thereof.

Article 9

The United States agrees that the ports at either entrance of the Canal and the waters thereof, and the Republic of Panama agrees that the towns of Panama and Colon shall be free for all time so that there shall not be imposed or collected custom house tolls, tonnage, anchorage, lighthouse, wharf, pilot, or quarantine dues or any other charges or taxes of any kind upon any vessel using or passing through the Canal or belonging to or employed by the United States, directly or indirectly, in connection with the construction, maintenance, operation, sanitation and protection of the main Canal, or auxiliary works, or upon the cargo, officers, crew, or passengers of any such vessels, except such tolls and charges as may be imposed by the United States for the use of the Canal and other works, and except tolls and charges imposed by the Republic of Panama upon merchandise destined to be introduced for the consumption of the rest of the Republic of Panama, and upon vessels touching at the ports of Colon and Panama and which do not cross the Canal.

The Government of the Republic of Panama shall have the right to establish in such ports and in the towns of Panama and Colon such houses and guards as it may deem necessary to collect duties on importations destined to other portions of Panama and to prevent contraband trade. The United States shall have the right to make use of the towns and harbors of Panama and Colon as places of anchorage, and for making repairs, for loading, unloading, depositing, or trans-shipping cargoes either in transit or destined for the service of the Canal and for other works pertaining to the Canal.

Article 10

The Republic of Panama agrees that there shall not be imposed any taxes, national, municipal, departmental, or of any other class, upon the Canal, the railways and auxiliary works, tugs and other vessels employed in the service of the Canal, store houses, work shops, offices, quarters for laborers, factories of all kinds, warehouses, wharves, machinery and other works, property, and effects appertaining to the Canal or railroad and auxiliary works, or their officers or employees, situated within the cities of Panama and Colon, and that there shall not be imposed contributions or charges of a personal character of any kind upon officers, employees, laborers, and other individuals in the service of the Canal and railroad and auxiliary works.

Article 11

The United States agrees that the official dispatches of the Government of the Republic of Panama shall be transmitted over any telegraph and telephone lines established for canal purposes and used for public and private business at rates not higher than those required from officials in the service of the United States.

Article 12

The Government of the Republic of Panama shall permit the immigration and free access to the lands and workshops of the Canal and its auxiliary works of all employees and workmen of whatever nationality under contract to work upon or seeking employment upon or in any wise connected with the said Canal and its auxiliary works, with their respective families, and all such persons shall be free and exempt from the military service of the Republic of Panama.

Article 13

The United States may import at any time into the said zone and auxiliary lands, free of custom duties, imposts, taxes, or other charges, and without any restrictions, any and all vessels, dredges, engines, cars, machinery, tools, explosives, materials, supplies, and other articles necessary and convenient in the construction, maintenance, operation, sanitation and protection of the Canal and auxiliary works, and all provisions, medicines, clothing, supplies and other things necessary and convenient for the officers, employees, workmen and laborers in the service and employ of the United States and for their families. If any such articles are disposed of for use outside of the zone and auxiliary lands granted to the United States and within the territory of the Republic, they shall be subject to the same import or other duties as like articles imported under the laws of the Republic of Panama.

Article 14

As the price or compensation for the rights, powers and privileges granted in this convention by the Republic of Panama to the United States, the Government of the United States agrees to pay to the Republic of Panama the sum of ten million dollars ($10,000,000) in gold coin of the United States on the exchange of the ratification of this convention and also an annual payment during the life of this convention of two hundred and fifty thousand dollars ($250,000) in like gold coin, beginning nine years after the date aforesaid.

The provisions of this Article shall be in addition to all other benefits assured to the Republic of Panama under this convention.

But no delay or difference of opinion under this Article or any other provisions of this treaty shall affect or interrupt the full operation and effect of this convention in all other respects. . . .

Article 18

The Canal, when constructed and the entrances thereto shall be neutral in perpetuity, and shall be opened upon the terms provided for by Section I of Article three of and in conformity with all the stipulations of the treaty entered into by the Governments of the United States and Great Britain on November 18, 1901.

Article 19

The Government of the Republic of Panama shall have the right to transport over the Canal its vessels and its troops and munitions of war in such vessels at all times without paying charges of any kind. The exemption is to be extended to the auxiliary railway for the transportation of persons in the service of the Republic of Panama, or of the police force charged with the preservation of public order outside of said zone, as well as to their baggage, munitions of war and supplies. . . .

Article 23

If it should become necessary at any time to employ armed forces for the safety or protection of the Canal, or of the ships that make use of the same, or the railways and auxiliary works, the United States shall have the right, at all times and in its discretion, to use its police and its land and naval forces or to establish fortifications for these purposes.

Article 24

No change either in the Government or in the laws and treaties of the Republic of Panama shall, without the consent of the United States, affect any right of the United States under the present convention, or under any treaty stipulation between the two countries that now exists or may hereafter exist touching the subject matter of this convention.

If the Republic of Panama shall hereafter enter as a constituent into any other Government or into any union or confederation of states, so as to merge her sovereignty or independence in such Government, union or confederation, the rights of the United States under this convention shall not be in any respect lessened or impaired.

Article 25

For the better performance of the engagements of this convention and to the end of the efficient protection of the Canal and the preservation of its neutrality, the Government of the Republic of Panama will sell or lease to the United States lands adequate and necessary for naval or coaling stations on the Pacific coast and on the western Caribbean coast of the Republic at certain points to be agreed upon with the President of the United States. . . .

PANAMA CANAL TREATY: 1977–1978

The United States of America and the Republic of Panama,

Acting in the spirit of the Joint Declaration of April 3, 1964, by the Representatives of the Governments of the United States of America and the Republic of Panama, and of the Joint Statement of Principles of February 7, 1974, initialed by the Secretary of State of the United States of America and the Foreign Minister of the Republic of Panama, and

Acknowledging the Republic of Panama's sovereignty over its territory,

Have decided to terminate the prior Treaties pertaining to the Panama Canal and to conclude a new Treaty to serve as the basis for a new relationship between them and, accordingly, have agreed upon the following:

Article I

Abrogation of Prior Treaties and Establishment of a New Relationship

1. Upon its entry into force, this Treaty terminates and supersedes:

        (a) The Isthmian Canal Convention between the

United States of America and the Republic of Panama, signed at Washington, November 18, 1903;

(b) The Treaty of Friendship and Cooperation signed at Washington, March 2, 1936, and the Treaty of Mutual Understanding and Cooperation and the related Memorandum of Understandings Reached, signed at Panama, January 25, 1955, between the United States of America and the Republic of Panama;

(c) All other treaties, conventions, agreements and exchanges of notes between the United States of America and the Republic of Panama concerning the Panama Canal which were in force prior to the entry into force of this Treaty. . . .

2. In accordance with the terms of this Treaty and related agreements, the Republic of Panama, as territorial sovereign, grants to the United States of America, for the duration of this Treaty, the rights necessary to regulate the transit of ships through the Panama Canal, and to manage, operate, maintain, improve, protect and defend the Canal. The Republic of Panama guarantees to the United States of America the peaceful use of the land and water areas which it has been granted the rights to use for such purposes pursuant to this Treaty and related agreements.

3. The Republic of Panama shall participate increasingly in the management and protection and defense of the Canal, as provided in this Treaty.

4. In view of the special relationship established by this Treaty, the United States of America and the Republic of Panama shall cooperate to assure the uninterrupted and efficient operation of the Panama Canal.

Article II

Ratification, Entry Into Force, and Termination

1. This Treaty shall be subject to ratification in accordance with the constitutional procedures of the two Parties. . . .

2. This Treaty shall terminate at noon, Panama time, December 31, 1999.

Article III

Canal Operation and Management

1. The Republic of Panama, as territorial sovereign, grants to the United States of America the rights to manage, oper-

ate, and maintain the Panama Canal, its complementary works, installations and equipment and to provide for the orderly transit of vessels through the Panama Canal. The United States of America accepts the grant of such rights and undertakes to exercise them in accordance with this Treaty and related agreements.

2. In carrying out the foregoing responsibilities, the United States of America may:

(a) Use for the aforementioned purposes, without cost except as provided in this Treaty, the various installations and areas (including the Panama Canal) and waters, described in the Agreement in Implementation of this Article, signed this date, as well as such other areas and installations as are made available to the United States of America under this Treaty and related agreements, and take the measures necessary to ensure sanitation of such areas;

(b) Make such improvements and alterations to the aforesaid installations and areas as it deems appropriate, consistent with the terms of this Treaty;

(c) Make and enforce all rules pertaining to the passage of vessels through the Canal and other rules with respect to navigation and maritime matters, in accordance with this Treaty and related agreements. The Republic of Panama will lend its cooperation, when necessary, in the enforcement of such rules;

(d) Establish, modify, collect and retain tolls for the use of the Panama Canal, and other charges, and establish and modify methods of their assessment;

(e) Regulate relations with employees of the United States Government;

(f) Provide supporting services to facilitate the performance of its responsibilities under this Article;

(g) Issue and enforce regulations for the effective exercise of the rights and responsibilities of the United States of America under this Treaty and related agreements. The Republic of Panama will lend its cooperation, when necessary, in the enforcement of such rules; and

(h) Exercise any other right granted under this Treaty, or otherwise agreed upon between the two Parties.

3. Pursuant to the foregoing grant of rights, the United States of America shall, in accordance with the terms of this Treaty and the provisions of United States law, carry out its responsibilities by means of a United States Government agency called the

Panama Canal Commission, which shall be constituted by and in conformity with the laws of the United States of America.

(a) The Panama Canal Commission shall be supervised by a Board composed of nine members, five of whom shall be nationals of the United States of America, and four of whom shall be Panamanian nationals proposed by the Republic of Panama for appointment to such positions by the United States of America in a timely manner.

(b) Should the Republic of Panama request the United States of America to remove a Panamanian national from membership on the Board, the United States of America shall agree to such request. In that event, the Republic of Panama shall propose another Panamanian national for appointment by the United States of America to such position in a timely manner. In case of removal of a Panamanian member of the Board at the initiative of the United States of America, both Parties will consult in advance in order to reach agreement concerning such removal, and the Republic of Panama shall propose another Panamanian national for appointment by the United States of America in his stead.

(c) The United States of America shall employ a national of the United States of America as Administrator of the Panama Canal Commission, and a Panamanian national as Deputy Administrator, through December 31, 1989. Beginning January 1, 1990, a Panamanian national shall be employed as the Administrator and a national of the United States of America shall occupy the position of Deputy Administrator. Such Panamanian nationals shall be proposed to the United States of America by the Republic of Panama for appointment to such positions by the United States of America.

(d) Should the United States of America remove the Panamanian national from his position as Deputy Administrator, or Administrator, the Republic of Panama shall propose another Panamanian national for appointment to such position by the United States of America. . . .

5. The Panama Canal Commission shall reimburse the Republic of Panama for the costs incurred by the Republic of Panama in providing the following public services in the Canal operating areas and in housing areas set forth in the Agreement in Implementation of Article III of this Treaty and occupied by both United States and Panamanian citizen employees of the Panama Canal Commission: police, fire protection, street maintenance,

street lighting, street cleaning, traffic management and garbage collection. The Panama Canal Commission shall pay the Republic of Panama the sum of ten million United States dollars ($10,000,000) per annum for the foregoing services. It is agreed that every three years from the date that this Treaty enters into force, the costs involved in furnishing said services shall be reexamined to determine whether adjustment of the annual payment should be made because of inflation and other relevant factors affecting the cost of such services.

6. The Republic of Panama shall be responsible for providing, in all areas comprising the former Canal Zone, services of a general jurisdictional nature such as customs and immigration, postal services, courts and licensing, in accordance with this Treaty and related agreements.

7. The United States of America and the Republic of Panama shall establish a Panama Canal Consultative Committee, composed of an equal number of high-level representatives of the United States of America and the Republic of Panama, and which may appoint such subcommittees as it may deem appropriate. This Committee shall advise the United States of America and the Republic of Panama on matters of policy affecting the Canal's operation. In view of both Parties' special interest in the continuity and efficiency of the Canal operation in the future, the Committee shall advise on matters such as general tolls policy, employment and training policies to increase the participation of Panamanian nationals in the operation of the Canal, and international policies on matters concerning the Canal. The Committee's recommendations shall be transmitted to the two Governments, which shall give such recommendations full consideration in the formulation of such policy decisions.

8. In addition to the participation of Panamanian nationals at high management levels of the Panama Canal Commission, as provided for in paragraph 3 of this Article, there shall be growing participation of Panamanian nationals at all other levels and areas of employment in the aforesaid commission, with the objective of preparing, in an orderly and efficient fashion, for the assumption by the Republic of Panama of full responsibility for the management, operation and maintenance of the Canal upon the termination of this Treaty. . . .

10. Upon entry into force of this Treaty, the United States Government agencies known as the Panama Canal Company and

the Canal Zone Government shall cease to operate within the territory of the Republic of Panama that formerly constituted the Canal Zone.

Article IV

Protection and Defense

1. The United States of America and the Republic of Panama commit themselves to protect and defend the Panama Canal. Each Party shall act, in accordance with its constitutional processes, to meet the danger resulting from an armed attack or other actions which threaten the security of the Panama Canal or of ships transiting it.

2. For the duration of this Treaty, the United States of America shall have primary responsibility to protect and defend the Canal. The rights of the United States of America to station, train, and move military forces within the Republic of Panama are described in the Agreement in Implementation of this Article, signed this date. The use of areas and installations and the legal status of the armed forces of the United States of America in the Republic of Panama shall be governed by the aforesaid Agreement.

3. In order to facilitate the participation and cooperation of the armed forces of both Parties in the protection and defense of the Canal, the United States of America and the Republic of Panama shall establish a Combined Board comprised of an equal number of senior military representatives of each Party. These representatives shall be charged by their respective governments with consulting and cooperating on all matters pertaining to the protection and defense of the Canal, and with planning for actions to be taken in concert for that purpose. Such combined protection and defense arrangements shall not inhibit the identity or lines of authority of the armed forces of the United States of America or the Republic of Panama. The Combined Board shall provide for coordination and cooperation concerning such matters as:

(a) The preparation of contingency plans for the protection and defense of the Canal based upon the cooperative efforts of the armed forces of both Parties;

(b) The planning and conduct of combined military exercises; and

(c) The conduct of United States and Panamanian

military operations with respect to the protection and defense of the Canal.

4. The Combined Board shall, at five-year intervals throughout the duration of this Treaty, review the resources being made available by the two Parties for the protection and defense of the Canal. Also, the Combined Board shall make appropriate recommendations to the two Governments respecting projected requirements, the efficient utilization of available resources of the two Parties, and other matters of mutual interest with respect to the protection and defense of the Canal.

5. To the extent possible consistent with its primary responsibility for the protection and defense of the Panama Canal, the United States of America will endeavor to maintain its armed forces in the Republic of Panama in normal times at a level not in excess of that of the armed forces of the United States of America in the territory of the former Canal Zone immediately prior to the entry into force of this Treaty.

Article V

Principle of Non-Intervention

Employees of the Panama Canal Commission, their dependents and designated contractors of the Panama Canal Commission, who are nationals of the United States of America, shall respect the laws of the Republic of Panama and shall abstain from any activity incompatible with the spirit of this Treaty. Accordingly, they shall abstain from any political activity in the Republic of Panama as well as from any intervention in the internal affairs of the Republic of Panama. The United States of America shall take all measures within its authority to ensure that the provisions of this Article are fulfilled.

Article VI

Protection of the Environment

1. The United States of America and the Republic of Panama commit themselves to implement this Treaty in a manner consistent with the protection of the natural environment of the Republic of Panama. To this end, they shall consult and cooperate with

each other in all appropriate ways to ensure that they shall give due regard to the protection and conservation of the environment. . . .

Article VII

Flags

1. The entire territory of the Republic of Panama, including the areas the use of which the Republic of Panama makes available to the United States of America pursuant to this Treaty and related agreements, shall be under the flag of the Republic of Panama, and consequently such flag always shall occupy the position of honor. . . .

Article IX

Applicable Laws and Law Enforcement

1. In accordance with the provisions of this Treaty and related agreements, the law of the Republic of Panama shall apply in the areas made available for the use of the United States of America pursuant to this Treaty. The law of the Republic of Panama shall be applied to matters or events which occurred in the former Canal Zone prior to the entry into force of this Treaty only to the extent specifically provided in prior treaties and agreements.

2. Natural or juridical persons who, on the date of entry into force of this Treaty, are engaged in business or non-profit activities at locations in the former Canal Zone may continue such business or activities at those locations under the same terms and conditions prevailing prior to the entry into force of this Treaty for a thirty-month transition period from its entry into force. The Republic of Panama shall maintain the same operating conditions as those applicable to the aforementioned enterprises prior to the entry into force of this Treaty in order that they may receive licenses to do business in the Republic of Panama subject to their compliance with the requirements of its law. Thereafter, such persons shall receive the same treatment under the law of the Republic of Panama as similar enterprises already established in the rest of the territory of the Republic of Panama without discrimination.

3. The rights of ownership, as recognized by the United States of America, enjoyed by natural or juridical private persons in buildings and other improvements to real property located in

the former Canal Zone shall be recognized by the Republic of Panama in conformity with its laws. . . .

11. The Parties shall conclude an agreement whereby nationals of either State, who are sentenced by the courts of the other State, and who are not domiciled therein, may elect to serve their sentences in their State of nationality.

Article X

Employment with the Panama Canal Commission

1. In exercising its rights and fulfilling its responsibilities as the employer, the United States of America shall establish employment and labor regulations which shall contain the terms, conditions and prerequisites for all categories of employees of the Panama Canal Commission. These regulations shall be provided to the Republic of Panama prior to their entry into force.

2. (a) The regulations shall establish a system of preference when hiring employees, for Panamanian applicants possessing the skills and qualifications required for employment by the Panama Canal Commission. The United States of America shall endeavor to ensure that the number of Panamanian nationals employed by the Panama Canal Commission in relation to the total number of its employees will conform to the proportion established for foreign enterprises under the law of the Republic of Panama.

(b) The terms and conditions of employment to be established will in general be no less favorable to persons already employed by the Panama Canal Company or Canal Zone Government prior to the entry into force of this Treaty, than those in effect immediately prior to that date.

3. (a) The United States of America shall establish an employment policy for the Panama Canal Commission that shall generally limit the recruitment of personnel outside the Republic of Panama to persons possessing requisite skills and qualifications which are not available in the Republic of Panama.

(b) The United States of America will establish training programs for Panamanian employees and apprentices in order to increase the number of Panamanian nationals qualified to assume positions with the Panama Canal Commission, as positions become available.

(c) Within five years from the entry into force of this Treaty, the number of United States nationals employed by the Panama Canal Commission who were previously employed by the Panama Canal Company shall be at least twenty percent less than the total number of United States nationals working for the Panama Canal Company immediately prior to the entry into force of this Treaty. . . .

6. With regard to wages and fringe benefits, there shall be no discrimination on the basis of nationality, sex, or race. Payments by the Panama Canal Commission of additional remuneration, or the provision of other benefits, such as home leave benefits, to United States nationals employed prior to entry into force of this Treaty, or to persons of any nationality, including Panamanian nationals who are thereafter recruited outside of the Republic of Panama and who change their place of residence, shall not be considered to be discrimination for the purpose of this paragraph.

7. Persons employed by the Panama Canal Company or Canal Zone Government prior to the entry into force of this Treaty, who are displaced from their employment as a result of the discontinuance by the United States of America of certain activities pursuant to this Treaty, will be placed by the United States of America, to the maximum extent feasible, in other appropriate jobs with the Government of the United States in accordance with United States Civil Service regulations. For such persons who are not United States nationals, placement efforts will be confined to United States Government activities located within the Republic of Panama. Likewise, persons previously employed in activities for which the Republic of Panama assumes responsibility as a result of this Treaty will be continued in their employment to the maximum extent feasible by the Republic of Panama. The Republic of Panama shall, to the maximum extent feasible, ensure that the terms and conditions of employment applicable to personnel employed in the activities for which it assumes responsibility are no less favorable than those in effect immediately prior to the entry into force of this Treaty. . . .

Article XI

Provisions for the Transition Period

1. The Republic of Panama shall reassume plenary jurisdiction over the former Canal Zone upon entry into force of this

Treaty and in accordance with its terms. In order to provide for an orderly transition to the full application of the jurisdictional arrangements established by this Treaty and related agreements, the provisions of this Article shall become applicable upon the date this Treaty enters into force, and shall remain in effect for thirty calendar months. The authority granted in this Article to the United States of America for this transition period shall supplement, and is not intended to limit, the full application and effect of the rights and authority granted to the United States of America elsewhere in this Treaty and in related agreements.

2. During this transition period, the criminal and civil laws of the United States of America shall apply concurrently with those of the Republic of Panama in certain of the areas and installations made available for the use of the United States of America pursuant to this Treaty, in accordance with the following provisions:

(a) The Republic of Panama permits the authorities of the United States of America to have the primary right to exercise criminal jurisdiction over United States citizen employees of the Panama Canal Commission and their dependents, and members of the United States Forces and civilian component and their dependents, in the following cases:

(i) for any offense committed during the transition period within such areas and installations, and

(ii) for any offense committed prior to that period in the former Canal Zone.

The Republic of Panama shall have the primary right to exercise jurisdiction over all other offenses committed by such persons, except as otherwise provided in this Treaty and related agreements or as may be otherwise agreed.

(b) Either Party may waive its primary right to exercise jurisdiction in a specific case or category of cases.

3. The United States of America shall retain the right to exercise jurisdiction in criminal cases relating to offenses committed prior to the entry into force of this Treaty in violation of the laws applicable in the former Canal Zone.

4. For the transition period, the United States of America shall retain police authority and maintain a police force in the aforementioned areas and installations. . . .

5. The courts of the United States of America and related personnel, functioning in the former Canal Zone immediately prior to the entry into force of this Treaty, may continue to func-

tion during the transition period for the judicial enforcement of the jurisdiction to be exercised by the United States of America in accordance with this Article. . . .

Article XII

A Sea-Level Canal or a Third Lane of Locks

1. The United States of America and the Republic of Panama recognize that a sea-level canal may be important for international navigation in the future. Consequently, during the duration of this Treaty, both Parties commit themselves to study jointly the feasibility of a sea-level canal in the Republic of Panama, and in the event they determine that such a waterway is necessary, they shall negotiate terms, agreeable to both Parties, for its construction.

2. The United States of America and the Republic of Panama agree on the following:

(a) No new interoceanic canal shall be constructed in the territory of the Republic of Panama during the duration of this Treaty, except in accordance with the provisions of this Treaty, or as the two Parties may otherwise agree; and

(b) During the duration of this Treaty, the United States of America shall not negotiate with third States for the right to construct an interoceanic canal on any other route in the Western Hemisphere, except as the two Parties may otherwise agree.

3. The Republic of Panama grants to the United States of America the right to add a third lane of locks to the existing Panama Canal. This right may be exercised at any time during the duration of this Treaty, provided that the United States of America has delivered to the Republic of Panama copies of the plans for such construction.

4. In the event the United States of America exercises the right granted in paragraph 3 above, it may use for that purpose, in addition to the areas otherwise made available to the United States of America pursuant to this Treaty, such other areas as the two Parties may agree upon. The terms and conditions applicable to Canal operating areas made available by the Republic of Panama for the use of the United States of America pursuant to Article III of this Treaty shall apply in a similar manner to such additional areas.

5. In the construction of the aforesaid works, the United States of America shall not use nuclear excavation techniques without the previous consent of the Republic of Panama.

Article XIII

Property Transfer and Economic Participation by the Republic of Panama

1. Upon termination of this Treaty, the Republic of Panama shall assume total responsibility for the management, operation, and maintenance of the Panama Canal, which shall be turned over in operating condition and free of liens and debts, except as the two Parties may otherwise agree. . . .

4. The Republic of Panama shall receive, in addition, from the Panama Canal Commission a just and equitable return on the national resources which it has dedicated to the efficient management, operation, maintenance, protection and defense of the Panama Canal, in accordance with the following:

(a) An annual amount to be paid out of Canal operating revenues computed at a rate of thirty hundredths of a United States dollar ($0.30) per Panama Canal net ton, or its equivalency, for each vessel transiting the Canal after the entry into force of this Treaty, for which tolls are charged. The rate of thirty hundredths of a United States dollar ($0.30) per Panama Canal net ton, or its equivalency, will be adjusted to reflect changes in the United States wholesale price index for total manufactured goods during biennial periods. The first adjustment shall take place five years after entry into force of this Treaty, taking into account the changes that occurred in such price index during the preceding two years. Thereafter, successive adjustments shall take place at the end of each biennial period. If the United States of America should decide that another indexing method is preferable, such method shall be proposed to the Republic of Panama and applied if mutually agreed.

(b) A fixed annuity of ten million United States dollars ($10,000,000) to be paid out of Canal operating revenues. This amount shall constitute a fixed expense of the Panama Canal Commission.

(c) An annual amount of up to ten million United

States dollars ($10,000,000) per year, to be paid out of Canal operating revenues to the extent that such revenues exceed expenditures of the Panama Canal Commission including amounts paid pursuant to this Treaty. In the event Canal operating revenues in any year do not produce a surplus sufficient to cover this payment, the unpaid balance shall be paid from operating surpluses in future years in a manner to be mutually agreed.

Article XIV

Settlement of Disputes

In the event that any question should arise between the Parties concerning the interpretation of this Treaty or related agreements, they shall make every effort to resolve the matter through consultation in the appropriate committees established pursuant to this Treaty and related agreements, or, if appropriate, through diplomatic channels. In the event the Parties are unable to resolve a particular matter through such means, they may, in appropriate cases, agree to submit the matter to conciliation, mediation, arbitration, or such other procedure for the peaceful settlement of the dispute as they may mutually deem appropriate.

DONE at Washington, this 7th day of September, 1977, in duplicate, in the English and Spanish languages, both texts being equally authentic.

TREATY CONCERNING THE PERMANENT NEUTRALITY AND OPERATION OF THE PANAMA CANAL: 1977–1978

The United States of America and the Republic of Panama have agreed upon the following:

Article I

The Republic of Panama declares that the Canal, as an international transit waterway, shall be permanently neutral in accordance with the regime established in this Treaty. The same regime of neutrality shall apply to any other international waterway that may be built either partially or wholly in the territory of the Republic of Panama.

Article II

The Republic of Panama declares the neutrality of the Canal in order that both in time of peace and in time of war it shall remain secure and open to peaceful transit by the vessels of all nations on terms of entire equality, so that there will be no discrimination against any nation, or its citizens or subjects, concerning the conditions or charges of transit, or for any other reason, and so that the Canal, and therefore the Isthmus of Panama, shall not be the target of reprisals in any armed conflict between other nations of the world. The foregoing shall be subject to the following requirements:

(a) Payment of tolls and other charges for transit and ancillary services, provided they have been fixed in conformity with the provisions of Article III(c);

(b) Compliance with applicable rules and regulations, provided such rules and regulations are applied in conformity with the provisions of Article III;

(c) The requirement that transiting vessels commit no acts of hostility while in the Canal; and

(d) Such other conditions and restrictions as are established by this Treaty.

Article III

1. For purposes of the security, efficiency and proper maintenance of the Canal the following rules shall apply:

(a) The Canal shall be operated efficiently in accordance with conditions of transit through the Canal, and rules and regulations that shall be just, equitable and reasonable, and limited to those necessary for safe navigation and efficient, sanitary operation of the Canal;

(b) Ancillary services necessary for transit through the Canal shall be provided;

(c) Tolls and other charges for transit and ancillary services shall be just, reasonable, equitable and consistent with the principles of international law;

(d) As a pre-condition of transit, vessels may be required to establish clearly the financial responsibility and guarantees for payment of reasonable and adequate indemnification, consistent with international practice and standards, for damages resulting from acts or omissions of such vessels when passing through the Canal. In the case of vessels owned or operated by a State or for which it has acknowledged responsibility, a certification by that State that it shall observe its obligations under international law to pay for damages resulting from the act or omission of such vessels when passing through the Canal shall be deemed sufficient to establish such financial responsibility;

(e) Vessels of war and auxiliary vessels of all nations shall at all times be entitled to transit the Canal, irrespective of their internal operation, means of propulsion, origin, destination or armament, without being subjected, as a condition of transit, to inspection, search or surveillance. However, such vessels may be required to certify that they have complied with all applicable health, sanitation and quarantine regulations. In addition, such vessels shall be entitled to refuse to disclose their internal operation, origin, armament, cargo or destination. However, auxiliary vessels may be required to present written assurances, certified by an official at a high level of the government of the State requesting the exemption, that they are owned or operated by that government and in this case are being used only on government noncommercial service.

2. For the purposes of this Treaty, the terms "Canal," "vessel of war," "auxiliary vessel," "internal operation," "armament" and "inspection" shall have the meanings assigned them in Annex A to this Treaty.

Article IV

The United States of America and the Republic of Panama agree to maintain the regime of neutrality established in this Treaty, which shall be maintained in order that the Canal shall remain permanently neutral, notwithstanding the termination of any other treaties entered into by the two Contracting Parties.

Article V

After the termination of the Panama Canal Treaty, only the Republic of Panama shall operate the Canal and maintain military forces, defense sites and military installations within its national territory.

Article VI

1. In recognition of the important contributions of the United States of America and of the Republic of Panama to the construction, operation, maintenance, and protection and defense of the Canal, vessels of war and auxiliary vessels of those nations shall, notwithstanding any other provisions of this Treaty, be entitled to transit the Canal irrespective of their internal operation, means of propulsion, origin, destination, armament or cargo carried. Such vessels of war and auxiliary vessels will be entitled to transit the Canal expeditiously.

2. The United States of America, so long as it has responsibility for the operation of the Canal, may continue to provide the Republic of Colombia toll-free transit through the Canal for its troops, vessels and materials of war. Thereafter, the Republic of Panama may provide the Republic of Colombia and the Republic of Costa Rica with the right of toll-free transit.

Article VII

1. The United States of America and the Republic of Panama shall jointly sponsor a resolution in the Organization of American States opening to accession by all nations of the world the Protocol to this Treaty whereby all the signatories will adhere to the objectives of this Treaty, agreeing to respect the regime of neutrality set forth herein.

2. The Organization of American States shall act as the depositary for this Treaty and related instruments.

Article VIII

This Treaty shall be subject to ratification in accordance with the constitutional procedures of the two Parties. The instruments of ratification of this Treaty shall be exchanged at Panama at the same time as the instruments of ratification of the Panama Canal Treaty, signed this date, are exchanged. This Treaty shall enter into force, simultaneously with the Panama Canal Treaty, six calendar months from the date of the exchange of the instruments of ratification.

DONE at Washington, this 7th day of September, 1977, in the English and Spanish languages, both texts being equally authentic.

Protocol to the Treaty Concerning the Permanent Neutrality and Operation of the Panama Canal

Whereas the maintenance of the neutrality of the Panama Canal is important not only to the commerce and security of the United States of America and the Republic of Panama, but to the peace and security of the Western Hemisphere and to the interests of world commerce as well;

Whereas the regime of neutrality which the United States of America and the Republic of Panama have agreed to maintain will ensure permanent access to the Canal by vessels of all nations on the basis of entire equality; and

Whereas the said regime of effective neutrality shall constitute the best protection for the Canal and shall ensure the absence of any hostile act against it;

The Contracting Parties to this Protocol have agreed upon the following:

Article I

The Contracting Parties hereby acknowledge the regime of permanent neutrality for the Canal established in the Treaty Concerning the Permanent Neutrality and Operation of the Panama Canal and associate themselves with its objectives.

Article II

The Contracting Parties agree to observe and respect the regime of permanent neutrality of the Canal in time of war as in time of peace, and to ensure that vessels of their registry strictly observe the applicable rules.

Article III

This Protocol shall be open to accession by all States of the world, and shall enter into force for each State at the time of deposit of its instrument of accession with the Secretary General of the Organization of American States.

Senate additions to Neutrality Treaty
March 16, 1978

Resolved (two-thirds of the Senators present concurring therein), That the Senate advise and consent to the ratification of the Treaty Concerning the Permanent Neutrality and Operation of the Panama Canal, together with Annexes A and B thereto and the Protocol relating thereto, done at Washington on September 7, 1977 (Executive N, Ninety-fifth Congress, first session), subject to the following—

(a) Amendments:

(1) At the end of Article IV, insert the following:

"A correct and authoritative statement of certain rights and duties of the Parties under the foregoing is contained in the Statement of Understanding issued by the Government of the United States of America on October 14, 1977, and by the Government of the Republic of Panama on October 18, 1977, which is hereby incorporated as an integral part of this Treaty, as follows:

" 'Under the Treaty Concerning the Permanent Neutrality and Operation of the Panama Canal (the Neutrality Treaty), Panama and the United States have the responsibility to assure that the Panama Canal will remain open and secure to ships of all nations. The correct interpretation of this principle is that each of the two countries shall, in accordance with their respective constitutional processes, defend the Canal against any threat to the regime of neutrality, and consequently shall have the right to act against any aggression or threat directed against the Canal or against the peaceful transit of vessels through the Canal.

" 'This does not mean, nor shall it be interpreted as, a right of intervention of the United States in the internal affairs of Panama. Any United States action will be directed at insuring that the Canal will remain open, secure, and accessible, and it shall never be directed against the territorial integrity or political independence of Panama.'."

(2) At the end of the first paragraph of Article VI, insert the following:

"In accordance with the Statement of Understanding mentioned in Article IV above: 'The Neutrality Treaty provides that the vessels of war and auxiliary vessels of the United States and Panama will be entitled to transit the Canal expeditiously. This is intended, and it shall so be interpreted, to assure the transit of such vessels through the Canal as quickly as possible, without any impediment, with expedited treatment, and in case of need or emergency, to go to the head of the line of vessels in order to transit the Canal rapidly.' "

(b) Conditions:

(1) Notwithstanding the provisions of Article V or any other provision of the Treaty, if the Canal is closed, or its operations are interfered with, the United States of America and the Republic of Panama shall each independently have the right to take such steps as each deems necessary, in accordance with its constitutional processes, including the use of military force in the Republic of Panama, to reopen the Canal or restore the operations of the Canal, as the case may be.

(2) The instruments of ratification of the Treaty shall be exchanged only upon the conclusion of a Protocol of Exchange, to be signed by authorized representatives of both Governments, which shall constitute an integral part of the Treaty documents and which shall include the following:

> "Nothing in the Treaty shall preclude the Republic of Panama and the United States of America from making, in accordance with their respective constitutional processes, any agreement or arrangement between the two countries to facilitate performance at any time after December 31, 1999, of their responsibilities to maintain the regime of neutrality established in the Treaty, including agreements or arrangements for the stationing of any United States military forces or the maintenance of defense sites after that date in the Republic of Panama that the Republic of Panama and the United States of America may deem necessary or appropriate.".

(c) Reservations:. . . .

(4) To carry out the purposes of Article III of the Treaty of assuring the security, efficiency, and proper maintenance of the Panama Canal, the United States of America and the Republic of Panama, during their respective periods of responsibility for Canal operation and maintenance, shall, unless the amount of the operating revenues of the Canal exceeds the amount needed to carry

out the purposes of such Article, use such revenues of the Canal only for purposes consistent with the purposes of Article III.

(d) Understandings:

(1) Paragraph 1(c) of Article III of the Treaty shall be construed as requiring, before any adjustment in tolls for use of the Canal, that the effects of any such toll adjustment on the trade patterns of the two Parties shall be given full consideration, including consideration of the following factors in a manner consistent with the regime of neutrality:

(A) the costs of operating and maintaining the Panama Canal;

(B) the competitive position of the use of the Canal in relation to other means of transportation;

(C) the interests of both Parties in maintaining their domestic fleets;

(D) the impact of such an adjustment on the various geographical areas of each of the two Parties; and

(E) the interests of both Parties in maximizing their international commerce.

The United States of America and the Republic of Panama shall cooperate in exchanging information necessary for the consideration of such factors.

(2) The agreement 'to maintain the regime of neutrality established in this Treaty' in Article IV of the Treaty means that either of the two Parties to the Treaty may, in accordance with its constitutional processes, take unilateral action to defend the Panama Canal against any threat, as determined by the Party taking such action.

(3) The determination of 'need or emergency' for the purpose of any vessel of war or auxiliary vessel of the United States of America or the Republic of Panama going to the head of the line of vessels in order to transit the Panama Canal rapidly shall be made by the nation operating such vessel.

(4) Nothing in the Treaty, in Annex A or B thereto, in the Protocol relating to the Treaty, or in any other agreement relating to the Treaty, obligates the United States of America to provide any economic assistance, military grant assistance, security supporting assistance, foreign military sales credits, or international military education and training to the Republic of Panama.

(5) The President shall include all amendments, conditions, reservations, and understandings incorporated by the Senate in this resolution of ratification in the instrument of ratification to be exchanged with the Government of the Republic of Panama.

U.S. Senate additions to Canal Treaty
April 18, 1978

Resolved (two-thirds of the Senators present concurring therein), That the Senate advise and consent to the ratification of the Panama Canal Treaty, together with the Annex and Agreed Minute relating thereto, done at Washington on September 7, 1977 (Executive N, Ninety-fifth Congress, first session), subject to the following—

(a) Reservations:

(1) Pursuant to its adherence to the principle of nonintervention, any action taken by the United States of America in the exercise of its rights to assure that the Panama Canal shall remain open, neutral, secure, and accessible, pursuant to the provisions of the Panama Canal Treaty, the Treaty Concerning the Permanent Neutrality and Operation of the Panama Canal, and the resolutions of ratification thereto, shall be only for the purpose of assuring that the Canal shall remain open, neutral, secure, and accessible, and shall not have as its purpose or be interpreted as a right of intervention in the internal affairs of the Republic of Panama or interference with its political independence or sovereign integrity.

(2) The instruments of ratification of the Panama Canal Treaty to be exchanged by the United States of America and the Republic of Panama shall each include provisions whereby each Party agrees to waive its rights and release the other Party from its obligations under paragraph 2 of Article XII of the Treaty.

(3) Notwithstanding any provision of the Treaty, no funds may be drawn from the Treasury of the United States of America for payments under paragraph 4 of Article XIII without statutory authorization.

(4) Any accumulated unpaid balance under paragraph 4(c)

of Article XIII of the Treaty at the date of termination of the Treaty shall be payable only to the extent of any operating surplus in the last year of the duration of the Treaty, and nothing in such paragraph may be construed as obligating the United States of America to pay, after the date of the termination of the Treaty, any such unpaid balance which shall have accrued before such date.

(5) Exchange of the instruments of ratification of the Panama Canal Treaty and of the Treaty Concerning the Permanent Neutrality and Operation of the Panama Canal shall not be effective earlier than March 31, 1979, and such Treaties shall not enter into force prior to October 1, 1979, unless legislation necessary to implement the provisions of the Panama Canal Treaty shall have been enacted by the Congress of the United States of America before March 31, 1979.

(6) After the date of entry into force of the Treaty, the Panama Canal Commission shall, unless otherwise provided by legislation enacted by the Congress of the United States of America, be obligated to reimburse the Treasury of the United States of America, as nearly as possible, for the interest cost of the funds or other assets directly invested in the Commission by the Government of the United States of America and for the interest cost of the funds or other assets directly invested in the predecessor Panama Canal Company by the Government of the United States of America and not reimbursed before the date of entry into force of the Treaty. Such reimbursement for such interest costs shall be made at a rate determined by the Secretary of the Treasury of the United States of America and at annual intervals to the extent earned, and if not earned, shall be made from subsequent earnings. For purposes of this reservation, the phrase "funds or other assets directly invested" shall have the same meaning as the phrase "net direct investment" has under section 62 of title 2 of the Canal Zone Code.

(b) Understandings:

(1) Before the first day of the three-year period beginning on the date of entry into force of the Treaty and before each three-year period following thereafter, the two Parties shall agree upon the specific levels and quality of services, as are referred to in paragraph 5 of Article III of the Treaty, to be provided during the

following three-year period and, except for the first three-year period, on the reimbursement to be made for the costs of such services, such services to be limited to such as are essential to the effective functioning of the Canal operating areas and the housing areas referred to in paragraph 5 of Article III. If payments made under paragraph 5 of Article III for the preceding three-year period, including the initial three-year period, exceed or are less than the actual costs to the Republic of Panama for supplying, during such period, the specific levels and quality of services agreed upon, then the Panama Canal Commission shall deduct from or add to the payment required to be made to the Republic of Panama for each of the following three years one-third of such excess or deficit, as the case may be. There shall be an independent and binding audit, conducted by an auditor mutually selected by both Parties, of any costs of services disputed by the two Parties pursuant to the reexamination of such costs provided for in this understanding.

(2) Nothing in paragraph 3, 4, or 5 of Article IV of the Treaty may be construed to limit either the provisions of the first paragraph of Article IV providing that each Party shall act, in accordance with its constitutional processes, to meet danger threatening the security of the Panama Canal, or the provisions of paragraph 2 of Article IV providing that the United States of America shall have primary responsibility to protect and defend the Canal for the duration of the Treaty.

(3) Nothing in paragraph 4(c) of Article XIII of the Treaty shall be construed to limit the authority of the United States of America, through the United States Government agency called the Panama Canal Commission, to make such financial decisions and incur such expenses as are reasonable and necessary for the management, operation, and maintenance of the Panama Canal. In addition, toll rates established pursuant to paragraph 2(d) of Article III need not be set at levels designed to produce revenues to cover the payment to the Republic of Panama described in paragraph 4(c) of Article XIII.

(4) Any agreement concluded pursuant to paragraph 11 of Article IX of the Treaty with respect to the transfer of prisoners shall be concluded in accordance with the constitutional processes of both Parties.

(5) Nothing in the Treaty, in the Annex or Agreed Minute

relating to the Treaty, or in any other agreement relating to the Treaty obligates the United States of America to provide any economic assistance, military grant assistance, security supporting assistance, foreign military sales credits, or international military education and training to the Republic of Panama.

(6) The President shall include all reservations and understandings incorporated by the Senate in this resolution of ratification in the instrument of ratification to be exchanged with the Government of the Republic of Panama.

Bibliographical Essay

General Works

Foreign Relations of the United States, published by the U.S. Department of State, is the indispensable primary source; it is cited in the book as *FRUS*, followed by year and, when necessary, volume number. Begun in 1861, its publication date was changed in the early twentieth century so a volume is published 20 years after the events it documents. The gap has grown to nearly 30 years, but the 1950 volumes are now published, and under the leadership of David Trask, the Historical Office of the State Department is planning to print volumes shortly on the 1950–54 years. The *FRUS* documents are, of course, only a small fraction of the total available. Scholars can use documents from the year most recently opened in the *FRUS* volumes (that is, 1950 at present). The documents are available at the National Archives in Washington, D.C., mostly in Record Group #59. These are cited in the book as NA, RG 59. Most of the documents through 1929 are available on microfilm.

Important periodicals are *Department of State Bulletin*, containing speeches of State Department officials and also some documents; *Latin America* (London), probably the best weekly newsletter in the 1960s and 1970s; *Latin American Report* (San Francisco), an informative monthly published by the World Affairs Council of Northern California; the United Nations' Economic Commission for Latin America, *Economic Survey of Latin America,* thorough and authoritative; the Organization of American States, *Alliance for Progress Weekly Newsletter,* published for the 1962 to 1973 years. Other periodical material can be found in *Reader's Guide* and *Social Science Index.*

Published documentary material on presidential pronouncements is found in James D. Richardson, *Messages and Papers of the Presidents* (New York, 1897–1914), and *Public Papers of the Presidents,* published by the Government Printing Office and covering every Chief Executive since Truman. The best sources for congressional work on Panama, other than the *Congressional Record,* are the publications of the Senate Foreign Relations Committee, the House Foreign Affairs (now International Relations) Committee, and the House Merchant Marine and Fisheries Committee, which has a Panama Canal Subcommittee that has made available masses of vital data and testimony.

The indispensable secondary source is Thomas E. Weil, *et al., Area Handbook for Panama* (Washington, D.C., 1972). Good surveys are Sheldon B. Liss, *The Canal: Aspects of United States-Panamanian Relations* (Notre Dame, Ind., 1967); and William D. McCain, *The United States and the Republic of Panama* (Durham, N.C.), a superb treatment of the 1903–36 years. Panamanian views are available in Ernesto J. Castillero Reyes, *Historia de Panama* (Panama, 1955); and Ernesto Castillero Pimental, *Politica Exterior de Panama* (Panama, 1961), a small handbook on the objectives and general bases of Panamanian foreign policy. Castillero Reyes' *El Canal de Panama* (no publisher, no date, but approximately mid-1960s) emphasizes the pre-1904 era. Lawrence O. Ealy has written two important accounts, *The Republic of Panama in World Affairs, 1903–1950* (Philadelphia, 1951), the best work in English on Panamanian foreign policy during those years; and *Yanqui Politics and the Isthmian Canal* (University Park, Pa., 1971), good on the North American political debates.

Some of the best analyses of Panama and its relations

with the United States can be found in articles: Jules B. Billard, "Panama, Link Between Oceans and Continents," *National Geographic,* CXXXVII (March 1970), 402–440, a splendid, well-illustrated introduction; Daniel Goldrich, "Panama," in Martin C. Needler, ed., *Political Systems of Latin America* (Princeton, 1964), an excellent survey by one of the best scholars of Panamanian affairs; Louis Harris, "Panama," in Ben G. Burnett and Kenneth F. Johnson, eds., *Political Forces in Latin America* (Belmont, Calif., 1968), an important analysis, especially on the 1960s; two articles by E. Bradford Burns, "Panama's Struggle for Independence," *Current History,* LXVI (January 1974); and "Panama: The Search for Independence," *ibid.*, LXXII (February 1977), especially important for the historical perspective this well-known scholar of Latin America brings to these essays; and Lester D. Langley, "The United States and Panama: The Burden of Power," *ibid.*, LVI (January 1969). Langley's work on U.S.-Panamanian relations is crucial; several of his essays, listed below, are standard on the years they cover. Note especially his "U.S.-Panamanian Relations Since 1941," *Journal of Inter-American Studies,* XII (July 1970). E. S. Costrell, *U.S.* Policy Towards Panama, 1903–Present," *Department of State Bulletin,* LXX (April 22, 1974), is an important chronology of recognition and intervention problems. A useful overview, stressing the post-1960 era, is Robert E. Looney, *The Economic Development of Panama* (New York, 1976); and the most recent account of United Fruit, with some material on Panama, is Thomas P. McCann, *An American Company: The Tragedy of United Fruit* (New York, 1976). McCann notes the extensive earlier work on United Fruit in Latin America. Standard on legal questions is R. R. Baxter, *The Laws of International Waterways, With Particular Regard to Interoceanic Canals* (Cambridge, Mass., 1964). Several general accounts of U.S.-Latin American policy put relations with Panama in proper perspective: Donald M. Dozer, *Are We Good Neighbors?* (Gainesville, Fla., 1959), especially good on the 1940s; J. Lloyd Mecham, *A Survey of United States-Latin American Relations* (Boston, 1965), useful for the 1940–64 years; Dexter Perkins's well-known *Hands Off: A History of the Monroe Doctrine* (Boston, 1963); J. Fred Rippy, *Globe and Hemisphere: Latin America's Place in the Postwar Foreign Relations of the United States* (Chicago, 1958), a classic on the post-1930s era.

Documents from the early nineteenth century through the 1955 treaty, including some private reports as well as the treaties and other agreements, are usefully compiled in Diogenes A. Arosemena G., *Documentary Diplomatic History of the Panama Canal* (Panama, 1961).

The Early Years (to 1904)

A well-written introduction for the Panamanian side is David Howarth, *Four Hundred Years of Dreams and Cruelty* (New York, 1966); and the most important scholarly work on Panamanian nationalism is by Ricaurte Soler, especially *Pensamiento Panameño y Concepción de la Nacionalidad durante el Siglo XIX* (Panama, 1954); and *Formas Ideológicas de la Nación Panameña* (San Jose, Costa Rica, 1972).

Nineteenth-century North American movement into Panamanian affairs is analyzed in Charles S. Campbell's excellent *The Transformation of American Foreign Relations, 1865–1900* (New York, 1976); Richard D. Challener's *Admirals, Generals, and American Foreign Policy, 1898–1914* (Princeton, 1973), a pioneering account of military strategy with a valuable chapter on isthmian intervention; and Kenneth J. Hagan's fine monograph, *American Gunboat Diplomacy and the Old Navy, 1877–1889* (Westport, Conn., 1973). The broad background through the 1903 revolution has been covered many times in superb accounts: Dwight C. Miner, *The Fight for the Panama Canal Route* (New York, 1940); Miles P. DuVal, *Cadiz to Cathay* (Stanford, 1940), especially useful for the Colombian side;

Gerstle Mack, *The Land Divided* (New York, 1944), exhaustive on the years to 1921; Lester D. Langley, *Struggle for the American Mediterranean: United States-European Rivalry in the Gulf-Caribbean, 1776–1904* (Athens, Ga., 1976), an excellent survey of interest in a canal placed within the international competition in the area; and two definitive articles by Charles D. Ameringer, "The Panama Canal Lobby of Philippe Bunau-Varilla and William Nelson Cromwell," *American Historical Review*, LXVII (January 1963); and "Philippe Bunau-Varilla: New Light on the Panama Canal Treaty," *Hispanic American Historical Review*, XLVI (February 1966). Much of this has now been synthesized in David McCullough's highly readable, *The Path Between the Seas: The Creation of the Panama Canal, 1870–1914* (New York, 1977), especially valuable for its pages on the engineering and medical problems solved by the North American builders. A most helpful biography is William Henry Harbaugh, *Power and Responsibility: The Life and Times of Theodore Roosevelt* (New York, 1961); and TR's letters are available in Elting E. Morison, ed., *The Letters of Theodore Roosevelt*, 6 vols. (Cambridge, Mass., 1951). Central figures are analyzed in Richard W. Leopold, *Elihu Root and the Conservative Tradition* (Boston, 1954); Stanford University Libraries, *Francis Butler Loomis and the Panama Crisis* (Stanford, Calif., 1965), although much remains to be done on Loomis; and the most helpful of several biographies on Hay (largely because the author obtained first-person evidence on the 1903 episode), is William Roscoe Thayer, *The Life and Letters of John Hay*, 2 vols. (Boston, 1915). Bunau-Varilla tells his story with all the considerable egomania, overstatement, and drama at his command in *Panama: The Creation, Destruction, and Resurrection* (London, 1913). An opponent of TR's work is defined in John R. Lambert, *Arthur Pue Gorman* (Baton Rouge, La., 1953); and public sentiments on both sides are given at length in *Public Opinion*, especially volumes 35 and 36 which cover 1903–1904; the opponents are also picked up in David S. Patterson, *Toward a Warless World: The Travail of the American Peace Move-*

ment, *1887–1914* (Bloomington, Ind., 1976), especially good on the Panama Tolls debate. A leading Panamanian historian provides his perspective and many little known vignettes of the 1903 revolution in Ernesto J. Castillero Reyes, *Episodios de la Independencia de Panama* (Panama, 1957); a Colombian historian gives his nation's view in Germán Arciniegas, *Caribbean: Sea of the New World* (New York, 1954); and the Latin American reaction to the U.S. involvement in the revolution—a reaction surprisingly benign—is analyzed in J. Patterson, "Latin-American Reactions to the Panama Revolution of 1903," *Hispanic American Historical Review*, XXIV (May 1944).

The 1904 policies are analyzed in Dana G. Munro, *Intervention and Dollar Diplomacy in the Caribbean, 1900–1921* (Princeton, 1964), also good on 1902–1903 events; G. A. Mellander, *The United States in Panamanian Politics; The Intriguing Formative Years* (Danville, Ill., 1971), a useful synthesis; two most important works by Ralph E. Minger, "Panama, The Canal Zone, and Titular Sovereignty," *Western Political Quarterly*, XIV (June 1961); and *William Howard Taft and United States Foreign Policy: The Apprenticeship Years, 1900–1908*; and William D. McCain's classic, *The United States and the Republic of Panama* (Durham, N.C., 1937).

Brief analyses of theories on colonialism are in Rupert Emerson, "Colonialism: Political Aspects," in David L. Sills, ed., *International Encyclopedia of the Social Sciences*. Vol. III (New York, 1968); and D. K. Fieldhouse, "Colonialism: Economic Aspects," *ibid.*

The Middle Years (1904–1960)

The best account is McCain, *U.S. and Republic of Panama*, cited above, which concludes in the mid-1930s. Wilsonian policy is well described in G. W. Baker, Jr., "The Wilson Administration and Panama, 1913–1921," *Journal of Inter-American Studies*, VIII (April 1966); Joseph Tulchin, *The Aftermath of War: World War I and U.S. Policy Towards Latin America* (New York, 1971), which has a short account of Hughes's dealings with the Panamanians; George Westerman, "Gold vs. Silver Workers in the Canal Zone," *Common Ground*, VIII (No. 2, 1948), by an eminent black Panamanian who traces racial discrimination in the Zone; Willis J. Abbot, *The Panama Canal: An Illustrated Historical Narrative* (New York, 1922), which stands apart from the usual traveler's account and seems to catch perfectly the growing tensions on the Isthmus; Frank Otto Gatell, "Canal in Retrospect—Some Panamanian and Colombian Views," *Americas*, XV (July 1958), a good essay on intellectual currents, particularly in early Panamanian textbooks; Harmodio Arias, *The Panama Canal: A Study in Institutional Law and Diplomacy* (London, 1911), a crucial analysis by one of the leading Panamanian political figures.

An excellent introduction to the 1920s and 1930s is R. L. Buell, "Panama and the United States," *Foreign Policy Reports*, VII (Jan. 20, 1932); material from the Henry Stimson diaries, Yale University, available on microfilm provides important primary documents. The pivotal work has been done by Lester Langley in two articles: "Negotiating New Treaties with Panama: 1936," *Hispanic American Historical Review*, XLVIII (May 1968); and "World Crisis and the Good Neighbor Policy in Panama, 1936–1941," *Americas*, XXIV (October 1967); Cordell Hull gives his view in *Memoirs*, 2 vols. (New York, 1948); while Roosevelt's views are best discovered in two primary sources: Edgar B. Nixon, ed., *Franklin D. Roosevelt and Foreign Affairs*, 3 vols. (Cambridge, Mass., 1969); and Samuel I. Rosenman, ed., *The Public Papers and Addresses of Franklin D. Roosevelt*, 13 vols. (New York, 1938–50).

The best introduction to the 1940s is David Green, *The Containment of Latin America* (Chicago, 1971); while a top State Department officer has second thoughts in Laurence Duggan, *The Americas* (New York, 1949). Important articles are Norman J. Padelford, "American Rights in the Panama Canal," *American Journal of International Law,*

XXXIV (July 1940); the short anaysis of 1944—48 in Austin F. Macdonald, *Latin American Politics and Government* (New York, 1949); Arthur P. Whitaker's superb article in *Inter-American Affairs, 1941* (New York, 1942), which Whitaker edited; A. R. Wright, "Defense Sites Negotiations Between the Unitd States and Panama, 1936—1948," *Department of State Bulletin*, XXVII (Aug. 11, 1952); and material in *Records of Meetings*, especially volume VI, at the Council on Foreign Relations in New York City.

For the 1950s one book stands alone; indeed it is the best available work on Panamanian politics in any era: Larry LaRae Pippin, *The Remón Era; An Analysis of a Decade of Events in Panama, 1947–1957* (Stanford, 1964). The growing economic crisis is traced in United Nations, *Economic Bulletin for Latin America*, IV (October 1959), the best analysis of the Panamanian economy, 1939—56; Pedro C. M. Teichert, *Economic Policy, Revolution and Industrialization in Latin America* (Oxford, Miss., 1959) is important; C. G. Fenwick, "Treaty of 1955 Between the United States and Panama," *American Journal of International Law*, IL (October 1955), provides the starting place, along with Pippin, for the treaty. For the background of the 1959 riots, see Milton S. Eisenhower, *The Wine Is Bitter. The United States and Latin America* (New York, 1963); Ricardo J. Alfaro, *Media Siglo de Relaciones entre Panama y los Estados Unidos* (Panama, 1959), for a key Panamanian view; and Martin B. Travis and James T. Watkins, "Time Bomb in Panama," *The Nation*, CXC (April 30, 1960).

The critical development of the middle class in Panama is traced in several works: the essays by Carolina de Campbell and Ofelia Hopper, and another by John Biesanz, in Theo R. Crevenna, ed., *Materiales para el estudio de la clase media en la América Latina*, vol. IV (Washington, D.C., 1950); John and Mavis Biesanz, *The People of Panama* (New York, 1955), which is a broad work of importance; John Biesanz and L. M. Smith, "Panamanian Politics," *Journal of Politics*, XIV (August 1952); Richard N. Adams, *Cultural Surveys of Panama, Nicaragua. . . .* (Washington,

D.C., 1957), important for its study of the *campesino* in the interior; and for the economic aspects, E. A. Cleugh, *Panama: Economic and Commercial Conditions. . . .* (London, 1955).

The Recent Years (post-1960)

An excellent overall introduction to the changing world of post-1956 is Geoffrey Barraclough, *Introduction to Contemporary History* (New York, 1965); also see John Gerassi, *The Great Fear; The Reconquest of Latin America by Latin Americans* (New York, 1963). On U.S.-Panamanian relations, the two standard studies are Kent Jay Minor, "United States-Panamanian Relations: 1958–1973," unpublished doctoral dissertation, Case Western Reserve University, 1974; and Lester D. Langley, "U.S.-Panamanian relations Since 1941," *Journal of Inter-American Studies,* XII (July 1970). The influence of Castro, or lack thereof, is mentioned in William E. Ratliff, *Castroism and Communism in Latin America, 1959–1976* (Washington, D.C., 1976); and Ernest A. Duff, *et al., Violence and Repression in Latin America* (New York, 1976), which emphasizes the cohesiveness in Panamanian society. Panama is not considered an integral part of Central America, as is made evident in C. F. Denton, "Interest Groups in Panama and the Central American Common Market, " *Inter-American Economic Affairs,* XXI (Summer 1967), important also for its material on interest groups; and Kenneth J. Grieb, "The United States and the Central American Federation," *Americas,* XXIV (October 1967). Some of the most important work on the 1960s has been done by Daniel Goldrich: *Sons of the Establishment: Elite Youth in Panama. . . .* (Chicago, 1966); "Requisites for Political Legitimacy in Panama," *Public Opinion Quarterly,* XXVI (Winter 1962); and "Developing Political Orientations of Panamanian Students," *Journal of Politics,* XXIII (February 1961). See also Organization of American States, *Latin America's Development and the Alliance for*

Progress (Washington, D.C., 1973), a key document on the 1960s and early 1970s.

The 1964 tragedy is anticipated in Mercer D. Tate, "The Panama Canal and Political Partnership," *Journal of Politics,* XXV (February 1963), an excellent overview; T. Armbrister, "Panama: Why They Hate Us; More Than One Torn Flag," *Saturday Evening Post,* CCXXXVII (March 7, 1964), is brilliant reporting on the causes; and Lyndon Johnson's view is given in his *The Vantage Point* (New York, 1971); to be tempered with Philip Geyelin, *Lyndon B. Johnson and the World* (New York, 1966), which remains the best analysis of Johnson's foreign policy; and Eric F. Goldman, *The Tragedy of Lyndon Johnson* (New York, 1969); primary materials are opening slowly at the Lyndon B. Johnson Presidential Library in Austin, Texas. The 1964 rioting is analyzed in detail in International Commission of Jurists, *Report on the Events in Panama, January 9–12, 1964* (Geneva, Switzerland, 1964); and Lyman M. Tondel, Jr., ed., *The Panama Canal: Background Papers and Proceedings of the Sixth Hammarskjold Forum* (Dobbs Ferry, N.Y., 1965); Jules Dubois, *Danger Over Panama* (Indianapolis, 1964), highly critical of Panama; J. Fred Rippy, "United States and Panama: The High Cost of Appeasement," *Inter-American Economic Affairs,* XVII (Spring 1964), required reading, as are all of Rippy's works on Latin America; and North American opinion can be found for this and other years in George H. Gallup, *The Gallup Poll: Public Opinion, 1935–1971,* 3 vols. (New York, 1972). The aftermath, and especially the inexorable economic problems, can be studied in Georgetown University Center for Strategic Studies, *Panama; Canal Issues and Treaty Talks* (Washington, D.C., 1967); Carl R. Jacobsen, "Basic Data on the Economy of the Republic of Panama," *Overseas Business Reports* (June 1968), published by the U.S. Department of Commerce; and especially Larry L. Pippin, "Challenge in Panama," *Current History,* L (January 1966).

For the 1970s a number of good articles are the starting point: Helen C. Low, "Panama Canal Treaty in Perspective," Overseas Development Council Monograph Series #29 (1976); Thomas M. Franck and Edward Weisband, "Panama Paralysis," *Foreign Policy*, No. 21 (Winter 1975–76); Stephen S. Rosenfeld, "The Panama Negotiations—A Close-Run Thing," *Foreign Affairs*, LIV (October 1975); Richard Hudson, "Storm Over the Canal," *New York Times Magazine*, May 16, 1976; E. J. Kahn, Jr., "Letter from Panama," *The New Yorker*, Aug. 16, 1976; Jan Morris, "A Terminal Case of American Perpetuity," *Rolling Stone*, No. 203 (Jan. 1, 1976), which has brilliant reporting; Roger S. Leeds, "The Panama Canal Treaty: Past and Present United States Interests," *Foreign Service Journal*, LIII (March 1976); and the context for the new Kissinger diplomacy is given critically in Ben S. Stephansky, " 'New Dialogue' on Latin America: The Cost of Policy Neglect," in Ronald G. Hellman and H. Jon Rosenbaum, eds., *Latin America: The Search for a New International Role* (New York, 1975).

Good introductions to General Omar Torrijos and the conditions which produced his kind of rule is in Graham Greene, "The Country with Five Frontiers," *New York Review of Books*, Feb. 17, 1977, mostly favorable; Martin C. Needler, "Omar Torrijos, The Panamanian Enigma," *Intellect*, CV (February 1977), quite critical; Omar Torrijos Herrera, *Una Revolution Diferente* (Panama, 1972), in which Torrijos speaks for himself through snippets from his many speeches; Steve C. Ropp's brilliant analysis in "Military Reformism in Panama: New Directions or Old Indications," *Caribbean Studies*, XII (October 1972); and a primary document is in Organization of American States, *Constitution of Panama, 1972* (Washington, D.C., 1974). Besides the Ropp article, the general circumstances which allow Torrijos (and others like him in Latin America) to rule are described in William H. Beezley, "Caudillismo: An Interpretive Note," *Journal of Inter-American Studies*, XI (July 1969); Eric R. Wolf and Edward C. Hansen, *The Human Condition in Latin America* (New York, 1972), especially its short analysis of populism; José Nun's pioneering "A Latin American Phenomenon: The Middle Class Military *Coup*," in

James Petras and Maurice Zeitlin, eds., *Latin America: Reform or Revolution* (New York, 1969); Edwin Lieuwen, *Arms and Politics in Latin America* (New York, 1961); and Roland H. Ebel, "Governing the City-State: Notes on the Politics of the Small Latin American Countries," *Journal of Inter-American Studies and World Affairs*, XIV (August 1972). Another major Panamanian figure speaks for himself in Marcos G. McGrath, "Ariel or Caliban?" *Foreign Affairs*, LII (October 1973); and the context is on pages 423–424 of J. Lloyd Mecham, *Church and State in Latin America* (Chapel Hill, 1966).

Panama's growth as an international banking center is examined in Harry Johnson, "Panama as a Regional Financial Center: A Preliminary Analysis of Development Contribution," *Economic Development and Cultural Change*, XXIV (January 1976); and Robin Pringle, "Panama—A Survey," *The Banker*, CXXV (October 1975); while T. V. Greer provides a fascinating survey in "Mercantile Potpourri Called Panama," *Journal of Inter-American Studies*, XIV (August 1972); and the overall picture is given in Looney, *Economic Development of Panama*, cited above; William C. Merrill, et al., *Panama's Economic Development; The Role of Agriculture* (Ames, Iowa, 1975).

The North American debate between 1973 and early 1977 can be found in "Controversy Over Proposed Panama Canal Treaty Revision, Pro and Con," *Congressional Digest*, LV (April 1976); while an earlier account is in *ibid.*, LI (November 1972); Charles Maechling, Jr., "The Panama Canal: A Fresh Start," *Orbis*, XX (Winter 1977), is a thoughtful criticism of the State Department position; Captain Paul Ryan, "Canal Diplomacy and U.S. Interests," *U.S. Naval Institute Proceedings*, CIII (January 1977), gives the military reasons for retaining the Canal; Daniel Flood's views can be found in "Projected Surrender of the U.S. Canal Zone," *Vital Speeches*, Aug. 1, 1975, as well as in the *Congressional Record*. The pro-treaty side is in Robert G. Cox, "Choices for Partnership or Bloodshed in Panama," in Kalman H. Silvert, ed., *The Americas in a Changing World*

(New York, 1975), a highly important analysis; Alan Riding, "Is America Giving Away the Panama Canal?" *Saturday Review*, July 24, 1976; Stanley Karnow, "The Politics of Bluster and Ballyhoo," *ibid.*; Commission on United States-Latin American Relations, *The United States and Latin America: Next Steps* (no publishing place, 1976), written by the Commission headed by Sol Linowitz; Xabier Gorostiaga, *Panama y la Zona del Canal* (Buenos Aires, 1975), a fact-filled Latin American analysis.

On the future of the Canal, an excellent, thorough treatment is Norman J. Padelford and Stephen R. Gibbs, *Maritime Commerce and the Future of the Panama Canal* (Cambridge, Md., 1975); and see the detailed study in U.S. Congress, House, Subcommittee of the Committee on Appropriations, 94th Cong., 1st Sess., *Department of Transportation and Related Agencies Appropriations for 1976,* especially Part 4 (Washington, D.C., 1975); the Leon M. Cole study deserves special notice.

Additional extensive bibliography, especially on Panamanian affairs, can be found in Thomas E. Weil, *et al., Area Handbook for Panama* (Washington, D.C., 1972).

Index